To You and Your Children

TO YOU &
YOUR CHILDREN

EXAMINING THE BIBLICAL DOCTRINE OF
COVENANT SUCCESSION

Edited by
Benjamin K. Wikner

CANON PRESS *Moscow, Idaho*

Benjamin K. Wikner (ed.), *To You and Your Children: Examining the Biblical Doctrine of Covenant Succession*
This collection © 2005 by Benjamin K. Wikner. Individual authors retain the copyright of their respective articles.

Published by Canon Press, P.O. Box 8729, Moscow, ID 83843
800-488-2034 / www.canonpress.org
Printed in the United States of America.
Cover design by Paige Atwood.

05 06 07 08 09 10   9 8 7 6 5 4 3 2 1

Library of Congress Cataloging-in-Publication Data

To you and your children : examining the biblical doctrine of covenant succession / edited by Benjamin K. Wikner.
    p. cm.
  Includes index.
  ISBN 1-59128-028-1
  1. Christian children—Religious life. 2. Covenants—Religious aspects—Reformed Church. 3. Parent and child—Religious aspects—Reformed Church. 4. Reformed Church—Doctrines. 5. Covenants—Biblical teaching. 6. Parent and child—Biblical teaching. I. Wikner, Benjamin K. II. Title.

  BT705.T6 2004
  248.8'45—dc22

                                        2004017672

This book is dedicated to my beloved wife, Erin, who has been my helper extraordinaire in life and in my ministry in the church and to our children. A father could not ask for a better mother for his children, nor a husband a better wife for himself. She is God's gift to me in nurturing our five children in the Lord. We have confidence together in the promises of God in Christ that our precious children will reap the heavenly reward of God's covenant blessings. Soli Deo Gloria.

Contents

Part II: Implications

Part III: Covenant Nurture

Foreword: The Children's Crusade

R. C. Sproul, Jr.

Because we are myopic, parochial, individualist Americans we tend to think that myopic, parochial, individualist Americans invented myopic, parochial individualism. The particular error of individualism isn't peculiar to Americans, nor is it peculiar to the modern age. We meet at least one such creature in the book of Acts. We are all familiar with the story. Paul and Silas languish in prison, guilty of "troubling the city." As the two men pray and sing, an earthquake comes, shaking the foundations of the prison, loosing everyone's chains and opening every door. The jailer awakes, sees the doors open, and decides life is no longer worth living. Paul calls out, "Do yourself no harm, for we are all here." The jailer comes, falls down before Paul and Silas, and exhibits both great wisdom and great folly by asking, "Sirs, what must I do to be saved?"

Though he doubtless was rather ignorant of the fullness of the answer, he did well to ask about his salvation. Where he erred is evident in the answer given him: *"Believe* on the Lord Jesus Christ, and you will be saved, *you and your household."* Before we seek to understand how the grace of God works in the lives of our children, and even before that grace is actually at work, we ought first to hope for our children. The jailer's problem was not that he was insufficiently covenantal in his theology, but that he was not sufficiently concerned for his family. He cared first and foremost for himself and his own salvation. Even before he prays the sinner's prayer, he is learning from Paul and Silas to care more for his family.

My own experience was rather the opposite. I was raised in the nurture and admonition of the Lord by believing parents. In fact, many Reformed folk have felt the pangs of jealousy toward me because of how lucky I was in the parent lottery. In, through, under, and around their covenant faithfulness and in, through, under, and around my heavenly Father's covenant faithfulness, I am an heir of the covenant. I do indeed believe on the Lord Jesus Christ.

To one degree or another, I'm ashamed to say, I took that grace for granted. I was "in," and was making a reasonable effort toward my sanctification the Calvinist way. That is, I equated learning more theology, which is a good thing, with growing in grace, which is likewise a good thing. But confusing the two is not such a good thing. Calvinists, and I am among them, tend to measure their own sanctification on a peculiar scale. You are a simple novitiate when God regenerates you and you trust in the finished work of Christ alone. You become a first-degree believer when you understand the difference between Calvinism and Arminianism. The next step is actually to read a Calvinist or two—Piper, Boice, or Sproul will do. The next steps up the ladder correspond to the relative difficulty and obscurity of what you are reading. Calvin is better than Piper, but Turretin is better than Calvin. The next plateau has you reading Beza, Bullinger, and Bucer. You become an officer when you can actually quote Van Til. You reach the thirty-third degree when you actually understand that quotation.

Everything was going along swimmingly in this stream of least resistance until God did something shocking—He blessed me with a child. Suddenly I knew I had to get serious about my sanctification, because now it had eternal consequences beyond myself. In the grace of God, I was more zealous for the soul of my little girl Darby than I was for my own soul, which in turn focused my attention back to my own soul. Suddenly that whole "getting in by the skin of my teeth" thing, which had looked so appealing when I was a single man, now horrified me because it meant that my own daughter could end up being wood, hay, and stubble. Because of the work of Christ on my behalf, God was covenantally faithful enough to me to make me realize that I had to be covenantally faithful to Him and my daughter if I wished Him to bless her covenantally.

Since that time God has so blessed me five more times. Each time my own heart bursts with the truth of God: "I have no greater joy than to hear that my children walk in the truth." We are, of course, to be singularly focused on pursuing the glory of God. We are to long for the fullness of God's blessing, for the beatific vision, for that day when we shall be like Him, for we will see Him as He is. But there can be no greater earthly desire, yearning, or passion than that which yields the greatest joy—knowing that not only we but also our children walk in the truth. If such doesn't enflame our hearts, I'm afraid we have no hearts to enflame.

The doctrine of covenant succession, then, misses the mark. It is not that the doctrine is false, but that it is false that it is merely a doctrine. We aren't here talking about competing theories of the nature of free will. We aren't dickering over what year John wrote his Apocalypse. We aren't fussing about whether the Spirit proceeds from the Father only or from the Father and the Son. We are talking about eternity, heaven, hell, and our children. We are talking about the pursuit of joy, the very substance of life.

Such doesn't mean, of course, that we should descend into sloppy sentimentalism. It would indeed be a deadly mistake to assume our children will be on our side of the great divide simply because we really want them to be there—which is why it is a good thing that Ben Wikner has assembled such a team of scholars to tackle the thorny questions of covenant succession, and why it is a good thing to read this book, and read it with all due care. But my prayer is that as you read, behind every argument, beneath every syllogism, you will see the radiant face of your own children, reflecting the radiant face of the Savior, as "He took them up in His arms, laid His hands on them, and blessed them" (Mk. 10:16).

Introduction

Benjamin K. Wikner

Not too long ago, as I was discussing this book project with a fellow minister, he warned me, "Be careful—the subject of parenting can be as sensitive and uncomfortable as discussing love-making technique." I was somewhat taken aback, if by nothing else than the discomfort of the analogy. Nevertheless, I must agree. Parenting *is* highly personal, involving one of the most precious and intimate parts of our lives—our children. Most parents have given the better part of their lives, and their fortunes, in the raising of their children. What parent, therefore, can be blamed for taking personally their children's well-being, and the outcome of their lives?

It's not only the parents' sacrifice—it's also their pride. The fact is, children are reflections of their parents. When a child's misbehavior becomes known, it is an embarrassment not only to him personally but to his parents as well. But inquiring into someone's parenting ability typically results only in defensiveness. We like to take pride in our children and in our raising of them, and most parents are jealous for the right to make the decisions and set the parenting program. The retort "Don't tell me how to raise my kids!" is never far from most parents' lips.

Yet the Word of God is clear that the wise man seeks counsel, even a multitude of godly counselors. Experience also shows us our need for help. We know only as much as we have learned, and much of what we have learned has been wrong, whether from worldly teachers or from the misguided (albeit well-intentioned) lessons of our own parents. All parents carry baggage into their parenting, some of which can be so burdensome that it overwhelms them and greatly hinders the spiritual progress of their children.

So is this another book on parenting technique? A how-to manual on raising your children, disciplining them, and generally keeping them out of trouble? Not exactly, though such things are addressed. This book offers no magical "blue pill" of parenting that will make parents perform their duties well and scientifically assure satisfying results in their families. Covenant nurture could never be so artificial or mechanical, especially when done biblically and spiritually. As in all things spiritual, God requires faith, obedience, and perseverance. For such things, there can never be a formula, pill, or methodology that will guarantee a particular result.

That said, covenant nurture begins with a promise—God's promise to us and to our children that He will be our God and we His people. In light of this promise, we see that *the nurture of our children begins with covenant succession.* Just as a builder cannot begin without a blueprint from the architect, so also the covenant nurture of children cannot properly be understood or applied without an understanding of covenant succession. The expectation of spiritual success in our covenant children comes by faith—faith in God's promises to us and to our children. Without such faith, we cannot please God.

The term *covenant succession* may not be altogether familiar to you. In past generations it may have been called *covenant expectation, the doctrine of children in the covenant,* or just simply *practical covenant theology.* Notably, it really had no specific title, in part because it was not a matter of particular controversy in Christian circles. It seems that only within the past century has the issue of the spiritual standing and expectation of covenant children been substantively assailed. Nowhere in the writings of the early magisterial Reformers will you find anything other than the full belief that children of believing parents were set apart as holy and expected to own the faith into which they were born. If anything, some may fault the early Reformed theologians for being *too* strenuous in their advocacy of children in the covenant (see Trouwborst's article for a full presentation of the historical progress—or regress—of the doctrine).

In the last century and a half, many have called into question and even upended the biblical (and historically Reformed) doctrine of children in the covenant. The influence of baptistic thought has casually entered into Reformed circles, even bringing about a generally recognized segment in the Reformed community called Reformed Baptists. The doctrines and practices of revivalism have also taken root and have further eroded the view that children have strong standing in the covenant. Additionally, the increasing exodus of covenant children away from the church and into unbelief has greatly heightened the practical relevance of the subject and influenced the pragmatic disposition against the historic doctrine.

Typically, when an issue becomes controversial, terminology tends to become more prolific and specific. The term *covenant succession* naturally results from the need to bring clarity to this discussion. Needless to say, this is no arcane, academic controversy. On the contrary, our children—who are the future of the church—are at stake in this discussion.

To be specific, *the doctrine of covenant succession presents the Scriptural teaching that the children of believers (covenant children) are expected to succeed in the faith of their parents, and this is accomplished through the divinely ordained means of covenant nurture.* While the term *covenant succession* has likely been used in this context in various writings, it was effectively cemented for our day in an article written by the first contributing author of this volume, Rob Rayburn, entitled "The Presbyterian Doctrines of Covenant Children, Covenant Nurture and Covenant Succession." In this article, he presented the doctrine in its historical context along with some of its implications and applications for the church and family. To the degree that this article led the way for the contemporary evolution of this discussion, we might consider Rayburn the modern patriarch of covenant succession thinking.

Much has happened since 1996 when Rayburn's article first appeared. The world continues to change. Theological discourse has evolved. Today, covenant succession has become embroiled in the justification controversy that has recently spread throughout Reformed denominations. This ought to come as no surprise. At the heart of this controversy is a renewed emphasis on salvation by faith alone. This is good. But this emphasis seems to discount or depreciate the instrumentality of works, the cause-and-effect relationship between obedience and consequence in the Christian life. No one in the present controversy (that I am aware of) suggests that we are saved by our works or that works are in any way meritorious. Neither do any advocates of covenant succession say that our works save our children. Instead, covenant succession merely applies the biblical teaching that our conduct as parents has real consequences and is instrumental according to the covenant promise.

Thus the topic of covenant succession has taken on much greater significance in the eyes of some than it did when it *merely* dealt with our children and nurture. Apparently, in the minds of some, upholding the doctrine of covenant succession undermines the pristine glory of the doctrine of justification by faith alone. You can follow the logic: If the children of the church are saved by a faith which is nurtured by diligent and faithful parenting, then they are saved not by faith *alone*, but by faith *and* the works of their parents! Thus (the argument goes) upholding the historic doctrine of salvation by faith alone means rejecting the doctrine of covenant succession (see the essays by Rayburn, Kloosterman, and Wilson for excellent treatments of this topic).

Assuredly, we must agree to uphold the historic doctrine of justification. But it is the *historic* doctrine of justification that we must uphold—a doctrine which does not sacrifice covenant consequences, the obedience of faith, and the spiritual succession of our children. It is a dreadful dilemma to contemplate sacrificing our covenant expectation for our precious children's spiritual success for the sake of upholding the doctrine of justification by faith! We certainly don't see such a dilemma in the writings of the magisterial Reformers when they wax eloquent on the glorious doctrine of justification. Truly, the doctrine of covenant succession should be much less controversial.

One is inclined to wonder, which was the cart and which the horse? What is the real issue? Is it that covenant succession really undercuts justification by faith alone, or is the doctrine of justification inadvertently (to put the best light on it) being used as a means to undercut covenant succession? Why is there the felt need to undermine such a precious and biblical doctrine? We suggest it stems from the modern church's already low expectation for her covenant children. But then, why would the church have such a low expectation for her children? Does it?

We answer sadly that in too many Reformed churches the answer is yes. The influences of non-Reformed theology and a fleshly culture have taken their toll. The path downward seems to be increasingly precipitous in its slope. Has there ever been a graver time for the families and children of believers? That's hard for us to answer, having lived only in our day. But based upon the memoirs and writings of past saints, and a comparison of their faith and their families to our own, we are convinced that the church needs a clarion call, a call faithful to the Bible and enriched by the covenant, to take captive her families and her children to the obedience of Christ. Thus the reason— nay, the necessity—for such a volume as this.

Any honest evaluation of our society's moral decay and general decline, especially of its youth, should give every Christian grave concern and lead to fervent prayer. But what is even more frightening is what is happening in our churches. Maybe we have made peace with the fact that the neighbor kids are going to be bad influences upon our children. Maybe we have resolved to separate from the mainstream of culture in order to protect our family and our faith. But we expect the church to be an oasis in a wilderness world. Here, at least, Christian parents should be able to let their guard down a little and receive inspiration and help with their children. Certainly the leadership of the church should be exemplifying such spirituality in their own homes and instructing others to do the same.

Herein lies the grave concern that I and each of the writers of this volume share. We write out of love and concern for the church of Jesus Christ, a church in which families and children are struggling to survive spiritually. How often do our churches suffer the loss of their beloved children—lost to sin, unbelief, and rebellion? How many Christian parents are grieving over a broken relationship with one of their children? How many right now feel the sinking despair and pounding desperation at the thought of losing one of their little ones to unbelief? How many have any idea what to do or are getting any real help in reclaiming one of these precious, wandering sheep?

This is the reality in our churches today, punctuated by the surprising nonchalance of so many Christian parents about the unbelieving state of their grown children. Yet this should come as no surprise considering the weak, unbiblical, and unfaithful teaching that exists in regard to our children and families. The expectation of faith has been replaced by the pragmatics of experience or even the passivity of an imbalanced theological perspective. "Who can know, who can say," we are told, "how one's children will turn out?" "We hope for the best and trust God for the rest." That sounds spiritual, but is in reality as shallow as "Let go and let God" or even the opposite extreme of "God helps those who help themselves."

Thus, concentrated instruction and diligent attention upon such practical and essential matters as family and parenting are often neglected. Instead, many pastors pound the pulpit on the fine points of justification, predestination, or whatever else gives them a sense of theological superiority over those "in error." Meanwhile, the families in our churches are flailing about for answers, the children are rebelling, and the spiritual well-being of the churches is disintegrating. Were it more predominately the case that the church's children were following in the footsteps of faith, this volume would not be needed, and the issue not nearly so controversial.

It is our contention that the scandal of apostate covenant youth is only surpassed by the scandal of church leaders and teachers who dismiss the problem, finding theological excuses for it. The church of

Jesus Christ is not well served by such (lack of) spiritual leadership. For the sake of Christ, His church, and our children, we offer this volume as both an alarm and a collection of positive instruction for the people of God.

This volume seeks to increase the church's faith. In order for this to happen, such faith must begin in the leadership of the church—pastors, elders, and teachers. The present crisis in the church is evident particularly in its leadership, for in the households of the church's leaders we see the direction of the church as a whole. If the men who lead a congregation as elders and overseers are men of little faith and piety, the members of the church will, like good sheep, follow in the same immature example. If the leaders' households, including their children, are in disarray, we cannot expect other families in the church to do any better. The Bible speaks to this principle very clearly: followers will not be greater than the leader, sheep not more spiritual than the shepherd.

As teachers and preachers in the church, we recognize the sensitivity of the subject matter. The clear implication of covenant succession is that if a child of Christian parents rejects the faith, there has been a failure of covenant nurture on the part of the parents as well as the church (particularly its leaders). Some will say that tender hearts which have already been broken by the spiritual loss of a child should not be put through the wringer of acknowledging their parental and covenantal failings, but this is well-intentioned sentimentalism. We don't say to the unbeliever who is suffering some terrible consequence of his sin, "It is enough that you are suffering. I won't mention the fact that you are a sinner who needs to repent and receive Christ." On the contrary, we recognize that the way to forgiveness and healing is confronting sin and repenting of it. The doctrine of covenant succession, properly understood and applied, not only lifts up believing families to greater expectation in faith but also to better obedience, not only when children are succeeding in the faith but also when they have rebelled.

So where do we begin? We begin at the foundation—the very

promises of God as proclaimed in the covenant made with Christ and His church. Without a grasp of these divine promises, we cannot comprehend what we should expect, or know what we should properly desire. To mitigate the promises is to limit the blessings. Thus the first part of this collection deals with the doctrine proper—what is the biblical, theological, and historical basis for the teaching of covenant succession? The second part presents some implications of the doctrine—what does covenant succession look like in the church? The third part covers some practical applications of the doctrine of succession by answering the question, "How do we implement covenant nurture in the home and church?"

The God who has been so gracious to His people and so beneficent to His children in the covenant is to be praised and thanked for allowing this volume to come together. It was just over a year ago that I happened to call Doug Jones of Canon Press, with whom I had previously never spoken or even met, to talk to him about some unrelated matter. We began to speak about the need to address the church on the topic of covenant succession. As I recall, I said, "A book needs to be written," and Doug responded, "Actually, we have been working on such a book for awhile now, but the project has stalled for lack of someone to take it on. Are you interested?" I was, of course, deeply interested —and also somewhat taken aback that Doug could make the offer on such a short acquaintance. (I don't think that is how he typically finds authors for the books Canon publishes!)

Now, a year and countless work hours later, I can guess why Doug was so eager to offer this project to someone—anyone—even one he barely knew. Despite its difficulty, it has been a labor of love, not so much for the work, but for the intended benefactor—the church of Jesus Christ. The church is composed of families which make up *the* family of God. The children of the church grow up to become the children of God in maturity. If Christ was willing to give Himself for His bride to sanctify her, cleanse her, and present her holy and unblemished to Himself, what are a few hours to me and the contributors of this volume to bless and beautify the bride of Christ?

That has indeed been the constant theme and character of this effort —each contributor has a deep and sincere love for the church, for her children and her future. In putting together a roster of writers and making the calls to ask for their participation, I was blessed to see how eager and united these ministers, scholars, and churchmen were towards this effort. That they were willing to entrust this project to a neophyte such as I shows their eagerness (or recklessness, but that is hardly possible considering the godly maturity of these men) to see it accomplished. Each in his own place of ministry had been thinking similar thoughts, expressing similar concerns, and seeing a similar vision for the improvement of Christ's church and kingdom. God has providentially brought us together to offer this book for the edification and improvement of the church.

Each one of the contributors is an ordained minister or elder in Christ's church, and together they have a combined ministry of some two hundred and fifty years and a joint family of fifty-six children and thirty grandchildren. We share a deeply-held love and conviction for the church, her families, and her children. It is our desire that having read these essays you will be inspired to faith by God's gracious promises to your children, both biological and covenantal, that you may be convicted of the need for humble reflection upon any previous sloth or error, that you will be equipped to implement faithful covenant nurture in your home and in your church, and finally, that you will be blessed to enjoy the godly fruit of your faithful nurture in your children and your children's children. The promise of covenant succession is to you and your children. May you, like the apostle John, be able to say, "I have no greater joy than this, to see my children walking in the truth" (3 Jn. 1:4).

I
The Doctrine

Parental Conditions and the Promise of Grace to the Children of Believers

Robert Rayburn

Everywhere we look in Holy Scripture, we find both destiny and contingency. We are well-used to the age-old problem created by the competing emphases of divine sovereignty and human responsibility, predestination and free will, election and covenant. But in whatever terms we describe this biblical polarity, there can be no question that these dialectical emphases lie face up and side by side on virtually every page of Holy Scripture.[1] The integration of these two themes is *the* problem of Christian soteriology. Numerous attempts have been made to harmonize them and provide an account of the Bible's theology of salvation in which they are reconciled, but in all such attempts one truth invariably suffers at the expense of the other. Arminianism, with its denial of sovereign grace, and hyper-Calvinism, with its diminishment of the place of the human will in the outworking of salvation, are but two examples of the failure to take with full seriousness both sides of the biblical revelation of salvation. Biblical soteriology will always be charged with some tension because Holy Scripture presents us with interacting ideas that, at least to finite minds, seem to be in conflict with one another, or at the very least seem impossible to harmonize.

---

[1] I use "polarity" in the sense of a system that exhibits opposite parts in opposite directions, and "dialectical" in the sense of the tension created between two interacting ideas.

3

The Bible itself recognizes the tension produced by its assertion of absolute predestination and the fully responsible exercise of the human will (Rom. 9:14, 19), but makes no effort to resolve it. It asserts; it does not explain. Reformed theology has, by and large, generally preferred simply to follow the Bible in its manner of teaching and to confess both destiny and contingency as equally essential to uphold. After centuries of sanctified reflection, it seems impossible to go beyond this:

> God from all eternity, did, by the most wise and holy counsel of His own will, freely, and unchangeably ordain whatsoever comes to pass; yet so, as thereby neither is God the author of sin, nor is violence offered to the will of the creatures; nor is the liberty or contingency of second causes taken away, but rather established. (WCF 3.1)

Lest anyone mistake the burden of that statement, it is an assertion, not an explanation—and far less a resolution. That is not to say, of course, that within Reformed theology there have not been many differences of presentation and emphasis.[2]

On this general point, in my judgment, Reformed preachers have often been clearer than the theologians. Spurgeon is typical:

> I believe in predestination, yea, even in its very jots and tittles. I believe that the path of a single grain of dust in the March wind is ordained and settled by a decree which cannot be violated; that every word and thought of man, every flittering of a sparrow's wing, every flight of a fly . . . that everything, in fact is foreknown and foreordained. But I do equally believe in the free agency of man, that man acts as he wills, especially in moral operations—choosing the evil with a will that is unbiased by anything that comes from God, biased only by his own depravity of heart and the perverseness of his habits; choosing the right too, with perfect freedom, though sacredly guided and led by the Holy Spirit. . . . I believe that man is

---

[2] John Murray, "Covenant Theology," in *Collected Writings* (Carlisle, Penn.: Banner of Truth, 1982), 4:216–240.

as accountable as if there were no destiny whatever. . . . Where these two truths meet I do not know, nor do I want to know. They do not puzzle me, since I have given up my mind to believing them both."[3]

Charles Simeon is better still. Speaking about the age-old controversy regarding grace and free will, he writes:

> I love the simplicity of the Scriptures; and I wish to receive and inculcate every truth precisely in the way, and to the extent, that it is set forth in the inspired volume. . . . I have a great jealousy on this head; never to speak more or less than I believe to be the mind of the Spirit in the passage I am expounding. . . . I would run after nothing and shun nothing. . . . [T]he truth is not in the middle, and not in one extreme, but in both extremes."[4]

Therefore, as we confess from the heart that man's salvation, from first to last, in all the links of the chain, is the gift and the work of God alone, so also we confess that in that salvation man is a free and

---

[3] *Metropolitan Tabernacle Pulpit,* 15:458; qtd. in Ian Murray, *Spurgeon v. Hyper-Calvinism: The Battle for Gospel Preaching* (Edinburgh: Banner of Truth, 1995), 82–83.

[4] H.C.G. Moule, *Charles Simeon* (London: InterVarsity, 1952), 77. Simeon goes on to say, "Of this [I am] sure, that there is not a decided Calvinist or Arminian in the world who equally approves of the whole of Scripture . . . who, if he had been in the company of St. Paul whilst he was writing his Epistles, would not have recommended him to alter one or other of his expressions" (79). The extraordinarily perceptive John Duncan, the celebrated "Rabbi" Duncan of nineteenth-century Scottish Presbyterianism, had a knack for putting things in a fresh and memorable way. On this point he remarked, "That God works half and man the other half, is false; that God works all, and man does all, is true" (W. Knight, ed., *Colloquia Peripatetica: Notes of Conversations with John Duncan* [Edinburgh, 1907], 29–30, qtd. in Murray, *Spurgeon v. Hyper-Calvinism*, 84). In another place Duncan explains the genius and the necessity of this biblical pedagogy that leaves us holding two truths in active tension. "Preach the antinomies of truth, and carry each out as far as it is possible to carry it. But don't attempt to reconcile them. These lines [and we are shown two lines that look almost parallel to one another] will meet if produced far enough. But if I try to make them meet, I give one or other of them a twist, and so reduce it from being a straight line. If the stones of the arch were to become animated and speak, the stones on the right hand would say, 'Right-hand pressure is right pressure;' and the stones on the left hand would say, 'left-hand pressure is right pressure;' but by pressing in opposite directions they keep up the keystone of the arch" (qtd. in A. Moody Stuart, *The Life of John Duncan* [Edinburgh: Banner of Truth, 1991], 212).

responsible agent whose faith, repentance, and perseverance are essential conditions of its fulfillment. As Augustine somewhere says, "Qui fecit nos sine nobis, non salvabit nos sine nobis."[5]

While the tension between divine sovereignty and human responsibility may be thought a commonplace of Reformed and covenantal theology, in my experience it is necessary to point out how emphatically the contingency that attaches to the gospel, the covenant, and the Christian life is taught in Holy Scripture. There is an entirely understandable fear that a pointed assertion of a real "if . . . then" in the covenant would subtly but inevitably undermine the church's confidence in the sovereignty of grace and reintroduce works through the back door. If we talk too much about what man must do "or else," if we hold before him the promises that will be fulfilled if and only if he is faithful, will it not be hard for us to continue to believe that God does and must do all? Furthermore, *sola gratia* is a doctrine so gloriously captivating that it is no surprise that a kind of spiritual prejudice would arise against teaching that in any way might be thought to diminish it. Genuine as those dangers are and justifiable as that allegiance to God's grace is, loyalty to Holy Scripture requires us to state the conditionality of the covenant in terms as absolute and unqualified as those used numerous times in the Bible itself.

> *There is an entirely understandable fear that a pointed assertion of a real if/then in the covenant would undermine the Church's confidence in the sovereignty of grace and reintroduce works through the back door.*

Everyone knows, of course, how often and through what large tracts of the Bible's teaching God is said to be dealing with man *according to what he has done*. But there is more. When the apostle Paul,

---

[5] "He who made us without us, will not save us without us" (qtd. in G. Wainwright, *Doxology: The Praise of God in Worship, Doctrine, and Life* [New York: Oxford Univ. Press, 1980], 490). Wainwright mentions in an associated note that "John Wesley liked to quote this (uncharacteristically?) augustinian phrase: see, for instance, the sermon 'On Working out Our Own Salvation,' I, i."

of all people, the champion of justification by faith, of the election of grace, and of the indefectibility of God's saving love, says that he beats his body and makes it his slave lest having preached to others he himself be disqualified for the prize (1 Cor. 9:27), or when he warns a community of believers not to receive the grace of God in vain (2 Cor. 6:1), or when he lays himself under great and solemn obligation so that "somehow" he might attain to the resurrection of the dead (Phil. 3:11), we are face to face with a spiritual viewpoint that every pastor knows is not adequately represented in his own heart or in the hearts of his congregation. When the scenes of the last judgment in the New Testament invariably cast the separation of human beings and the discrimination between them within their respective classes in terms of their behavior (e.g. Mt. 7:21–23; 25:1–46; Jn. 5:28–29; 1 Cor. 3:10–15; 2 Cor. 5:10; Phil. 4:17; Rev. 20:13; 22:12), no honest reader of the Bible will deny the considerable weight that is placed by Holy Scripture on the importance of faith and obedience for the issue of life. And when, time and again, the Bible traces spiritual outcomes back to the faithfulness or unfaithfulness of an individual or people, we can scarcely deny that real contingency is woven into human life and that human actions are real causes. When strong emotions are attributed to the Lord in response to the fidelity or infidelity of His people or the wickedness of unbelievers (Gen. 6:6; Eph. 4:30), we are forbidden to treat the Bible's universal assertion of the real contingency of human life, within or without the covenant, as a mere artifice.

If the sovereignty of divine grace, and the absolute dependence of sinners upon it, is sometimes stated in the Bible in terms so unqualified that they seem almost calculated to offend, no less is this true of human responsibility. What are we to think when a book that lays all men in the dust, pronounces them guilty before a holy God, affirms they are hopeless apart from God's mercy joined with God's power, and relentlessly exposes the continuing sinfulness of even the most devout—what are we to think when this same book artlessly describes believers as "righteous" (2 Pet. 2:8), "blameless" (Ps. 26:1), "worthy of the kingdom of God" (Lk. 20:35; 2 Thes. 1:5; Rev. 3:4), and "deserving" of the gospel (Mt. 10:13)?

Contingency and Covenant Succession

It should not surprise us, then, that the doctrine of covenant succession, as a division of biblical soteriology, inevitably partakes of this same divine/human polarity. The salvation of the church's children occurs as much in the interplay between a divinely ordered destiny and the believer's exercise of his responsibility as does the salvation of adults drawn out of the unbelieving world. There can be no doubt that the children of believers owe their salvation ultimately to the same divine election, the same predestined grace, and the same discriminating love of God that reaches down to deliver any other human being from sin and death (Rom. 9:10–13). But it is made equally certain in the teaching of the Word of God that the salvation of those children is suspended on conditions to be met first by their parents (together with their ministers and churches) and then by the children themselves as they grow up to responsible adulthood. In other words, the doctrine of covenant succession, as a subset of biblical soteriology, is entirely characteristic. Here too, free will is the *modus operandi* of destiny.

The Bible describes the way of salvation in many dimensions and with many terms, providing a diverse witness to the real contingency of the covenanted gospel as it embraces the children of the church. There are a great many texts that set forth the obligations of parental nurture (e.g., Deut. 6:7–9; Eph. 6:4), but no obligations are ever laid down in the covenant for which there are no corresponding blessings promised to those who live faithfully. And so, not unexpectedly, there are many more texts that explicitly connect the fulfillment of those parental obligations to the salvation of children, both positively (e.g., Gen. 18:19; Deut. 5:29; Ps. 78:1–8; 112:1–2; Prov. 22:6; Is. 59:19–21) and negatively (e.g., Exod. 20:5; 1 Sam. 2:29; 1 Kgs. 1:6; Tit. 1:6).

Even the layered contingency we encounter in this material is typical of the pattern of biblical soteriology. That others may bear a portion of the responsibility for the belief or unbelief of another, who still retains primary responsibility, is a biblical commonplace. That parents bear a responsibility for the salvation of their children, parental nurture is an instrumentality of that salvation, and divine promises attach to parental faithfulness are truths very like the direct connection the Bible repeatedly draws between faithful ministry and the salvation of God's people (e.g., Mal. 2:6; 1 Tim. 4:16) or the necessity of witness and preaching for the ingathering of God's elect (e.g., Rom. 10:14). The want of the instruments does not excuse unbelief and rebellion, but it is not the case that only the faith of the individual is a necessary condition of his or her salvation (e.g., Mk. 2:5).[6]

> *No obligations are ever laid down in the covenant for which there are no corresponding blessings promised to those who live faithfully.*

This real contingency or conditionality in the covenant as it bears on the salvation of the church's children is stated so categorically, so frequently, and is elaborated in so many different ways that, understandably, in robustly biblical Reformed theology the assertion of some connection between means and ends has not been in itself controversial. That conditions are laid upon parents to nurture their children in the faith, that the salvation of covenant children is in some way suspended upon the fulfillment of those conditions, that the connection between faithfulness on the part of parents and the salvation of their children is illustrated both positively and negatively

---

[6] In the Reformed system, faith is the only condition of justification not the only condition of salvation (holiness, perseverance, etc.) even for the individual believer. My point here, of course, is that in the economy of God the work of others can be a necessary condition of salvation (the parent's nurture, the preacher's preaching, the witness's gospel presentation, and so on). To say that faith in Jesus Christ is the condition of a sinner's justification before God, as Paul says in Romans 10:5–13, is not to say that the proclamation of the gospel is not essential to summoning up that faith in the hearts of the elect, as Paul goes on to say in verses 14–15.

in the Bible can scarcely be denied and is not denied by our Reformed authorities. Quite the contrary: the assertion of the sacred respon-sibility of parents in the covenant to raise their children in the nur-ture and admonition of the Lord is a characteristic of Reformed spiritual writing. You can find it in the magisterial reformers, the scholastics, the men of Dutch and English Puritanism, and the Ameri-can Presbyterians. It was the inevitable consequence of the Reformed doctrines of church membership of covenant children, the prospect of the seed of faith already planted in the hearts of covenant infants, the presumption of their salvation, and the practice of infant bap-tism.[7]

Contingency Denied or Diminished

Problems and hesitations surface, however, when it is felt necessary to reconcile this contingency, however emphatically taught in the Bible, with the counter-emphasis on sovereign grace. Does suspend-ing the salvation of the church's children on the faithfulness of their nurture betray *sola gratia*? Does making parents in some way account-able for the salvation of their children amount to a reintroduction of works through the back door? Given that the tension produced by the Bible's double emphasis on divine grace and human accountability is inevitable because of the polarity in the presentation of salvation in Holy Scripture, it should come as no surprise that it surfaces here, as it surfaces at every other point where grace and freedom are coun-terpoised. Nor should it be surprising that the concerns that arise out of that tension concerning the salvation of the church's children are those very concerns that inevitably surface at the intersection of di-vine grace and human responsibility.

---

[7] A summary of Reformed views on this point can be found in H. Bavinck, *Gerefor-meerde Dogmatiek*, vol. 4 (Kampen: J. H. Kok, 1918), 31–35; 42–48; 116; A. Kuyper, *Dictaten Dogmatiek,* vol. 4, (Kampen: J. H. Kok, n.d.), 136–151; E.C. Gravemeijer, *Leesboek over de Gereformeerde Geloofsleer,* vol. 3 (Utrecht: H. Ten Hoove, 1894), 429–434; and Lewis Bevens Schenck, *The Presbyterian Doctrine of Children in the Covenant* (New Ha-ven: Yale Univ. Press, 1940).

In Reformed theology there has always been the intention to be faithful to the Bible's double emphasis on destiny and contingency, but how to state the biblical teaching and how to understand the interrelationship of these two realities have been matters of long-standing disagreement. No wonder, then, that there should be similar debates in Reformed theology regarding the nature and ground of infant baptism and the nature of the conditions of the covenant as it embraces children born into it.[8] If the history of theology proves anything, it is that destiny and contingency are spark and powder. It is impossible to deny that God's covenant with His people, to be their God and the God of their children, as an instrument mediating salvation, has both destiny and contingency thoroughly woven through it. Nothing is more characteristic of the revelation of God's covenant of grace in Holy Scripture than its origin and foundation in the discriminating grace of God and the immutable love of God for His chosen people. But the Bible is no less emphatic in insisting upon the necessity of our meeting the conditions of the covenant in order to obtain its benefits. We are left, as the great preachers always left us, needing to confess salvation *sola gratia* on the one hand and the reality of a real *arbitrium liberum*, a genuine and consequential accountability, on the other.

We certainly do not wish to deny that grace comes first, or that it is precisely the consciousness of this divine grace in the heart that animates a believer's faith and obedience as God's covenant partner.

---

[8] In recent years, the discussion of this doctrine of covenant succession in American Reformed circles has been largely inchoate; there is little literature and the doctrine has not surfaced as a matter of serious dispute. This has not been so in Dutch Reformed Christianity, in which the debates concerning this doctrine in its various parts have been conducted at length, with learning, and to the considerable unrest of the churches. See E. Smilde, *Een Eeuw van Strijd over Verbond en Doop* (Kampen: J. H. Kok, 1946) and J. van Genderen, *Verbond en Verkiezing* (Kampen: J. H. Kok, 1983); the latter has been translated by C. Pronk as *Covenant and Election* (Neerlandia, AB: 1995). For the American debate, which largely ended as a matter of public interest in the nineteenth century, see Schenck, *Children in the Covenant*. The Dutch have done the heavy lifting necessary to lay the foundation, build the structure, and even finish the doctrine properly, though nothing like a consensus has been reached. The Americans have much catching up to do.

However, no less can we deny the real "if . . . then" by which the blessings of the covenant are limited to those who are faithful. And among those conditions that must be met are some that bear directly and absolutely on the fulfillment of the promise of God's covenant that He would be the God of His people's children.

That there is such a promise to be claimed was put "more fear-lessly" by the earlier representatives of covenant theology.[9] A less "fearless" approach is often taken by Reformed writers and preach-ers today. Conscious of the fact, also comprehensively demonstrated in the Bible, that all covenant children are not eventually saved, many now prefer to say only that there is a holy seed to be found among the seed of believers and it is for those elect children only for whom the covenantal promises hold without limitation.[10]

---

[9] G. Vos, "The Doctrine of the Covenant in Reformed Theology" in *Redemptive History and Biblical Interpretation,* ed. by Richard B. Gaffin, Jr. (Phillipsburg: Presbyterian and Reformed, 1980), 263.

[10] Vos, "The Doctrine of the Covenant," 264. Vos cites the seventeenth-century Zurich theologian J. H. Heidegger, whose opinion was, "Not to all the children of believers particularly, but only to the elect, baptism seals regeneration and the total contents of spiritual grace. Though it is good and proper to hope for the best for each one in par-ticular according to the judgment of love, it is not permitted in regard to all collectively." By itself, that judgment might be taken as nothing more than a truism. Obviously not all covenant children are saved. However, once it is admitted that precisely the same could be said of adult Christians (and certainly of all who enter the church in adulthood by profession of faith)—i.e., that they are to be treated as Christians as a class on the basis of their membership in the church but that no one can say for certain that any or all of them are in fact regenerate and in possession eternal life (a point Heidegger him-self acknowledges in the same place)—what has been said? Certainly nothing to sug-gest that the connection between means and ends is less certain in the case of covenant children than adult professors. Certainly nothing to suggest that the promise made to covenant children is of a different class, or that it possesses some lesser measure of cer-titude, than the promise made to adults who profess faith. Charles Hodge wrote of cov-enant children, "We do not assert their regeneration, or that they are true members of Christ's body; we only assert that they belong to the class of persons whom we are bound to regard and treat as members of Christ's Church. This is the only sense in which even adults are members of the Church, so far as men are concerned" ("The General Assem-bly," *Biblical Repertory and Princeton Review* 20: 351). On the whole, however, we do not accept that the Bible teaches us to regard the promises of the covenant as limited by unmentioned qualifications. The promise of salvation is made to believers and to their children. But its fulfillment, in the case of both, is suspended upon the meeting of various

Plainly, the Scripture does not explicitly say this. The promise given and often repeated is that God will be our God and the God of our children. "To be our God" is the Bible's way to comprehend the whole of eternal salvation in the fewest words (Eph. 2:12; Rev. 21:3). In its other characteristic formulations, the promise to believers' children is emphatically a promise of salvation. God promises to extend to them His righteousness (Ps. 103:17), His Spirit (Is. 59:21), His forgiveness (Acts 2:38–39), and His salvation (Acts 16:31). The covenant that embraces our children is the covenant *of grace.*

A less "fearless" approach to covenant theology is often taken by Reformed writers and preachers today.

As we would expect, however, conditions are attached to the fulfillment of this promise along the way. God's promises in the Bible are, almost without exception, condition-laden. It would seem, therefore, more faithful to the teaching of the Bible simply to say that the promises of the covenant hold for those who meet the conditions attached to them.[11] That such conditions can be met only

---

conditions. This is the nature of the gospel and the covenant from beginning to end. It is upon the real contingency of the fulfillment of those promises that biblical emphasis so often falls. It is certainly easy enough to demonstrate that Reformed theology in its formative period held that baptism was to be given to covenant infants precisely because, according to the covenant, the things signified therein belonged or pertained to them. See, for example, Calvin's *Institutes* (Philadelphia: Westminster, 1960), IV.xvi.5, 19, 20; and Turretin's *Institutes* (Philadelphia: Presbyterian and Reformed, 1992) vol. 3, XIX.xx (pp. 415–416).

[11] "It is to be remembered that these promises are conditional. God has never promised to make no distinction between faithful and unfaithful parents, between those who bring up their offspring in the nurture of the Lord, and those who utterly neglect their religious training. The condition, which from the nature of the case is implied in the promise, is in many cases expressly stated. His promise is to those who keep his covenant, and to those who remember his commandments to do them. It is involved in the very nature of a covenant that it should have conditions. And although in one important sense, the conditions of the covenant of grace have been performed by Christ, still its promises are suspended on conditions to be performed by or in his people. And this is expressly declared to be the case with regard to the promise of the divine blessing to the children of believers. They must keep his covenant. They must train up their children for God. They must use the means which he has appointed for their conversion and sanctification or the promise does not apply to them" (Charles Hodge, "Bushnell on

by divine grace is not to be doubted, but that is not the point here. The question is whether there is a real promise made to all believers and to all their children that may be claimed by faith and obedience. Those who answer that there is not must argue in one of several ways that God has made no sure promise of salvation to all covenant children.

Those who deny a real promise of salvation made in the covenant to every child born to Christian parents argue in one of three ways. Some hold that the promise of the covenant is made, in fact, only to elect infants and not to Christians' children generally. Others maintain that the promise made in the covenant is not a promise of salvation but only of privilege. Finally, others argue that the promise is to be taken as a generality, that is, that it holds in many, if not most cases, but cannot be claimed to hold in all. The first is the recourse of hyper-Calvinists of whom Herman Hoeksema is a recent representative. The second is a view made popular among Southern Presbyterians, having been championed by James Henley Thornwell and Robert Dabney. The third is the view of a number of popular writers and has the support of Charles Hodge.

In the first instance the argument offered is a deduction from the fact of sovereign grace and is of a piece with the practical denial of real contingency everywhere in the covenant of grace, and so also is of a piece with the denial of the free offer of the gospel. They reason that to argue that God has promised anything to children who do not come to faith and go to heaven is to open the door to Arminianism. To suspend the fulfillment of salvation on the faithfulness of man is to deny both man's inability and God's grace. God's

---

Christian Nurture," *Biblical Repertory and Princeton Review* 19, no. 4: 505–506). "He will be true to his own covenants. It is in Zion that the children of the Church are born to newness of life. Since He has promised to be their God, it is in training them as if they were his; as if it were alone congruous with their position to walk as his children in faith, love, hope, and all holy obedience, that we are to look for that inworking Spirit, and outworking holiness, commensurate with their years, which shall seal them as sons and daughters of the Lord Almighty" (Lyman Atwater, "The Children of the Church and Sealing Ordinances," *Biblical Repertory and Princeton Review* 29, no. 1: 16–17).

grace is always particular and so, therefore, must be His promises.[12] The promise must be ultimately unconditional. If there are no conditions then there is no real offer made to parents or to children, except in the case of the elect. It lies beyond the province of this essay to offer a critique of such views of the covenant and its promise to children.[13] It is enough to say that this view has always remained a decidedly minority position in the Reformed church precisely because it does not faithfully reproduce the Bible's own way of speaking. The promise is universally given in Holy Scripture to believers and their children. A summons is attached. The fulfillment of the promise is suspended upon the fulfillment

> *If there are no conditions then there is no real offer made to parents or children, except in the case of the elect.*

of the conditions. That is everywhere the Bible's approach. Divine grace does not abolish conditions; rather, it sees to their fulfillment. Grace is necessary *precisely because* conditions must be fulfilled. In Holy Scripture people *in the church* are lost not because no promise was made to them, but because they failed to obtain what was promised for want of faith and obedience (e.g., Heb. 3:12, 18–19; 4:1–11).

Thornwell and Dabney, on the other hand, operating with an understanding of salvation shaped by the Great Awakening, see the promise as one not of salvation *per se* but of privilege, the privilege

---

[12] Hoeksema's argument reduces to this: "The promise of God in the preaching of the gospel is either unconditional, or it is impossible of realization" (qtd. in A. C. De Jong, *The Well-Meant Gospel Offer: The Views of H. Hoeksema and K. Schilder* (Franeker: T. Wever, 1954), 43. See Hoeksema's *Believers and their Seed* (Grand Rapids: Reformed Free Publishing Association, 1971).

[13] For a critique of such views consult De Jong, *The Well-Meant Offer*; John Murray and Ned Stonehouse, *The Free Offer of the Gospel* (Nutley, N.J.: Presbyterian and Reformed, 1977); C. Veenhof, *Prediking en Uitverkiezing* (Kampen: J. H. Kok, 1959); J. van Genderen, *Verbond en Verkiezing*; Murray, *Spurgeon v. Hyper-Calvinism*. It is interesting and important to observe how closely bound together are the questions of the well-meant gospel offer and the nature of the promise made to children in the covenant. The answer one gives to the former is often the same answer one gives to the latter, wittingly or unwittingly, because both depend in the same way on how one construes the relationship between promise and conditions in the covenant or gospel.

of growing up in the church, under the Word, surrounded by Christian influences. Once again, election trumps covenant. So much is this the case that in this view, contrary to the central tradition of Reformed theology descending from Calvin, the children of Christians are not even to be regarded as Christians until they profess faith. The presumption that covenant children are *unregenerate* until they prove the contrary cannot but mean that the covenant offers salvation to the church's children in only some seriously marginalized way. That baptized covenant children should be described, as Thornwell describes them, only as *quasi*-members of the church, that they should be regarded as *in* the church but *of* the world, and that evangelism and not nurture should be the paradigm of their upbringing turns the simple and straightforward instruction of the Bible on its head. The promise is thus offered with one hand and withdrawn with the other.[14]

This is, however, in my judgment, the most common view held in Reformed churches at present. I don't say that it is a view consciously chosen or one likely to be thoughtfully defended. It is simply where one is left if a commitment to paedobaptism is jointly held with a revivalist and voluntarist view of salvation. If one thinks of salvation in terms of a conversion experience, as most of American evangelicalism does, including that of the Reformed type, it becomes difficult to maintain the special place of covenant children in the church and hard to imagine just what might be meant by a promise of salvation made to infants. There is a promise in the covenant, but it is a vague promise of uncertain meaning, not the same definite promise embraced by the adult believer. Somehow, it is thought, provision must be made for the covenant children who

> *Divine grace does not abolish conditions; it sees to their fulfillment.*

---

[14] For a presentation and critique of the views of Thornwell and Dabney, see Schenck, *Children in the Covenant*; R. S. Rayburn, "The Presbyterian Doctrines of Covenant Children, Covenant Nurture, and Covenant Succession," *Presbyterion* 22, no. 2 (fall 1996): 76–109.

grow up in unbelief and are not saved. The best way to do this, so it seems, is to reconstrue the promise to children as a promise of a privileged upbringing only, not as the promise of eternal life.

Because, however, precisely the same problem applies to the case of adult professors, some of whom likewise will not attain to eternal life, this solution solves nothing. We are still left with a promise that is suspended upon conditions. When the conditions are met the promise is fulfilled, whether we are talking about the nurture of children in a covenant home or an adult responding to the offer of salvation in the gospel. At least the hyper-Calvinistic approach to the promise of salvation in the covenant has the advantage of taking the promise in the same way for children and adults. After all, the Bible puts it in the very same words and the very same breath to both adults and infant children. For Hoeksema, for example, it is the same whether we are speaking of adults or children: there is a real promise made only to the elect. Thornwell and Dabney, however, treat the promise to children in a different way than the promise to adults. The same words spoken in the same way in the Bible—"I will be a God to you and to your children"—mean salvation for the adult who believes, but merely a privileged upbringing for the infant child of Christian parents.

There is a third way to qualify or relativize the apparent contingency that attaches to the promise of the covenant. Rather than limit the scope of the promise to the elect or the substance of the promise to that of privilege only, the real contingency of gospel and covenant, so far as the children of believers are concerned, is diminished by *generalizing* the promise and its conditions. In this case, the conditions for the fulfillment of the covenant promise regarding covenant children are distinguished from other such gospel conditions and treated proverbially. It is not denied that the condition of faithful parental nurture is attached to the covenant promise, but it is argued that while faithful parental nurture is *an* instrument by which children are in many cases and perhaps usually brought to living faith, it is not uniformly the case that such nurture always secures that happy result.[15] It is certainly true that the importance of the godly nurture of covenant children is an emphasis in Proverbs and that the connection between means and ends is stated there quite frankly. It is also true that sometimes the proverbs are in fact statements that are only *proverbially true*. It is not, for example, by the Bible's own express testimony, invariably true that "When a man's ways are pleasing to the Lord, he makes even his enemies live at peace with him" (16:7). While that may be proverbially true, the life of the Lord Jesus and that of the martyrs is proof that it is not always true. So, it is argued, we should think similarly of "Train a child in the way he should go, and when he is old he will not turn from it" (22:6) or "Punish him with the rod and save his soul from death" (23:14). In this way it is possible to argue that the faithful nurture of children is very important and may well contribute to their salvation, and it is

---

[15] Such is the way in which the conditions are treated in popular works such as Bruce Ray's *Withhold Not Correction* (Phillipsburg: Presbyterian and Reformed, 1978), 67; and John R. De Witt's *Amazing Love* (Edinburgh: Banner of Truth, 1981), 23–24. Interestingly, Charles Hodge, Thornwell's opponent in the discussions about the place of the children of the covenant in the economy of grace that took place in nineteenth-century American Presbyterianism, at some points took a similar position. He too argued, very inconsistently in my judgment, that the promise "is general; expressing what is to be the general course of events, and not what is to be the result in every particular case." He offers two proofs. First, "when God promised that summer and winter, seed time and harvest should succeed each other to the end of time, he did not pledge himself that there never should be a failure in this succession, that a famine should never occur, or that the expectations of the husbandman should never be disappointed." But that is to mistake the nature of the promise God made in Gen. 8:22. He is not promising there unending harvests, but rather the uninterrupted continuation of times and seasons, the continuation, that is, of human history until the end of the world. There will never again be such a judgment as a flood. There is nothing "general" about that promise. It is absolute, it is not suspended upon conditions, and has been proved so ever since. It is very hard to see how, taking the promise of Gen. 8:22 as merely "general," any promise of God's Word can be understood to hold in all cases. Hodge's second argument is taken from Prov. 22:6 and thus amounts to a begging of the question ("Bushnell on Christian Nurture," 505–506). The fact remains that no other gospel promise, no other promise of salvation such as is made in the covenant to believers and their seed, is taken to be merely "general," that is, expressing "the tendency and ordinary result" of faithfulness on man's part. This is not the way the Bible provides for the failure to obtain the promise. It does not "generalize" the promise; it suspends it upon conditions.

possible to accept that there is a basis for the Bible's connecting a failure of nurture to the spiritual death of certain children *without having to argue that such a connection exists in every case.*

However, it is by no means true that all or even most of the teaching of Proverbs is proverbial in the sense of being only widely or generally true. That is especially the case with those proverbs that contain what we might call *theological* truth, that is, truth that is taught first and foremost in those parts of the Bible that set forth its doctrine regarding God, man, and salvation. For example, it is certainly no mere proverb that "the lot is cast into the lap, but its every decision is from the Lord" (16:33) or that "the Lord works out everything for his own ends—even the wicked for a day of disaster" (16:4). We know those statements are not merely proverbial truths—that is, usually but not necessarily always true—because absolute divine sovereignty is taught everywhere

> *Do we dare say that there is such a thing as blameless nurture? This is the great scandal of the doctrine of covenant succession.*

in the Bible and is an important feature of its doctrine of God and His works. In the same way, the material regarding covenant children, their nurture, and the hope that springs from that nurture is taught everywhere in the Bible and especially in those great texts which lay down the Bible's doctrine of the covenant, the place of our children in the covenant, and the promise and the means of their salvation.

What is more, no one proposes to treat as merely proverbial other gospel or covenantal promises with their conditions. No one suggests that it would be faithful to Holy Scripture to say to the unsaved: "Believe on the Lord Jesus Christ and *there is a strong possibility* that you and your house will be saved," or "If you confess with your mouth, 'Jesus is Lord,' and believe in your heart that God raised Him from the dead, *there is a great likelihood* that you will be saved." This is not the way the Bible makes its promises of life; it is not the way the Bible connects those promises to their conditions. What all these alternative proposals lack is any clear biblical demonstration. What we see in the Bible, repeatedly and emphatically, positively and negatively, consistently and systematically, is a real promise of salvation made to believers and their children, a promise suspended upon the fulfillment of conditions.

The Faithful Nurture of Covenant Children

But, it will be asked, how can one speak of the fulfillment of such a condition? How can it be imagined that any parent, Christian though he or she be, is adequate for these things? Can we imagine that parents have really nurtured their children so well that they have fulfilled the divine summons to raise their children in the nurture and admonition of the Lord and have, for that reason, obtained what was promised? Is not every devout parent all too conscious of his failures, in how many ways he has not taught or disciplined his children as he should have, in how many ways he has not set the example of godliness for his children that he should have? Does not every devout parent cringe when he thinks of how many ways he has failed his children? Do we dare say that there is such a thing as blameless nurture? Would anyone dare claim to

> *If we deny the possibility of a faithful nurture of covenant children, we have embraced a way of thinking that must prove fatal to our entire understanding of salvation and the gospel.*

have provided it? If there is such a thing, does it imply in some way that parents have "earned" their children's salvation? Are we not then resting the salvation of covenant children on the "goodness" of their parents? I have been asked these questions so often that it has become clear to me that, practically speaking, this is the great scandal of the doctrine of covenant succession.[16] It is also proof to me that a super-

---

[16] I use the term "scandal" in the sense that the scandals of the doctrine of sovereign grace are the perceptions of God's injustice and the nullification of the human will, or that the scandal of the doctrine of justification by faith is its seeming consequence of undermining holy living.

ficial understanding of the conditionality of the gospel and the covenant is a significant defect in contemporary Reformed preaching and spirituality. For the fact is that if we deny the possibility of a faithful nurture of covenant children, we have embraced a way of thinking that must prove fatal to our entire understanding of salvation and the gospel.

First, the problem of such a blameless nurture of covenant children, that is, a nurture that satisfies the condition laid down in the covenant for the fulfillment of its promise, is the problem we encounter with every gospel condition. We take this one so seriously and imagine its burden to be so intolerable perhaps only because we have been allowed to consider the others too superficially. In fact, whether we are talking about the faith that obtains justification or the holiness necessary "to see the Lord," the devout are faced with the same problem. Who is adequate for these things? The godly man knows very well how imperfectly, inconstantly, and half-heartedly he believes. He knows how often it is not obvious that faith is the animating principle of his life. What faithful Christian does not regret that he does not live moment by moment in the sure and certain conviction of the Lord's presence, immutable love, and forgiveness, as well as the prospect of eternal joy, the inevitable reckoning when he must stand before the judgment seat of Christ and give an account of the deeds done in the body, whether good or evil, and receive what is due him (2 Cor. 5:10)? Where, we must ask all too often, is our faith? And, regarding holiness of life, what believer has not staggered before the Lord's warning that "Not everyone who says to me, 'Lord, Lord,' will enter the kingdom of heaven, but only he who does the will of My Father who is in heaven" (Mt. 7:21)? Similar responsibilities are laid upon us when it comes to the salvation of others. What faithful minister thinks himself to have so closely watched his life and his doctrine that he has become a fit instrument of the salvation of his hearers (1 Tim. 4:16)? What minister is ready to say with Paul that he is innocent of the blood of all men, so faithfully, tirelessly, and zealously has he conducted his ministry among them? To nurture covenant children in faith, hope, and love is a gospel condition no more demanding than the other conditions laid upon us in the covenant of grace. If it is impossible of fulfillment, so are they.

Second, the condition of faithful parental nurture is, like all other conditions by which the promises of God's covenant are realized, *a gospel condition*. That is, what believers do in obedience to God's summons is made effective not by the perfection of their obedience but by the condescension of God. The faithful nurture of children, as blameless faith or blameless obedience, is not perfect by any means. When David appeals to God for vindication because he has lived in integrity (Ps. 26:1; 2 Sam. 22:21–25), he is certainly making no claim to sinlessness. And when it is said that an elder must be above reproach, it is certainly not suggested that such a man does not remain a sinner. It is not sinless nurture any more than the faith by which we obtain the forgiveness of our sins is sinless faith or the holiness by which we see

> *It is undeniable that many devout people have been unfaithful parents.*

God is a sinless holiness. The entire Bible bears witness to the fact that God counts as living faith and true obedience what is manifestly very far from sinless or perfect faith and obedience. The Lord, in His grace, treats this imperfect faith and obedience a great deal better than they deserve.

Third, the faithful people of God can fail at one place or another in the Christian life while succeeding at others. When we are told in Holy Scripture that David had been a faithful man "except in the case of Uriah the Hittite" (1 Kgs.15:5), we are being taught that a devout life can be marred by discrete failures and the consequences that ensue. Faithful Christians can fail miserably at marital faithfulness or sexual purity, at the stewardship of money or the controlling of one's temper, at telling the truth or moderating one's appetite. Surely they can also fail in ways that bear directly on the nurture that believing parents are to provide for their covenant children. They can be indifferent teachers and let the culture have its way with their children.

They can be ineffective or harsh disciplinarians. They can teach and discipline consistently but set a bad example. Such failures are pointed out in the cases of Isaac, Jacob, Eli, David, and, I would say, Hezekiah, and are directly connected to horrific consequences in the lives of the children of these devout men. When we are told that to be qualified for the office of elder a man must have believing children, we are given to understand that otherwise good men may be disqualified for a particular failure on their part.[17] It is undeniable that many devout people have been unfaithful parents. The Bible says so often enough to require us to accommodate this fact into our understanding of the covenant and its consequences in the lives of our children.

Fourth, the Lord's judgment of life is an impenetrable mystery. He judges the motives and the actions of each of His children with an infinite knowledge and perfect justice. When the Lord says, "to whom much is given, much is required," we learn that His judgment of any believer's behavior is adjusted to reflect factors that bear on the measure of his accountability. While the general principles of faithful covenant nurture are common to all parents, specific parental

---

[17] In Titus 1:6 (see also Hagopian's essay in this volume for a fuller look at this important verse) Paul uses the adjective *pistos* (faithful, believing) rather than the participle. The authorities almost universally agree that, as used in Titus 1:6, it means "believing (in Christ)" or "simply means 'Christian'" (Walter Bauer, *A Greek-English Lexicon of the New Testament and Other Early Christian Literature*, trans. William F. Arndt and F. Wilbur Gingrich [Chicago: Univ. of Chicago Press, 1979], 665; and Rudolf Bultmann, *Theological Dictionary of the New Testament*, 10 vols., ed. Gerhard Kittel and Gerhard Friedrich, trans. Geoffrey W. Bromiley (Grand Rapids: Eerdmans, 1988 [1968]), 6:215, n. 311). Almost all modern English versions render Paul's meaning as "children who believe" or "children who are believers" (NIV, NASB, NEB, RSV, ESV). The case for reading the adjective in the passive sense as "faithful" and taking it to mean "obedient" and "submissive" is given by George Knight, who argues that the parallel statement in 1 Timothy 3:4 ("He must see . . . that his children obey him with proper respect") defines the meaning of *pistos* in Titus 1:6. He points out that the meaning "faithful" is attested in the Pastoral Epistles as well, for example 2 Timothy 2:2 (*The Pastoral Epistles: A Commentary on the Greek Text,* NIGTC [Grand Rapids: Eerdmans, 1992], 289–290). First, were the apostle's intention to say merely that a man must have obedient and submissive children, terms were ready at hand that would have conveyed that meaning in a more precise and natural way than *pistos*. Indeed, he said exactly that in both 1 Timothy 3:4 and Titus 1:6 ("not open to the charge of being wild and disobedient"), but even some faithful children can be open to that charge. The cognate adverb of the noun "wildness" or "loose-

behavior that may constitute faithful nurture in one case may not in another. It remains utterly beyond the ability of even the wisest Christian to calculate the faithfulness of any parental nurture in the way that infinite knowledge, wisdom, goodness, justice, and love can. In my experience it is the fear of the assignment of blame more than anything else that dogs the discussion of covenant succession in the contemporary Reformed church. That Christian parents might in some significant measure be responsible for the spiritual death of their own children is a prospect so fearful and repugnant that it is not surprising to find an unwillingness to face it. Thus we observe a preference for theological (de)constructions of the covenant that seek to mitigate the connection between the faithfulness of parental nurture and the spiritual outcome of a child's life. I have had more than one

---

living" is used in Luke 15:13 of the prodigal's "riotous living." Far more importantly, such a usage of *pistos* is supremely unlikely, because it is against the entire drift of Paul's philosophy of life that he would describe the children of a Christian family as "faithful" who refused to subscribe to the Christian faith and who were, therefore, unsubmissive to their parents at the only ultimately important point, however outwardly dutiful they might otherwise appear. No use of the adjective faithful in Paul or the rest of the New Testament suggests that Paul would employ it of unrepentant, unbelieving children of Christian parents, whose unbelief is now a visible quality of life. Certainly it is not employed in 2 Timothy 2:2 in such a denatured sense. Alford is surely correct that *pistos* implies that these children were not only led to the faith but were established in the faith (*The Greek New Testament*, vol. 3, 5th ed. [Grand Rapids: Baker, 1980], 410). On the other hand, even if the statements regarding a man's children in the two lists of qualifications for the eldership are virtual equivalents, I say again that Paul should not be taken even in 1 Timothy 3:4 to mean that children who "obey [their father] with proper respect" might well be children who have no spiritual interest and display a filial obedience that is mere good manners and not a true submission to their Christian father's rule. Is mere outward docility what an elder is to seek and maintain in the behavior of Christians in the church? "And therefore let us marke that in this place, when hee speaketh of children, it is to the ende wee should marke whether a man be meete to governe the people of God, and to rule his house and his Church wel, and have shewed ye effect of it in his own house. Therefore if a man do not onely shew that he walketh in the fear of God, and absteineth from all evill, but also causeth them that are in his charge to serve and honour God . . . then we know that hee is watchfull, and hath a zeale of God, and wisedome and gravitie in him. . . . will hee bee able to bring strangers to the faith, when hee hath not brought his owne?" (Calvin, *Sermons on the Epistles to Timothy and Titus* [Edinburgh: Banner of Truth, 1983 (1579)], 1070–1071). "For he who could not bring his children to the faith, how shall he bring others?" (Bengel, *Gnomon Novi Testamenti*, editio tertia [Tübingen: 1855], 849). A man who is to oversee the faithfulness of the Christian church should have produced that faithfulness in his own house first.

minister balk at the very point where it becomes clear that the responsibility of nurture carries with it an inevitable accountability for the result. My experience in speaking of this matter with Christian people has confirmed many times that this is and will always remain a stumbling block in the way of embracing the Bible's doctrine of the succession of grace in the lines of generations.

The Bible, however, directly assigns this accountability to parents. What is more, it commends parental faithfulness as the appointed means for the spiritual blessing of their children. There is always the unmistakable implication that the failure to provide a proper nurture will be attended by the forfeiture of that blessing. What is everywhere implied is often enough directly asserted. However, many things we cannot judge. The Bible teaches that the individual is himself, first and foremost, accountable for his faith and life, no matter the faithfulness or unfaithfulness of his parents (Ezek. 18). Ministers and church leaders are also responsible for the nurture of the church and the spiritual welfare of her children (Jer. 2:8–9).[18] The condition of the church as a whole bears mightily on the spiritual outcome of an individual life (Judg. 2:10; 3:5–6).

In my experience it is the fear of the assignment of blame that more than anything else dogs the discussion of covenant succession in the contemporary Reformed church.

That many may share responsibility for the spiritual life or death of a covenant child does not mean, however, that those with the most immediate accountability should fail to acknowledge their primary

---

[18] In my judgment, the Christian ministry may regularly be more accountable for the loss of the church's children than the parents themselves, because it has not faithfully taught the parents of the church that there are promises to claim by faith on behalf of their children, and it has not taught them what faithful nurture consists of. It is worth noting that often in the Bible the blame for the spiritual declension of God's people is assigned generally to the ministry rather than to parents. It is true, of course, that blame is assigned to parents. But I have too often been told by Christian parents grieving the rebellion of one of their children that had they known then what they know now, they would never have raised their child the way they did.

responsibility. How God weighs each of these factors in the judgment of a life—a parent's life, a minister's life, or a child's life—is entirely beyond our knowing. Nevertheless, it is no part of godliness for a believer to seek to shift or to diminish his share of the responsibility laid upon him in God's covenant. When Eli, hearing of the impending judgment on his family and recognizing his complicity in the sins of his sons, says only, "He is the Lord; let Him do what is good in His eyes," we should learn that a parent's godliness in the face of the rebellion of his children takes the form of penitent submission, not quibbling over the apportionment of blame. It would be the worst sort of irony, and protest carried to its most dismal end, if the cherished hope, the rich comfort, and the motivation of love conveyed to us in the covenant's promise regarding the salvation of our children should be abandoned for fear that we may be blamed for a rebellious child.

Fifth, the Bible does in fact state unequivocally that this condition of faithful nurture is met and has often been met (e.g., Gen. 18:9, Tit. 1:6). Indeed, the simple implication of large tracts of the Bible's teaching on this theme is that multitudes upon multitudes of God's people have, through the ages, received just that sort of faithful nurture in their Christian homes. That

Most Christians in the history of the church have become Christians by means of faithful covenant nurture.

nurture was made, as promised in the covenant, the instrument of their coming to or growth in faith and their obtaining eternal life. Surely it is safe to say that most Christians in the history of the church have become Christians by this means.

In the Bible, the promises of the gospel are attached to conditions and the fulfillment of those promises is suspended upon the meeting of those conditions. This is true whether we are speaking of an adult believer or a covenant child. These conditions, perfectly suited to our nature as creatures made in the image of God, requiring the exercise of mind, heart, and will, are the divinely appointed means by which salvation comes to God's elect in a manner agreeable to the will of God. Divine grace ensures that the conditions are met on behalf of and by those who are being saved. *Soli Deo gloria!* That fact, however, does not in any way diminish the genuine contingency of the gospel and covenant, the real culpability of those who fail to meet the responsibilities laid upon them in the covenant, or the obvious importance of the fact that God intends His children's children to be saved *through* the godly nurture they receive in their homes.

Proverbs 22:6 and Covenant Succession: A Study of the Promissory Character of Biblical Wisdom

Nelson D. Kloosterman

When discussing the significance of the covenant of grace for child-rearing, Lewis Bevens Schenck summarized two biblical principles: (1) God expects that the faith of Christian parents will govern and direct family life, and (2) if parents are unfaithful (i.e., fail to fulfill this obligation of the covenant), then they have no right to expect any divine blessing and benefit.[1] The converse of (2) is that if parents are faithful in child-rearing, then they may, on the basis of God's own promise, expect His blessing upon their children. At the heart of this covenant relationship is the divine gift of grace, which alone creates and sustains the response of faith. Moreover, this continual trusting in God's promises is God's ordained route along which grace produces fruit in the believer's life, and this outworking of grace in human life is blessed, wholesome, integrative, and shalomic.

These observations are neither novel nor limited to child-rearing. Schenck himself said as much when he wrote:

> The same requirement [of faith-directed obedience] is true with respect to all the means of grace, all the ordinances and institutions of religion, and all the promises of God's Word. These imply that

---

[1] Lewis Bevens Schenck, *The Presbyterian Doctrine of the Children in the Covenant: An Historical Study of the Significance of Infant Baptism in the Presbyterian Church in America,* Yale Studies in Religious Education (Eugene, Ore.: Wipf and Stock, 2001 [1940]), 121.

those who avail themselves of them must do so in good faith, with sincerity and honesty, with faith in God, and with a full purpose to comply with the conditions annexed.[2]

Promise and obligation (or demand)—these are the constitutive elements of every relationship God ever established.[3] Together these elements help to define *covenant* and to produce *blessedness*. Separated, they spell *apostasy* and yield *accursedness*. As such, these elements belong to the heart of what is called "covenant succession," that doctrine which teaches that the Lord works out His gracious purposes in history through the faithful administration of the means of grace, which serve to advance His covenant (via baptized children of believers) and to expand His covenant (through the church's baptizing and discipling new believers and their children).

It is the *connection* between these two elements of promise and demand that we wish to explore in this essay, in relation to biblical wisdom in general and to covenant succession in particular, the latter with the help of Proverbs 22:6. How do promise and demand fit together? Is their sequence important? How can we relate their connectedness to the teaching of covenant succession? What happens in Christian families where promise and demand are isolated from each other? What happens when one or the other is preferred? How must we explain either the promise remaining unfulfilled though the demand has been met, or the promise being fulfilled without the demand having been met?

> *Promise and obligation are the constitutive elements of every relationship God ever established.*

We begin by setting forth a brief analysis of Proverbs 22:6, "Train up a child in the way he should go; even when he is old he will not depart from it" (ESV). We will then move outward in order to work

---

[2] Schenck, *Children in the Covenant,* 121–22.

[3] For an important discussion of this claim, see S. A. Strauss, "Schilder on the Covenant," in *Always Obedient: Essays on the Teachings of Dr. Klaas Schilder,* ed. J. Geertsema (Phillipsburg, N.J.: Presbyterian & Reformed, 1995), 19–33.

back from the circumference toward the center, from the general description of biblical wisdom to conclusions regarding its specific embodiment in Proverbs 22:6. Several reasons warrant this approach. First, a tendency exists to isolate this proverb from its broader biblical context, and the resulting misconstrual of the proverb's meaning wreaks havoc in our families and our hearts. Second, if we are to convey properly the Bible's teaching about covenant succession expressed in this proverb, then we must carefully examine its various parts to study the life pulsating through this divine word of promise and demand.[4]

1. Proverbs 22:6

Of all the proverbs on child-rearing, this one is among the most familiar aphorisms in the book of Proverbs. Many other proverbs dealing with child-rearing focus on discipline (13:24; 19:18; 22:15; 23:13–14; 29:17).

Part of this proverb's uniqueness in relation to its subject is its opening verb, *hanok,* used in connection with dedicating a house (Deut. 20:5), the temple (1 Kgs. 8:63; 2 Chr. 7:5), and an image (Dan. 3:2), with its noun form referring to the dedication of an altar (Num. 7:10; 2 Chr. 7:9) and of Jerusalem's walls (Neh. 12:27). The Hebrew root seems to include the notion of setting aside, narrowing, or hedging in, suggesting by its usage here in Proverbs 22:6 that child-rearing involves narrowing or hedging in a child's conduct in a way that sets the child walking in a particular direction. In post-biblical Hebrew this root denoted what the Christian church has come to call "catechesis," since the phrase *sefer hanok* is the usual title of catechisms for youth.[5]

---

[4] For a helpful discussion of this subject, see Edward N. Gross, *Will My Children Go to Heaven? Hope and Help for Believing Parents* (Phillipsburg, N.J.: Presbyterian and Reformed, 1995).

[5] F. Delitzsch, *Proverbs, Ecclesiastes, Song of Solomon,* Commentary on the Old Testament in Ten Volumes, vol. 6 (Grand Rapids: Eerdmans, n.d.), 87; Matthew Henry, *Matthew*

The recipient of this nurture is a *na'ar,* a term used eight times in the book of Proverbs, generally referring to a young man of any age. The suggestion that the term refers primarily to a royal squire who is being apprenticed in wisdom in order to assume royal responsibilities consistent with his status[6] is not certain, given that the term *na'ar* can mean both "servant" and "youth."[7]

The measure or standard of this nurture is indicated by the phrase *'al-pi darko,* which could be rendered literally, "upon the mouth of his way." The Hebrew idiom "upon the mouth of" means "according to" or "in accord with" his way. But what does "his way" mean? Basically two interpretations have emerged, one involving duty (the way a child ought to go, in terms of divine precepts), the other aptitude (the way a child is suited to go, by virtue of personality, age, and ability). Perhaps elements of both interpretations provide the best understanding, namely, that the training and teaching of youth in the Lord's precepts ought to fit the nature of youth, in terms of manner and method, as well as content of instruction.[8]

The proverb's promise is expressed negatively: "He will not turn aside" from that way he was taught. The words "from it" *(mimenah)* refer to this nurture of youth, which by adulthood will have become a matter of reflex, imprinted upon the personality, one's customary conduct.

In summary, Proverbs 22:6 encourages parents to direct actively the formation of their child, nurturing with proper teaching suited to the child's capacity. The stimulus behind this encouragement is the promise that a child thus formed will become an adult who lives consistently with that nurture.

Henry's Commentary on the Whole Bible: Complete and Unabridged in One Volume (Peabody, Mass.: Hendrickson, 1996), s.v. Prov. 22:6.

[6] Ted Hildebrandt, "Proverbs 22:6a: Train up a Child?" *Grace Theological Journal* 9, no. 1 (1988): 10–14.

[7] Raymond C. Van Leeuwen, *Proverbs,* The New Interpreter's Bible, vol. 5 (Nashville: Abingdon Press, 1997), 198.

[8] Delitzsch, *Proverbs, Ecclesiastes, Song of Solomon,* 86–87; Randy Jaeggli, "Interpreting Proverbs 22:6," *Biblical Viewpoint* 33, no. 2 (November 1999): 41–48.

Keeping this proverb in mind, we now broaden the scope of our attention to examine how Proverbs 22:6 relates to covenant succession within the wider context of biblical wisdom.

2. Wisdom and Divine Creation

All proverbs may be classified as belonging to "wisdom," a term used variously to describe a kind of literature, or intergenerational traditions, or a school of thought. We begin our analysis by distinguishing between Wisdom and wisdom, the former referring to how God created and continues the world (let's call this "God's Wisdom"), the latter to the human apprehension and application of life-lessons drawn from studying Wisdom (let's call this "our wisdom"). A proper understanding of God's Wisdom and our wisdom in general, and of Proverbs 22:6 in particular, requires that we locate them within a worldview, a matrix of Bible-nurtured convictions regarding God, creation, history, and humanity. For our purposes in what follows, we define a worldview as a comprehensive framework and an integrated system of basic beliefs and values that provide a pattern for meaningful living.[9]

2.1: Creation's Beginning

Understanding this relationship between Wisdom and creation is essential to biblical conduct. God created the world "by wisdom" (Ps. 104:24; Prov. 3:19), which indicates not divine agency or instrumentality, but the attribute that God manifested in His created work.[10] We begin to understand God's Wisdom as creational structure when we perceive its embeddedness in creation. Citing Old Testament

---

[9] For a shorter definition and longer discussion of the term, see Albert M. Wolters, *Creation Regained: Biblical Basics for a Reformational Worldview* (Grand Rapids: Eerdmans, 1985), 2.

[10] Gordon D. Fee, "Wisdom Christology in Paul: A Dissenting View," in *The Way of Wisdom: Essays in Honor of Bruce K. Waltke,* ed. J. I. Packer and Sven K. Soderlund (Grand Rapids: Zondervan, 2000), 261.

scholar James Fleming, Albert Wolters reminds us that "wisdom . . . was wrought into the constitution of the universe," such that human wisdom entails arranging one's ways according to God's knowable creational order. In light of Proverbs 8:22–23, 27–30, we learn that God's Wisdom was the "scale model" or blueprint according to which God fashioned the universe; it is the master plan or purpose of God which undergirds the cosmos and gives it coherence and meaning.[11] This Wisdom imparts structure, order, and objectivity to the creation, and to this Wisdom must correspond human wisdom, the human skill of discerning and living according to the order which God has revealed in creation.[12]

One of the most helpful definitions of human wisdom is "the art of living purposefully in the fear of God, according to the order he has revealed in Scripture and creation, for our own well-being."[13] Biblical human wisdom is the search for God's Wisdom, for the order needing to be observed, an order integrating various spheres of human activity (familial, economic, societal), an order in which moral demands belong to the "natural" laws of created existence just as much as do physical laws. Fully recognizing and following such "laws" requires the fundamental disposition provided by the fear of the Lord who has revealed Himself in Scripture.[14] Throughout the opening chapters of Proverbs, those who seek to be wise are motivated by appeals to observation and reason simply because biblical wisdom is

> The goal of right living is to live in harmony with God's revelation in the created order.

---

[11] Wolters, *Creation Regained,* 25–27; Fee, "Wisdom Christology in Paul," 261–62; G. B. Caird, *New Testament Theology,* completed and edited by L. D. Hurst (Oxford: Clarendon, 1995), 334.

[12] Daniel J. Estes, *Hear, My Son: Teaching and Learning in Proverbs 1–9,* New Studies in Biblical Theology (Grand Rapids: Eerdmans, 1997), 26.

[13] F. van Deursen, *Spreuken,* De voorzeide leer (Barendrecht: Drukkerij Liebeek & Hooijmeijer B.V., 1986), 52.

[14] R. E. Clements, "Wisdom and Old Testament Theology," in *Wisdom in Ancient Israel: Essays in Honour of J. A. Emerton,* ed. John Day, Robert P. Gordon, and H. G. M. Williamson (Cambridge: Cambridge Univ. Press, 1995), 280.

rooted in a worldview which teaches that a personal, communicating, communion seeking God created an ordered universe.[15]

Thus the goal of right living is to live in harmony with God's revelation in the created order. After the entrance of sin into human history, God gave the Ten Commandments to Israel, commands that clearly reflect the uprightness of God and the ordered integrity of His creational design. "Thus the ethos of the orders of creation is the ethos of the law and both form the ethos of wisdom."[16] Wise living respects the way God has made things to work. He has structured created life to function according to laws of various kinds, including laws of physics, economics, biology, statecraft, and morality. One lives wisely by respecting all of these laws and ordering life according to them. This is the route to wholeness and happiness in this world, as people live before the face of God, in the fear of the Lord.

2.2: Creation's Continuation

To undergird the Wisdom which God has embedded in creation, God has also embedded within creation the impulse of continuation, an ongoing-ness manifested in an unfolding variegated sequence we know as *history*. This impulse is not an autonomous force, nor a watchmaker's unwinding spring; rather, it is God's purposive power, usually called *providence*, beautifully described by the Heidelberg Catechism in question and answer 27:

Q. What do you understand by the providence of God?
A. The almighty, everywhere-present power of God, whereby, as it were by His hand, He still upholds heaven and earth with all creatures, and so governs them that herbs and grass, rain and drought, fruitful and barren years, meat and drink, health and sickness, riches

---

[15] Estes, *Hear, My Son*, 111.

[16] Walter C. Kaiser, Jr., *Toward Old Testament Ethics* (Grand Rapids: Zondervan, 1983), 304; see the fulsome discussion of creation order and Christian ethics in Oliver O'Donovan, *Resurrection and Moral Order: An Outline for Evangelical Ethics*, 2nd ed. (Grand Rapids: Eerdmans, 1994).

and poverty, indeed, all things come not by chance, but by His fatherly hand.

In other words, both creational Wisdom and human wisdom imply and entail history, a sequence of interrelated events and occurrences. The Lord directs all history to suit His glory and to encompass human responsibility. Part of this divinely personal and purposive impulse is the correlative principle of cause and effect, to which we shall return below.

This embedded creational impulse of personal and purposive historical ongoing-ness (some might say "development") lies at the heart of both covenant and wisdom. For the word *covenant* describes the relationship between God, humanity, and creation, and this relationship forms the context of history, supplies its texture, marks its progress, and defines its goals and outcomes. In the Bible, wisdom is the human discernment of, and conduct according to, the structures of this history. To possess such wisdom requires first the knowledge of God

> *Apart from God and the Bible, we can neither know true wisdom nor do it.*

and of His special revelation, since this wisdom is rooted in the fear of the Lord (Prov. 1:7, 9:10, 14:27, 15:33, 19:23), which is described as keeping His commandments (Eccl. 12:13). Moreover, due to the scope of sin, with its blinding and paralyzing effects upon human intellect and will, God and the Bible are more than noetic necessities for the expedition that goes in search of wisdom; they are ethical prerequisites for the trip. Apart from God and the Bible, we can neither *know* true wisdom nor *do* it. To enjoy God in creation and in history (which is to say, to live in covenant with Him), we must see *that* all of life relates to Him, and we must learn *how* all of life relates to Him.

This creational impulse of personal and purposive historical ongoing-ness comes to expression in the *sanctions* (rewards and punishments, blessings and curses) that God has built into creation and history. From the beginning of history God has revealed Himself as one who actively, personally blesses obedience and punishes disobedience. This means, among other things, that eschatology, which includes attention to the ultimate or final administration of sanctions, is not a supplement to creation nor a divine afterthought. Creation and history are inherently eschatological, that is, purposive, goal-directed, and outcome-oriented. Human morality, because it shares the purposive, goal-directed, outcome-oriented nature of all creation, *requires* sanctions. The biblical doctrine of sanctions validates the absolute seriousness of human conduct and character.[17]

2.3: Wisdom, Creation, and Covenant Succession

Let us pause here to consider the significance of these observations for our understanding and use of Proverbs 22:6: "Train up a child in the way he should go; even when he is old he will not depart from it." We could say that the Lord has built into creation the "law" of child-rearing, such that lessons one learns when young are generally lived when old. Although this proverb is not an immutable decree (no person is trapped by his upbringing), it fits well with how God has created human personality to reflect Himself. The consistency between character and conduct that belongs to the triune God is replicated in human beings created to reflect the same consistency. One important difference is that whereas human character (the constellation of moral virtues) is not already given at birth but is cultivated over time, God's character is eternal and immutable. Human personality as created is subject to change and development, but God's is not. (I assume that a newborn infant has no character, but does have a nature. In contrast to human character, human *nature* is sinful already at birth, and comes to gradual expression in the character under development. Unless sin is overcome by the power of divine grace, human nature inevitably comes to expression in a character governed by vice rather than virtue.)

---

[17] Bernard L. Ramm, *The Right, the Good and the Happy* (Waco: Word, 1971), 30.

Parents need this proverb, then, for the encouragement it provides. Parenting is much more than a biological relationship; in fact, we might say that biology is just the beginning of parenting! Effective parenting is a whole-personed relationship between parents and their offspring, second only to marriage. Wise parenting, therefore, is purposive, outcome-oriented, character-forming parenting. So that parents may spend the needed time and energy teaching their child lessons and cultivating their child's character, the Lord stimulates them with the prospect that their nurture will bear fruit. What godly parent would not understand and covet John's exuberant testimony: "I rejoiced greatly to find some of your children walking in the truth, just as we were commanded by the Father" (2 Jn. 4).

Parents also need this proverb for the warning it provides. Parental failure to bind the Lord's precepts upon their child's heart will generally result in an adult who is morally inept, confused, or weak. Children are quite adept at learning morals from other teachers (television, school, peers), but none of these teachers has the capacity that parents have to integrate these lessons into the child's character through personal cultivation and persistent demonstration.

This piece of creational and biblical child-rearing wisdom was employed by the apostles Paul and John in relation to the churches and believers they served. As spiritual parents speaking to their spiritual children, these apostles assumed that the gospel of Jesus' death and resurrection could interrupt the human cycle of "lessons learned when young are generally lived when old." So much of their apostolic ministry was devoted to teaching the churches to observe what

> *Wise parenting, therefore, is purposive, outcome-oriented, character-forming parenting.*

Jesus had commanded, in order that having learned Christ, they might so walk in Him (Col. 1:9–10; cf. Eph. 4:20–24; 2 Tim. 3:14; Phil. 4:9; 2 John 4). The apostles labored in confident dependence on the prudential truth that spiritual lessons learned when young (as believers) are generally lived when old. Thus, the New Testament writings themselves and the living church they sustain constitute an abiding demonstration of the truth of Proverbs 22:6.

3. A Proverb's Wisdom

Perhaps the question is elementary, but we shall ask it nonetheless: Just how does a proverb "work," anyway? What makes it tick? To figure this out, let us briefly consider several important features of biblical proverbs.

Biblical wisdom clearly rests upon Torah (Deut. 4:6; Prov. 28:7). The Bible's wise men knew the covenant stipulations from Leviticus 26 and Deuteronomy 28, which were echoed often throughout the book of Proverbs as divine blessings upon obedience and divine curses upon disobedience (for a sample, see Lev. 26:5 cf. Prov. 1:33, 18:10; Lev. 16:6 cf. Prov. 3:24, 6:22; Deut. 28:8 cf. Prov. 3:9-10; Deut. 28:12 cf. Prov. 22:7). Moreover, the commandments comprising the so-called second table of the Decalogue are repeated often throughout Proverbs. Because it arises from reflection on revelation (both special and general), biblical wisdom is not natural wisdom in the sense that it might be thought to arise merely from a careful use of reason. Since wisdom begins

> *A biblical proverb looks back, looks around, and looks ahead.*

with the fear of the Lord, human wisdom is a gift from God. Nor are the Bible's proverbs supra-temporal religious aphorisms. Wisdom is closely related, then, to God and His law, and proverbs are intimately tied to concrete, historical human living.

A biblical proverb (1) rests on conclusions drawn from observing the past, (2) proffers guidance for conduct in the present, and (3) reaches out for something expected in the future. Here, then, is our initial description of how a proverb works. A biblical proverb looks *back*, looks *around*, and looks *ahead*. We shall seek to unpack this claim with the help of several observations about the nature of biblical proverbs in general.

3.1: Wisdom Looks Back

First, wisdom looks back, analyzing the experiences of former generations and reviewing the cumulative life-understanding inherited from ancestors. In comparing the past and the present, a biblical proverb is a piece of casuistry and thus operates by way of analogy and comparison. In its quest to apply general principles to specific situations (which is casuistry), wisdom searches for analogies by which to live. A proverb links two realms and two ages.[18] In Proverbs 27:17–18, for example, metallurgy and arboriculture supply illustrations for how to conduct human relationships: "Iron sharpens iron, and one man sharpens another. Whoever tends a fig tree will eat its fruit, and he who guards his master will be honored." The natural order parallels the social/moral order, and the past provides analogies to the present. Past experience has taught the present truth that "a faithful man will abound with blessings, but whoever hastens to be rich will not go unpunished" (Prov. 28:20). Since it proceeds by way of comparison, analogy is the primary tool of all forms of casuistry (jurisprudence, ethics, polity, etc.). Surveying similarities and discerning differences between situations is the *modus operandi* of casuistry. Continuity within history makes analogy possible, while discontinuity within history makes analogy necessary.[19]

3.2: Wisdom Looks Around

Second, wisdom looks around, studying biblical texts, present circumstances, human personalities and needs. In this sense, a biblical proverb is situationally true, not absolutely true. For a proverb to be true, it needs to relate properly to its surroundings. The epigrammatic

---

[18] James L. Crenshaw, *Old Testament Wisdom: An Introduction,* rev. ed. (Louisville: Westminster/John Knox, 1998), 55–57.

[19] Nelson D. Kloosterman, "Casuistry as Ministerial Ethics: A Plea for Rehabilitating Moral Nurture in the Church," in *Nuchtere noodzaak. Ethiek tussen navolging en compromis. Opstellen aangeboden aan prof. dr. J. Douma,* ed. J. H. F. Schaeffer, J. H. Smit, and Th. Tromp (Kampen: J. H. Kok, 1997), 106–16; and O'Donovan, *Resurrection and Moral Order,* 181–203.

nature of proverbs means that they are partial utterances, unpro-
tected by qualifications expressed with words like *often* or *usually*,[20]
A proverb is this-worldly wisdom, situational truth, not an oracle
dropped from heaven. This is not to say that a proverb's truth value
is situationally *determined*, only that its truth value is situationally *related*. Circumstances affect the relevance and usefulness of a proverb,
as we learn from Proverbs 26:4–5: "Answer not a fool according to
his folly, lest you be like him yourself. Answer a fool according to his
folly, lest he be wise in his own eyes." Wisdom knows when to answer a fool according to his folly and when not to. "Proverbs are situ-
ation-sensitive. We must not apply them mechanically or absolutely.
Experience, observation, instruction, learning from mistakes and,
most importantly, revelation—all these lay the groundwork for reading the text, reading people, and reading the situation."[21] It was Job
who encountered, perhaps most fearsomely, the dangers of
absolutizing wisdom and misapplying it to human living, when he
suffered under the counsel of friends who failed to discern this feature of wisdom adequately.

3.3: Wisdom Looks Ahead

Third, in looking ahead, *a biblical proverb entails a promised benefit and
is therefore future-oriented*. A proverb offers us a condition to be met
and a result to be expected. Many proverbs can be cast as conditional
statements in the form of "if *x,* then *y*." Grammarians call the "if"
clause the *protasis,* and the "then" clause the *apodosis*. Interestingly, the
very word *apodosis* is derived from the Greek noun whose verbal root
means "to give back, to restore, to return, to render what is due, to
reward or recompense."[22]

---

[20] Bruce Waltke, "Does Proverbs Promise Too Much?" *Andrews University Seminary Studies* 34, no. 2 (1996): 326.

[21] Tremper Longman III, *How to Read Proverbs* (Downers Grove: InterVarsity, 2002), 57;
see also F. van Deursen, *Spreuken,* 24–25.

[22] Johannes P. Louw and Eugene Albert Nida, *Greek-English Lexicon of the New Testament
Based on Semantic Domains,* 2nd ed (New York: United Bible Societies, 1996), LN 38.16;
H. G. Liddell, Robert Scott, and Henry Stuart Jones, *A Greek-English Lexicon* (Oxford:
Clarendon Press, 1940).

Take, for example, the proverb "A penny saved is a penny earned." We may recast it to say, "If you save a penny, then you will have earned that penny." "Haste makes waste" we may reformulate to say, "If you hurry, then you will lose something important." "People in glass houses shouldn't throw stones" is a rather complex proverb containing several conditionals, among them, "If you live in public view, then your criticism of others should be restrained" and "If you live in public view and if your criticism of others is not restrained, then your own life will be negatively affected."

As conditionals, then, proverbs supply us either implicitly or explicitly with promises and demands. A protasis is nothing less than a demand or condition needing to be fulfilled in order for the apodosis or promise to come true. (Notice that a proverb may contain a negative promise or threat.) Fulfilling the condition of not hurrying ordinarily results in not losing something important. Limiting their criticism of others is the condition whose fulfilling will let people who live as "public persons" live happily.

This can be illustrated with biblical proverbs just as easily. "A wise son makes a glad father, but a foolish son is a sorrow to his mother" (Prov. 10:1) can be restated as two conditionals: "If you are wise, then your father will be glad," and "If you are foolish, then your mother will be sad." "A word fitly spoken is like apples of gold in a setting of silver" (Prov. 25:11) means "If you speak appropriately to the situation, then people will admire and treasure your words."

In this connection, it is vitally important to distinguish between a promise and a guarantee. A promise entails a personal relationship, with all its contingencies, its twists and turns. A guarantee expresses a contractual relationship, arranged in terms of a *quid pro quo* (something for something). No one thinks of a wedding vow as a guarantee, but rather as a promise. This distinction is rooted in the nature and purposes of a covenant-keeping God, who personally governs human history in ways that suit His glory and encompass human responsibility.

3.4: Looking Back, Around, and Ahead with Proverbs 22:6

Our Scripture guided observation of the past has taught us the truth that children who have been well-taught in the way they should live generally follow that path in adulthood. Skilled parents will devote themselves to diligent thinking about child-rearing techniques that have worked and those that haven't, seeking to learn why. Skilled parents will devote themselves to studying their child's personality in order to apply appropriate, studied nurturing techniques that fit that unique child. Such continual interaction with past and present stimulates hope and expectation for the future, when parents apply lessons from the past as they provide nurture in the present that will in the future bring forth the fruit of this child's thankfully obedient living.

This proverbial truth about child-rearing is, however, a generalization to which there can be exceptions. Sometimes the inconsistencies of God-fearing parents vitiate their good instruction, at which point self-examination, confession, and repentance are required. Sometimes children either resist being taught the way they should live or, once taught, reject it in their adult years. The promise of Proverbs 22:6 is not a guaranteed

> *A promise entails a personal relationship. A guarantee expresses a contractual relationship, arranged in terms of a* quid pro quo.

outcome because of the presence of sinfulness and suffering in our world. God-fearing parents must learn to read Proverbs 22:6 in the company of Job and Qoheleth (Ecclesiastes), both of whom agonized, in faith, over the reality of broken connections between righteousness and blessing.

4. A Proverb's Dynamic

"Train up a child in the way he should go; even when he is old he will not depart from it" (Prov. 22:6). "The plans of the diligent lead surely to abundance, but everyone who is hasty comes only to poverty"

(Prov. 21:5). Why are these proverbs true? What makes life, as we say, "work out" this way? Why does it happen that a properly trained child usually grows up to walk the right path, or that a diligent person usually succeeds while one who lives carelessly ends up poor?

Put another way, what provides the connection between the "if" clause and the "then" clause of a proverb? What is the connection between the demand or condition expressed in the protasis, and the promise or recompense issued in the apodosis? This question brings us to the heart of the matter of covenant succession in light of Proverbs 22:6.

4.1: A Proverb as a Promise

We have already learned that the internal structure of many biblical proverbs is the form of a conditional statement, with a protasis and an apodosis. A proverb contains a demand and a promise, and thereby shares the fundamental features of a truly covenantal ethic.

Before going any further, we must recall that in the Bible, the Lord gave His law and its wisdom to His people in the context of grace. He had liberated Israel from Egypt, and later at Sinai gave her the law for the protection of that liberty. Along with the law the Lord supplied promises of blessing and of cursing (sanctions) as encouragement unto obedience and life. This redemptive-historical context is essential and quite relevant for our study of proverbs. A proverb's "if" clause is not God's *first* word to His children, as though He were waiting for them to initiate events or to empower the promise. The Lord has already spoken and shown grace to His children, so that the protasis "kicks in" as His appeal that they be faithful in response to this grace in light of the promised benefit. Careful readers will sense how easily this notion of conditionality can be misconstrued. Here, we are seeking to unfold its significance in line with the thought of John Calvin.[23]

---

[23] See Peter A. Lillback, *The Binding of God: Calvin's Role in the Development of Covenant Theology,* Texts and Studies in Reformation and Post-Reformation Thought (Grand Rapids: Baker, 2001), 162–75, 264–75; and Francis Turretin, *Institutes of Elenctic Theology,*

Now, it lies within the *nature* of a biblical promise to provide the "offer" of an outcome, in order to stimulate faith, hope, and love, and thereby stimulate a receptive attitude and obedient living in the light of the promise. The faith whereby one nurses the hope of receiving the promised blessing is empowered by the promise to fulfill the accompanying demand.

In the Bible, this conditional structure appears not only in many proverbs, but also throughout the entire Old and New Testaments. This is true because the covenant relation between God and people is conditional, and both Old and New Testaments are covenantal in content and form. In fact, this conditional structure characterizes the very gospel itself, "which God himself first revealed in Paradise, afterwards proclaimed by the holy Patriarchs and Prophets, and foreshadowed by the sacrifices and other ceremonies of the law, and finally fulfilled by his well-beloved Son" (Heidelberg Catechism, answer to question 19). It is a *promissory* gospel, by which we mean that the gospel announces the new reality (past, present, and future) that God has brought about in Jesus Christ and demands that all people respond with a faith-walk that springs from this new reality.

> *Within the nature of a biblical promise is the "offer" of an outcome, in order to stimulate faith, hope, and love.*

Like the proverbs found in the Old Testament, the gospel can be formulated biblically as a conditional "if *x*, then *y*." In his Pentecost sermon, Peter said to his listeners, "Repent and be baptized every one of you in the name of Jesus Christ for the forgiveness of your sins, and you will receive the gift of the Holy Spirit. For the promise is for you and for your children and for all who are far off, everyone whom the Lord our God calls to Himself" (Acts 2:38–39). *If you repent and are baptized, then you will receive the forgiveness of sins and the Holy Spirit.* Similarly, late one night an earthquake rattled open the

ed. James T. Dennison, Jr., trans. George Musgrave Giger (Phillipsburg, N.J.: Presbyterian and Reformed, 1994), 2:597, 710–24.

prison doors in Philippi, and "he [the jailer] brought them [Paul and Silas] out and said, 'Sirs, what must I do to be saved?' And they said, 'Believe in the Lord Jesus, and you will be saved, you and your household'" (Acts 16:30–31). *If you believe in the Lord Jesus, then you will be saved.* You will find quite similar if/then constructions in Matthew 10:22 and 24:13, Mark 13:13 and 16:16, John 10:9, and Romans 10:9 and 10:13.

4.2: A Proverb as a Filial Promise

We will not properly understand how a proverb works unless we position it correctly within the relationship for which it was designed. That relationship, as the book of Proverbs so clearly indicates, is between father or mother and son. From its opening instruction ("Hear, my son, your father's instruction, and forsake not your mother's teaching") to its closing echoes ("The words of King Lemuel. An oracle that his mother taught him"), we are overhearing a family conversation around the kitchen table, in the backyard garden, or in the family sedan.

We have a word to describe this relationship. The beautiful English adjective *filial* is derived from the Latin *filius*, which means "son." The fact that the book of Proverbs contains so many filial appeals is significant on two levels. Family living was, and still is, the context in which fathers and mothers teach their offspring lessons for life. For us, filiality is first experienced in human family. But more broadly still, filiality originally characterized the Creator's relationship with Adam (Luke 3:38). This filiality, marred and broken by sin, is precisely what Jesus Christ came to repair and restore, such that *adoption* belongs to the heart of the gospel experienced by those united to Christ by faith. This restored relationship between God and His children is *filial*, not *servile*. Servants are governed by contracts with payments and penalties, but children are regulated by covenants with promises and blessings. "For you did not receive the spirit of slavery to fall back into fear, but you have received the Spirit of adoption as sons, by whom we cry, 'Abba! Father!'" (Rom. 8:15). The basis and beauty of this filial relationship are described forcefully in Galatians 4:1–7.

No theologian has integrated the significance of adoption for Christian living within the whole of biblical teaching better than John Calvin.[24] The Bible's teaching on adoption—that filial relationship within which precepts and proverbs are given for guidance—provides the best orientation for understanding the nature and function of divinely-promised rewards for our obedience. In his *Institutes* 3.18.1–10, Calvin sets forth the relationship between our good works and God's promised reward and recompense.

> First, let us be heartily convinced that the Kingdom of Heaven is not servants' wages but sons' inheritance [Eph. 1:18], which only they who have been adopted as sons by the Lord shall enjoy [cf. Gal. 4:7], and that for no other reason than this adoption [cf. Eph. 1:5-6]. . . . Even in these very passages where the Holy Spirit promises everlasting glory as a reward for works, by expressly terming it an 'inheritance' he is showing that it comes to us from another source [i.e., other than our works].[25]

Scripture teaches us, Calvin warns, not to credit everlasting blessedness to our own works, but to our adoption by God. Augustine's dictum lives on: In crowning the works of His children, God is but crowning His own gifts. In this connection, notice the sequence and priority of divine activity in Calvin's appeal to Augustine:

[24] Some explorations of Calvin's thought on the subject of adoption can be found in Tim J. R. Trumper, "The Theological History of Adoption I: An Account," *Scottish Bulletin of Evangelical Theology* 20, no. 1 (spring 2002): 4–28; Tim J. R. Trumper, "The Theological History of Adoption II: A Rationale," *Scottish Bulletin of Evangelical Theology* 20, no. 2 (autumn 2002): 177–202; and B. A. Gerrish, *Grace and Gratitude: The Eucharistic Theology of John Calvin* (Minneapolis: Fortress, 1993). For similar discussions, see Richard B. Gaffin, Jr., *Resurrection and Redemption: A Study in Pauline Soteriology,* 2nd ed. (Phillipsburg, N.J.: Presbyterian and Reformed, 1987); Nigel Westhead, "Adoption in the Thought of John Calvin," *Scottish Bulletin of Evangelical Theology* 13, no. 2 (autumn 1995): 102–15; and Francis Turretin, *Institutes of Elenctic Theology,* 2:666–69.

[25] John Calvin, *Institutes of the Christian Religion,* 2 vols., trans. Ford Lewis Battles, The Library of Christian Classics (Philadelphia: Westminster, 1960), 3.18.2.

To whom should the righteous Judge have awarded the crown if the merciful Father had not bestowed grace? And how could there be righteousness unless the grace that "justifies the ungodly" had gone before? And how could these things now be awarded as due unless things not due had previously been given?[26]

In Christ, the Father bestows grace, mercy, and blessing upon those united to Christ by faith, so that God's fulfilling His promise is cemented to our fulfilling its related demand *by the very word-keeping character of God Himself*. Nothing external to this filial relationship can account for the "working" of a proverb.

4.3: A Proverb as a Powerful Promise

In the past several years, a number of evangelical authors have furnished us with challenging biblical reflections about the dynamics of Christian living and spirituality, especially about how the gospel works in the life and experience of the believer—specifically, I have in mind various writings by John Piper, Scott Hafemann, Sinclair B. Ferguson, and D. A. Carson.[27] Among the more helpful insights is the connection several of these writers draw between eschatology and Christian living, specifically, the power for Christian living supplied by divine promises in Scripture. The promises of divine grace and our faith-embrace of those promises exhibited in deeds of loving obedience are inherently future-oriented, whereby God draws (rather than pushes) His children forward from grace to grace.

Let me try to formulate this insight from the somewhat unusual angle of Greek grammar. There is within Christian biblical ethics a prominent emphasis on the relationship between the *indicative* and

---

[26] Ibid., 3.18.5.

[27] John Piper, *The Purifying Power of Living by Faith in Future Grace* (Sisters, Ore.: Multnomah, 1998). Scott J. Hafemann, *The God of Promise and the Life of Faith: Understanding the Heart of the Bible* (Wheaton, Ill.: Crossway, 2001). Sinclair B. Ferguson, *The Holy Spirit,* Contours of Christian Theology (Downers Grove, Ill.: InterVarsity, 1996). D. A. Carson, "When is Spirituality Spiritual? Reflections on Some Problems of Definition," *Journal of the Evangelical Theological Society* 37, no. 2 (June 1994): 381–94.

the *imperative*.[28] These terms come from the world of grammar, and they refer to *moods* or modes of verbal expression. The indicative mood describes a real state of affairs, while the imperative mood expresses a potential reality stronger than a wish—basically a command.

Applied to Christian ethics, this is usually said to mean that the indicative tells us what God has done in Christ Jesus, while the imperative arising out of that indicative tells us what we must do in response to, or as a result of, that divine action. The indicative discloses our status; the imperative describes our calling. For example, Paul writes, "You have been set free from sin" (Rom. 6:22) and exhorts his readers, "Let not sin therefore reign" (Rom. 6:12). To the Corinthians Paul writes, "Cleanse out the old leaven, as you really are unleavened" (1 Cor. 5:7). This sequence of "what God has done, therefore what you must do" is seen by many

> *By means of the promised benefit and outcome, God powerfully encourages and induces godly parents unto faithfulness.*

to form the structure of many Pauline epistles, such that the first part sets out the doctrine, followed by the second section which presents the ethics arising from that doctrine. (This exegetical conclusion is seriously flawed, however, since the epistles generally weave exhortation [imperatives] into the presentation of divine activity [indicative].)

In the usual description of the relationship between the indicative and the imperative, however, one small but significant shift has occurred that is worth observing. Notice that the indicative is usually

---

[28] This was originally outlined by Rudolf Bultmann, "The Problem of Ethics in Paul," trans. Christoph W. Stenschke, in *Understanding Paul's Ethics: Twentieth Century Approaches,* ed. Brian S. Rosner (Grand Rapids: Eerdmans, 1995), 195–216; see also William D. Dennison, "Indicative and Imperative: The Basic Structure of Pauline Ethics," *Calvin Theological Journal* 14, no. 1 (April 1979): 55–78; Allen D. Verhey, *The Great Reversal: Ethics and the New Testament* (Grand Rapids: Eerdmans, 1984), 104–06; and Michael Parsons, "Being Precedes Act: Indicative and Imperative in Paul's Writing," in *Understanding Paul's Ethics*, 217–47.

explained in terms of *the past tense*: what God *has done* in Christ Jesus. But we all know that the indicative *mood* has several *tenses*, among them (in the Greek) the present, imperfect, future, aorist, perfect, pluperfect, and future perfect tenses.

The point is that in the Bible, the indicative mood does indeed constitute the basis, the source, and the power for the imperative—but it is not just the past indicative, but also the *future* indicative! The indicative-imperative formula is not exhausted by saying "God has done *x*, therefore you must do *y*"—the formula also includes "God will do *x*, therefore you must do *y*."

More attention needs to be given to the moral motive-power of divine promises for godly living, and biblical proverbs provide us with exactly the material needed. The Lord supplies His children with strength for obedience, He motivates them unto holiness, with a certain declaration of *what He will do* in response to their faithful obedience. With respect to Proverbs 22:6 and covenant succession, this means that parents derive *power* for faithful child-rearing from the *promise* of divine blessing upon that nurture. Because the Lord has promised to do *x*, therefore parents should be diligent in doing *y*. By means of the promised benefit and outcome, God powerfully encourages and induces godly parents unto faithfulness.

4.4 A Proverb and Moral Causality

What accounts for how a proverb "works" is not an external or impersonal force, but rather the dynamic belonging to the filial relationship between God and His children. This dynamic, moreover, is the antidote against at least two toxic forms of moralism. The first is a mechanistic moralism, the second a decretal moralism.

In recent decades, students of Old Testament wisdom have been debating what has come to be called the *deed-consequence nexus* found in biblical wisdom teaching.[29] The issue, formulated most provocatively

---

[29] Klaus Koch, "Is There a Doctrine of Retribution in the Old Testament?" in *Theodicy in the Old Testament,* ed. and with introduction by James L. Crenshaw, Issues in Religion and Theology, vol. 4 (Philadelphia: Fortress, 1983), 57–87; Clements, "Wisdom and Old

by Klaus Koch, concerns whether an action contains its own consequence. Koch objected against the notion that reward or punishment
is brought from outside the action according to a previously established norm. According to him,
the inherent connection between deed and consequence in
the moral realm is captured by
the metaphors of sowing and
reaping, tree and fruit. Words
like "retribution" and "reward"
suggest an arbitrarily and externally applied standard. By contrast,
Koch argued, just as a seed "contains" its own grain and a tree its own
fruit, so every deed is pregnant with its own consequences, and the
Lord functions as a midwife who assists in their birthing.

> *This dynamic is the antidote against at least two toxic forms of moralism. The first is a mechanistic moralism, the second a decretal moralism.*

Many Old Testament scholars have criticized Koch's conclusions
as too mechanistic, insisting upon the Lord's personal, covenantal
involvement with all of creation and its history, a feature which characterizes the entire Old Testament worldview.

In its extreme form, the deed-consequence syndrome removes the
deity from activity in the world. According to this view, the consequence follows the deed of itself, and Yahweh, whose power is limited, is directly involved merely as a midwife or a chemical catalyst,
although indirectly involved as creator, who set into motion the
deed-consequence syndrome.[30]

Testament Theology," 278–80; Roland E. Murphy, *Proverbs*, Word Biblical Commentary,
vol. 22 (Nashville: Thomas Nelson, 1998), 265; Bruce K. Waltke and David Diewert,
"Wisdom Literature," in *The Face of Old Testament Studies: A Survey of Contemporary Ap-
proaches*, ed. David W. Baker and Bill T. Arnold (Grand Rapids: Baker, 1999), 298–99;
B. Janowski, "Die Tat kehrt zum Täter zurück. Offene Fragen im Umkreis des 'Tun-
Ergehen Zusammenhangs,'" *Zeitschrift für Theologie und Kirche* 91, no. 3 (1994): 247–71;
Douglas A. Knight, "Cosmogony and Order in the Hebrew Tradition," in *Cosmogony and
Ethical Order: New Studies in Comparative Ethics*, ed. Robin W. Lovin and Frank E. Reynolds
(Chicago: Univ. of Chicago Press, 1985), 133–57.

[30] E. F. Huwiler, "Control of Reality in Israelite Wisdom," Ph.D. dissertation (Duke
University, 1988), 64; Raymond C. Van Leeuwen, "Wealth and Poverty: System and
Contradiction in Proverbs," *Hebrew Studies* 33 (1992): 25–36.

This relationship between act and outcome is embedded within the universe, related ultimately to God's own righteous character. Teachers of wisdom move from observing *what* happens in creation (including history) to interpreting *why* it happens, yielding the formulation of predictable results in the form of proverbs. "The question of causality assumes that the world possesses inherent order, which is a prerequisite for rational thinking. . . . The wisdom teachers attempt to understand how the order in Yahweh's world functions, so that they can define the relation between acts and consequence."[31] However, as Job and his friends learned, God remains sovereign and cannot be ensnared by His own creation or its "laws" of moral cause and effect.[32] So, then, we are rightly warned against a mechanistic view of history, a kind of automatism where God gets swallowed up by history.

The other extreme allows history to be swallowed up in God. This may be termed decretal moralism, by which we mean that human responses to divine promises and commands are ultimately meaningless because they are determined by God's predestinating decree governing history. In relation to Proverbs 22:6, the matter can be stated rather crassly this way: "Whether a child grows up to believe in Jesus Christ and receive eternal life is really only up to God." Though in a certain sense this is true, the use to which this truth is put in this context tends to twist it, for the inescapable conclusion of this use of the doctrine of divine sovereignty is that parents really, genuinely have nothing to do with the outcome envisioned by Proverbs 22:6. The connection, then, between the proverb's protasis (if you train up a child in the way he should go) and its apodosis (then when he is old he will not depart from it) evaporates into fiction. Such argument emphasizes divine sovereignty at the expense of human responsibility—a construal contrary to Scripture.

---

[31] Estes, *Hear, My Son,* 32–33.

[32] J. H. Sailhamer, "Wisdom," in *New Dictionary of Christian Ethics and Pastoral Theology,* ed. David J. Atkinson, David H. Field, Arthur F. Holmes, and Oliver O'Donovan (Downers Grove, Ill.: InterVarsity, 1995), 896–97.

In contrast to both these views, we would plead for an understanding of moral causality that is truly covenantal, by which we mean one that takes seriously the collaboration of the Lord and godly parents, a cooperation wherein the Lord is fully sovereign and parents are fully responsible in the realization of Proverbs 22:6.

A mechanistic moralism tends to immanentize the connection between a proverb's protasis and apodosis, thereby obscuring God's personal sovereignty in administering Proverbs 22:6. This means that God becomes subject to history and its laws of cause and consequence, such that He no longer interacts personally with His children. Thus, as we said above, God gets swallowed up by history. A decretal moralism tends, by contrast, to transcendentalize the connection between protasis and apodosis, thereby obscuring parental responsibility in fulfilling Proverbs 22:6. This means that human moral conduct becomes ultimately and wholly irrelevant to the unfolding of history, such that there are no *historical* causes and consequences. Both views ignore history's significance as the covenantal concourse between a personal, promise-making, and promise-keeping God and His children who, being sinful yet redeemed, find in His promises the needed purpose and power for the filial obedience which they are called to render en route to receiving the Lord's promised blessings.

5. Jesus Christ, the "Wisdom of God," and Covenant Succession

In order to offer a textured portrait of biblical wisdom, we need to pause here to sketch some lines of development between Old and New Testaments, by paying all-too-brief attention to the person and work of Jesus Christ in relation to Proverbs 22:6 and covenant succession.

5.1 Christ as the Realization of Creation by Redemption

In itself, a creational worldview is an inadequate context for understanding biblical wisdom, for we live as fallen creatures in a fallen creation. Only God's redemptive work, within creation and in history, accomplished through the person and work of Jesus Christ, supplies a sufficient foundation for biblical wisdom.[33]

If Wisdom is God's structured plan and purpose for the universe, then this Wisdom finds perfect historical embodiment in Jesus Christ, the eternal Son of the Father, conceived by the Holy Spirit and born of the virgin Mary. As the last Adam (1 Cor. 15:45), Jesus Christ came to do what the first Adam failed to do, a failure that rendered all his posterity unable and unwilling—apart from intervening grace—to live wisely according to Wisdom. His divine authority joined with compassionate love to rescue the created order from its emptiness and foolishness (Rom. 8:20–21), restoring to those given to share His authority in this creation the capacity to love wisely, by discerning the order of things and delighting in their existence.[34]

Further, in Jesus Christ this divine Wisdom was perfectly manifested for all the world to see. By His obedience, Jesus Christ became for us God's wisdom, righteousness, sanctification, and redemption (1 Cor. 1:30–31), by fulfilling in history the divine plan for redemption. More than that, Christ Himself *is* God's plan for the world, for in Him "are hidden all the treasures of wisdom and knowledge" (Col. 2:3). In Jesus Christ, unlike any human being before Him, the Wisdom of creation's purpose and order is met by the responsive wisdom of filial obedience, a response characterized by perfect harmony, discernment, and blessing.

As Son of the Father, Jesus became incarnate to learn obedience through what He suffered (Heb. 5:8), which included growing in wisdom, that is, in living fully in accord with God's creational order

---

[33] Jonathan R. Wilson, "Biblical Wisdom, Spiritual Formation, and the Virtues," in *The Way of Wisdom: Essays in Honor of Bruce K. Waltke,* ed. J. I. Packer and Sven K. Soderlund (Grand Rapids: Zondervan, 2000), 305, n. 9.

[34] O'Donovan, *Resurrection and Moral Order,* 26.

(Mk. 6:2; Lk. 2:40, 52). His was a wisdom He sought to impart by summoning all people to believe in Him as the Father's Sent One, to have a faith demonstrated by becoming His disciple-learner, by following Him. Following Jesus by obeying His words now becomes the path wisdom takes throughout all of life, and along this route one receives protection in the context of judgment (taught in the parable of the wise builder, Mt. 7:24–27). The wisdom that springs from grace-produced faith in Jesus practices faithfulness in the present by looking ahead to the master's return, preparing for still greater service in the kingdom of God (taught in the parable of the faithful servant, Mt. 24:44–51; Lk. 12:42–48). This wisdom learns the laws of lamp-burning and fuel consumption in order to be ready, with wicks trimmed and burning, to welcome the bridegroom upon His sudden arrival (parable of the wise maidens, Mt. 25:1–13).

This message of Jesus Christ became the preaching of the apostles. Turning in faith and repentance to Jesus Christ is, according to the apostolic gospel, the only route to discerning and living out God's wisdom (see Rom. 1:16–32). To discern God's wisdom requires having the mind of Christ (see 1 Cor. 1:19–2:16; Phil. 2:5), a mind set on the Spirit (Rom. 8:6), a mind renewed in its capacity to discern God's perfect will (Rom. 12:2).

As both the power and the wisdom of God (1 Cor. 1:24; 2:7; Eph. 3:10), this incarnate, humiliated, crucified, and risen Savior imparts a wisdom antithetical to the world's wisdom. For Jesus Christ demonstrated that the route to cosmic authority entailed self-denial, the path to life passed through death, and gaining everything required losing all for God's sake.

5.2 Jesus Christ and Covenantal Causality

Earlier we claimed that the twin dangers of mechanistic moralism and decretal moralism can be averted by a covenantal explanation of moral causality, one that accounts for full divine sovereignty and full human responsibility within the same moral act. We have reached the point now where we must show that this covenantal connection between act and consequence, between protasis and apodosis, has been forged finally and fully in Jesus Christ alone.

Another way to frame the issue is to ask what change has occurred, with the coming of Jesus Christ, to the covenantal sanctions supplied by the Lord to His people Israel in the Old Testament? The limits of this essay permit only a brief, introductory suggestion in answering this important question. That suggestion is to point the reader to the apostolic confession in 2 Corinthians 1:20: "For all the promises of God find their 'Yes' in Him. That is why it is through Him that we utter our 'Amen' to God for his glory."

In Jesus of Nazareth, the promises of God and the fulfillment of their related obedience are united. He is the Mediator of the covenant, in whom is fulfilled everything written about the Messiah in the law, the prophets, and the psalms (Lk. 24:44). All the covenant promises given to Abraham and his descendants find fulfillment in this Seed (Gal. 3:16). As the ultimate content of all the Old Testament promises, Jesus Christ is the Father's "Yes." As the Head and Savior of the church, He conducts the church's responsive "Amen." The believing "Amen" of all our prayers and petitions—including our prayers for our baptized children—is established by the person and work of Christ. Expressing continuity between the New Testament church and the Old Testament people of God, the Hebrew word *amen*

conveys the idea of *firmness* and *reliability*, and the utterance of 'Amen' in public or private worship after prayers and thanksgivings expresses confidence in the faithfulness of God and the certainty of His promises. It is, in short, the voice of faith, setting to its seal that God is true (Jn. 3:33).[35]

Both the "Yes" that proceeds from God and the "Amen" that we return to Him are mediated by Christ; God has fulfilled all His prom-

---

[35] Philip Edgcumbe Hughes, *Paul's Second Epistle to the Corinthians: The English Text with Introduction, Exposition and Notes,* NICNT (Grand Rapids: Eerdmans, 1962), 37.

ises *in* Christ and we respond with the obedience of faith *through Christ.* [36]

This suggests that Proverbs 22:6 also finds in Jesus Christ—the true Adam, the power and wisdom of God—both its enablement (to satisfy the demand of its protasis) *and* its fulfillment (to enjoy the promise of its apodosis). "Train up a child in the way he should go; even when he is old he will not depart from it." To meet the daunting challenges connected with child-rearing, Christian parents look to Jesus Christ for wisdom and power to keep their vows made at their child's baptism. And while they work and pray with their children, Christian parents rest in God's liberating consolation promised them at their child's baptism: "I will be God to you and to your offspring after you" (Gen. 17:7). "For all the promises of God find their 'Yes' in [Christ]. That is why it is through Him that we utter our 'Amen' to God for His glory."

> *All God's promises find their "Yes" in Christ, so through Him we utter our "Amen" to God for His glory.*

Conclusion

"For we are God's fellow workers; you are God's field, God's building," wrote the apostle Paul (1 Cor. 3:9). This metaphorical description of the ministry of Paul and Apollos contains the phrase "God's fellow workers," which originally referred to the apostles themselves but may legitimately be extended to all of God's people (a similar emphasis may be found in Mark 16:20 and 2 Corinthians 6:1). The same apostle expresses this bilateral reality in Philippians 2:12–13: "Therefore, my beloved, as you have always obeyed, so now, not only as in my presence but much more in my absence, work out your own salvation with fear and trembling, for it is God who works in you, both to will and to work for His good pleasure."

---

[36] Paul Barnett, *The Second Epistle to the Corinthians,* NICNT (Grand Rapids: Eerdmans, 1997), 109.

This real partnership, initiated and sustained by divine grace, serves as the basis for God's appeal to His children that they walk before Him responsibly—which means embracing His promises with faith in Jesus Christ, who through His Spirit empowers us to fulfill the requirements God has attached to them. This reality accounts for human responsibility as an essential element of the covenant.[37]

As God's fellow workers, God-fearing parents lean upon Jesus Christ, both for the strength and wisdom to train their child in the way he should go, and for the assurance that even when he is old he will not depart from it. Living in Jesus Christ, godly parents find the reliable "Yes" of every divine promise, so that through Jesus Christ, they lift up their filial "Amen" with each family prayer, each household lesson, each instance of painful discipline.

> Blest the man that fears Jehovah,
> Walking ever in His ways;
> By thy toil thou shalt be prospered
> And be happy all thy days.
>
> Joyful children, sons and daughters,
> Shall about thy table meet,
> Olive plants, in strength and beauty,
> Full of hope and promise sweet.
>
> Lo, on him that fears Jehovah
> Shall this blessedness attend,
> For Jehovah out of Zion
> Shall to thee His blessing send.[38]

---

[37] Strauss, "Schilder on the Covenant," 26–27.

[38] Psalm 128, *Trinity Hymnal*, rev. ed. (Suwanee, Ga.: Great Commission Publications, 1990), no. 717, stanzas 1, 3, and 4.

From Covenant to Chaos: The Reformers and Their Heirs on Covenant Succession

Thomas Trouwborst

Not only covenant theologians are concerned about the passing of the faith to coming generations. Retired Brigadier General T. C. Pinckney appealed to his fellow Southern Baptists, "We are losing our children. Research indicates that seventy percent of teens who are involved in a church youth group will stop attending church within two years of their high school graduation. . . . We are losing our youth."[1] This observation is frightening but true. Why is this the case, despite the assurances in Scripture that God will be a God to us *and* to our children?[2]

A succinct summary of the question before us is *the choice between covenant succession or chaos*. Has God given promises concerning the faithfulness of children born to covenant families? If so, has He graciously equipped the covenant community to cultivate this faithfulness systematically in our seed? Or is passing the faith to successive generations accidental, haphazard, arbitrary, indiscriminate, and hit-or-miss? The church has given the latter answer for far too long, but this has not always been the case, as this essay will set forth. Consistent with a Reformational understanding, the great Charles Hodge

---

[1] T. C. Pinckney, "We are Losing Our Children," remarks to the Southern Baptist Convention Executive Committee (Nashville, Tenn., September 18, 2001).

[2] For example, Gen. 17:7; Exod. 3:15, 17:16, 20:6, 34:7; Deut. 4:37, 5:29, 7:9; 1 Chr. 16:15; Neh. 1:5; Ps. 22:30, 90:16, 102:28, 103:17; Jer. 32:18; Lk. 1:50; Acts 2:3.

wrote in 1847, "Where is the parent whose children have turned aside from God, whose heart will not rather reproach him, than charge God with forgetting his promise?"[3]

Our Lord has used Lewis Bevens Schenck's *The Presbyterian Doctrine of Children in the Covenant* to awaken many from their "dogmatic slumber" in reviving the historic Presbyterian and Reformed view concerning covenant children. We should praise God for Schenck's work—it is essential reading in our day—yet we need further theological and historical analysis. And although we may not find the term "covenant succession" until quite recently, much has been written in the historic, Reformed tradition about the subject in theological discussions, catechisms, and sermons, from which we can glean and learn.

> *"We are losing our youth."*

A study of our fathers in the faith will help us to understand better what has brought about this catastrophic failure, our inability to pass the faith to our children. Some say a study of history is unnecessary: "Just show me in the Bible." Of course the Scriptures are our final authority, but this attitude is in essence to deny the *covenant* in covenant succession. We should not be surprised when our children say no to the commands of their fathers when their parents (and the church) refuse to respect and learn from their fathers in the faith. The individualistic spirit prevails when we reject either our paternal *or* our theological fathers—there is more than one way to apply Anabaptist thought.[4] We have much to learn as we see the subtle and not-so-subtle changes in theology and practice concerning covenant children since the Reformation.

This study begins with a summary of the views of five Magisterial Reformers, prominent and leading men of the Reformation, and

---

[3] Charles Hodge, "Bushnell on Christian Nurture," *The Princeton Review* 19, no. 4 (October 1847): 507.

[4] My references to Anabaptists, Baptists, Reformed Baptists, etc., should not be taken pejoratively. And although these brothers in the Lord certainly share a common noncovenantal view of children, I do grant that there are significant theological differences amongst them.

a general assessment of sixteenth-century Reformed theology on this issue. The norm was to view and treat covenant infants as forgiven saints and to have confidence that they would continue as such. Upon this foundation, we will observe a select number of subsequent changes in theology and practice. Understanding of the covenant in the seventeenth and eighteenth centuries became deficient for some, often radically so (even among our beloved Puritans), which caused the church many difficulties in knowing how to regard and train the next generation. Our covenantal shortcomings did not begin with certain excesses in the First Great Awakening, nor did they originate with Charles Finney and his "anxious bench" tactics in the Second Great Awakening, nor with the Southern Presbyterian James Henry Thornwell, who spoke of viewing and treating our children "as slaves" to be "dealt with as the Church deals with all the enemies of God."[5] While many continued in the covenantal perspective of the Reformers, we simultaneously find a paradigm revolution in the seventeenth century that laid the foundation and set the stage for the Great Awakenings. The Princeton theology of the nineteenth century and the Dutch Reformed presence helped us to regain (partially) and promote the fully covenantal view of the Magisterial Reformers. And although this study is certainly not exhaustive in its efforts to review the Reformers or the changes subsequent to that period, it will allow us to make various theological assessments before we conclude.

Vital pastoral and parental issues are at stake. The radical changes to be noted have had radical implications for the passing on of the faith. The Reformers assumed covenant succession specifically because their theology of covenant children included them as part of God's people from the time of their conception onward. The grace of God was primary, from first to last. In contrasting the different theologies in this essay, we will see that *the way we view our covenant children directly affects the way we raise them, and thus the way they view themselves.* This is undeniable.

---

[5] James Henry Thornwell, *Ecclesiastical Writings,* vol. 4 of *The Collected Writings of James Henry Thornwell,* (Carlisle, Penn.: Banner of Truth, 1986), 348.

The Magisterial Reformers, and many who followed them, viewed and treated their children covenantally as full members of the covenant with all appropriate rights (excepting paedocommunion controversies), obligations and warnings. *This approach, coupled with faithful training and full trust and belief in the promises of the God of all mercy, will lead them in a growing faith according to their maturity.* Consequently, "when [a child] is old he will not depart

---

The way we view our covenant children affects the way we raise them, and thus the way they view themselves.

---

from it" (Prov. 22:6). Conversely, to treat children as partial members or external members only (as did many Puritans and as is common in our generation), or worse, as "enemies of God," *will encourage them to reject the faith that has first rejected them.* Further, to inculcate in them a penchant for doubt will not spur them on to greater faith. For us today, these seemingly theoretical discussions descend to the realm of the beautifully (or painfully) practical as we raise our children unto the Lord. The stakes are enormous.

The Sixteenth Century Considered

To the modern ear, the following quotes from the Magisterial Reformers may sound odd at best and unorthodox at worst. The fact that their views are so foreign to us should alert us to the chasm between our theology and theirs. Undoubtedly, to understand *covenant succession*, one must first comprehend the term *covenant*: the relationship that God has with His people—a corporate body, infants and children included. Because of the covenant, our fathers understood our young ones as having glorious privileges including the forgiveness of sins, even as infants.

Further, before we survey their views on covenant children, we must recognize some nuances of the Reformational position regarding the conversion and regeneration of covenant children. For the Reformers, regeneration was lifelong and all-inclusive. Berkhof writes, "Calvin also used the term in a very comprehensive sense as a designation of the whole process by which man is renewed."[6] William W. Heyns argues, "After the Reformation period regeneration began to be conceived of as including the first implanting of new life" and he goes on to write, "Regeneration is generally presented as a momentary act. This, of course, is a result of the later conception of regeneration. . . . But according to the original conception of regeneration, held by the Reformers, it is not true."[7] In his classic work on the history of Christian doctrine, William Cunningham speaks about regeneration being used in a "limited" versus a "wider sense"[8] while John Murray also differentiates its use "in later Reformed theology."[9] Herman Hoeksema writes that our fathers "spoke of a regeneration in a still broader sense of the word, as including the continued process of sanctification"[10] and argues that the Belgic Confession reflects this framework. Turretin speaks of "habitual regeneration."[11] Conversion for the Reformers was, as Paul Althaus notes, "a perpetual act beginning with baptism."[12]

Although the idea is problematic to many today, the Reformers saw our children as fully redeemed, even from infancy. Again, Louis Berkhof writes this in his standard systematic theology about the common position of the Reformers:

> That infants of believers are baptized, because they are in the covenant and are as such heirs of the rich promises of God including a

---

[6] Louis Berkhof, *Systematic Theology* (Grand Rapids: Eerdmans, 1974), 466.

[7] William W. Heyns, *Manual of Reformed Doctrine* (Grand Rapids: Eerdmans, 1926), 246, 249.

[8] William Cunningham, *Historical Theology* (Edinburgh: Banner of Truth, 1994 [1862]), 1:617.

[9] John Murray, *Systematic Theology,* vol. 2 of *The Collected Writings of John Murray* (Edinburgh: Banner of Truth, 1996 [1977]), 172.

[10] Herman Hoeksema, *Reformed Dogmatics* (Grand Rapids: Reformed Free Publishing Association, 1966), 464.

[11] Francis Turretin, *Institutes of Elenctic Theology*, ed. James T. Dennison, Jr., trans. George Musgrave Giger (Phillipsburg, N. J.: Presbyterian and Reformed, 1994), 2:546.

[12] As quoted by Rev. Arie W. Blok, "The Heidelberg Catechism and the Dutch Puritans" (Chatham, Ontario: n. p., 2000), 12.

title, not only to regeneration, but also to all the blessings of justification and of the renewing and sanctifying influence of the Holy
Spirit.[13]

He is unquestionably correct in his assessment, as we shall demonstrate.

Bullinger

The Swiss Reformer Henry Bullinger writes, "Therefore it is certain,
that infants are partakers of purification and remission of sins through
Christ."[14] His language is consistently forceful when speaking about
covenant children. Although covenant infants are clearly sons of
Adam and sinners by nature, this does not mean that God holds their
sins against them, "for by their nature and birth they are unclean, and
sinners; but for Christ's sake they are purified."[15] Of course, this
claim does not deny the necessity of the Holy Spirit's work. In arguing for infant baptism, Bullinger notes:

> Children are God's; therefore they have the Spirit of God. Therefore,
> if they have received the Holy Ghost, as well as we; if they be ac-
> counted among the people of God, as well as we that be grown in
> age; who, I pray you, can forbid these to be baptized with water in
> the name of the Lord?[16]

Bullinger believed that God has included our children in the body of
Christ and hence they have the benefit of the Holy Ghost. His view
is not a denial of original sin or a Pelagian view of children:

> But we, which condemn both Pelagius and Pelagians, do affirm both
> those things which they deny; to wit, that infants are born in original

---

[13] Berkhof, *Systematic Theology,* 639.

[14] Henry Bullinger, *The Decades of Henry Bullinger* (Cambridge: Cambridge Univ. Press,
1852), 4:384.

[15] Ibid., 384.

[16] Ibid., 390.

sin, and therefore that the sanctification of Christ is necessary unto them, without which they are not saved. Again we defend and maintain, that the same infants ought to be baptized, if it be possible, though by the right of the covenant they belong to the body of Christ and are sanctified by the blood of Christ. [17]

It is crucial that we see how Bullinger comes to this conclusion. It is "by right of the covenant" that he has confidence that Jesus' blood washes covenant children.

Infants are unable to exercise faith, at least as usually defined by modern theologians in a theologically precise manner, which has led many present-day Reformed Christians to doubt or to be agnostic about an infant's salvation. This is the same argument that the Anabaptists made during the sixteenth century. Bullinger replies to such thinking:

> As easily is that objection confuted, that baptism profiteth not infants, if we still say that sacraments without faith profit not; for infants have no faith. Thus they babble. We answer first, That the baptism of infants is grounded upon the free mercy and grace of God, who saith: "I will be thy God, and the God of thy seed;" and again: "Suffer children to come unto me; for of such is the kingdom of God," &c. Infants therefore are numbered and counted of the Lord himself among the faithful; so that baptism is due unto them, as far forth as it is due unto the faithful. For by the imputation of God infants are faithful. [18]

Elsewhere he writes concerning young children, "For he accounteth these as his own of his mere grace and free promise, without their confession." [19]

---

[17] Ibid., 376.
[18] Ibid., 343–344.
[19] Ibid., 388.

Olevianus and Ursinus

Bullinger's covenantal view of children is normative among the Magisterial Reformers. Lyle D. Bierma translates and summarizes the writings of Caspar Olevianus, the co-author of the Heidelberg Catechism, as follows:

> When a baby is baptized in the name of Jesus Christ, the parents should be assured that just as certainly as the water cleanses his or her body, so certainly does the Father through the Holy Spirit seal in his or her heart *gemeynschafft* [community, fellowship, or common identity] with the body and blood of Christ and, through that communion, the double benefit of the covenant—the forgiveness of sins and the beginnings of righteousness and holiness. [20]

He undoubtedly sees our children in terms of the covenant and, unlike what some will eventually argue, sees their blessings as including the forgiveness of sins and communion with Christ. Olevianus writes this so parents will be "assured" of these things. Elsewhere, we read, "To be sure, these children are conceived in sin, but even before their baptism they are justified by the power of the covenant promise." These are powerful statements. "Salvation, therefore, is not by baptism but solely by grace (the promise of the covenant) and by faith (the parents' belief in the promise)."[21] Are our children Christian? "So, too, can Christian parents today be confident that their children are Christians."[22]

Christian parents can be confident that their children are Christians.

The other co-author of the Heidelberg Catechism, Zacharias Ursinus, is just as clear in expressing what our covenant children possess in infancy:

---

[20] Lyle D. Bierma, *German Calvinism in the Confessional Age: The Covenant Theology of Caspar Olevianus* (Grand Rapids: Baker, 1996), 99.

[21] Ibid., 101.

[22] Ibid., 100.

Those are not to be excluded from baptism, to whom the benefit of the remission of sins, and of regeneration belongs. But this benefit belongs to the infants of the church; for redemption from sin, by the blood of Christ and the Holy Ghost, the author of faith, is promised to them no less than to the adult. . . .

Those unto whom the things signified belong, unto them the sign also belongs. . . .

Baptism ought to be administered to infants also; for they are holy; the promise is unto them; the kingdom of heaven is theirs.[23]

Are they members of the church? Yes, "Since the infant children of Christians are also included in the church."[24]

Perhaps the most pressing and disturbing question for some who read the above statements is whether they in any way deny the necessity of regeneration. Ursinus continues, "Infants have the Holy Ghost, and are regenerated by him." Regarding baptized infants he says, "All, and only those who are renewed or being renewed, receive baptism lawfully, being baptized for those ends for which Christ instituted this sacrament."[25] He held that we baptize infants because they are "renewed." Hence, the Reformers consistently saw the need for, and the fact of, our children's regeneration. Rather than denying the necessity of the Spirit's work in regeneration, they *believed* and had *faith* that God was already at work in a child's heart from his earliest days, based on the promises of the covenant.

Ursinus and Olevianus also had confidence concerning the future of these young ones. In calling them *saints*, they were also stating that they would *persevere as saints*. Under Lord's Day 20 in the Heidelberg Catechism, we read that the Holy Ghost "comforts me; and shall abide with me forever."[26] They taught children to learn, memorize

---

[23] Zacharias Ursinus, *The Commentary on the Heidelberg Catechism,* 2nd ed., trans. W. Williard (Phillipsburg: Presbyterian and Reformed, n.d. [reprint of 1852 Second American Edition]), 366–367.

[24] Ibid., 373.

[25] Ibid., 370–373.

[26] Heidelberg Catechism, question and answer 53.

and believe the questions of the Catechism, written self-consciously to instruct the youth, a point we must be sure to emphasize. As they became able to understand, parents and church impressed upon covenant children that they would, "Hereafter, in eternity, reign with Him over all creatures."[27] Concerning the church, the children learned to say, "I am, and forever shall remain, a living member of the same."[28] From the earliest ages, a child was to believe the answer to the first question of the Heidelberg Catechism, including this: "Because I belong to Him, Christ, by His Holy Spirit, assures me of eternal life and makes me whole-heartedly willing and ready from now on to live for Him." These men surely demonstrated a confidence with respect to our children, not only of God's love for them as infants, but of His continued presence with them.

Guido de Brès

Guido de Brès, the author of the Belgic Confession, had a similar perspective. "The Scriptures teach that all children . . . are by nature children of wrath. . . . The wrath of God remains upon all those who are not obedient to the Son . . . which remains on us and our children as long as we are not found to be in his covenant and congregation."[29] If someone is in covenant, we are to have confidence that God's wrath is no longer on him. We read in the Belgic Confession, "And indeed Christ shed His blood no less for the washing of the children of believers than for adult persons."[30] As one writer has said,

One sees that the Belgic Confession was clearly composed from an internal holiness view[31] of covenantal holiness. The baptism of infants of believers rested on assumed election and assumed internal

[27] Heidelberg Catechism, Lord's Day 12, Q & A 32.

[28] Heidelberg Catechism, Lord's Day 21, Q & A 54.

[29] Qtd. in Jonathan Neil Gerstner, *The Thousand Generation Covenant: Dutch Reformed Covenant Theology and Group Identity in Colonial South Africa, 1652–1814* (Leiden: E. J. Brill, 1991), 16.

[30] Belgic Confession, Article 34.

[31] That is, regenerated and forgiven.

holiness. The children of believers were separate from the children of the world internally as well as externally.[32]

Thus we find a consistent testimony in both the Belgic Confession and the Heidelberg Catechism.

John Calvin

One could write an entire work alone on Calvin's views on this subject. While we cannot here visit every source or answer every potential objection, it is clear that Calvin argued for a view of covenant children similar to the views of his fellow Magisterial Reformers. That is, we are to understand that children with God-fearing parents in a faithful church are fully Christian, having the forgiveness of sins, and are thus legitimate members of the church of Christ. Moreover, we ought to have confidence that they will continue as such.

We read in Calvin's catechism for the church of Geneva that baptism is a "kind of entrance into the Church."[33] After noting that baptism consists in "forgiveness of sins" and "spiritual regeneration," he continues that it is more than simply a figure. "I understand it to be a figure, but still so that the reality is annexed to it; for God does not disappoint us when He promises us His gifts. Accordingly, it is *certain* that both pardon of sins and newness of life are offered to us in baptism and *received by us*."[34] Is this true for children? "The force, and so to speak, the substance of baptism are common to children."[35]

> *Calvin argues that we are to understand covenant children as fully Christian.*

---

[32] Gerstner, *Thousand Generation Covenant,* 16.

[33] John Calvin, "Catechism of the Church of Geneva," *Treatises on the Sacraments, Catechism of the Church of Geneva, Forms of Prayer, and Confessions of Faith, Tracts by John Calvin,* trans. Henry Beveridge (Ross-shire, Great Britain: Christian Focus Publications, 2002), 86.

[34] Ibid., 87. Emphasis mine.

[35] Ibid., 89.

It should be of special interest that this catechism was written with the intention "to see that children should be duly instructed in the Christian religion"[36] and the principal reason for publishing this catechism was "concerning posterity."[37] We should note that Calvin does not speak here of the necessity of a covenant child's "conversion" in the manner that has become so common today. For such a concept, arguably a vital issue for both church and parents, to be absent from an agreed-upon, standard, historic catechism *for children* is telling and very significant.

We see this confirmed in Calvin's Strasbourg Catechism, which is similar to other catechisms of the era:

> Q. Are you, my son, a Christian in fact as well as in name?
> A. Yes, my father.
> Q. How do you know yourself to be?
> A. Because I am baptized in the name of the Father and of the Son and of the Holy Spirit.[38]

Hughes Oliphant Old writes of the Reformers' views, "Baptism is the fact, Christian instruction is the explanation of that fact, and the saying of the catechism is its acceptance."[39]

Further, in the "Form of Administering Baptism at Geneva" (for infants), we read concerning their salvation:

> All these graces are bestowed upon us when he is pleased to incorporate us into his Church by baptism; for in this sacrament he attests the remission of our sins. And he has ordained the symbol of water to figure to us, that as by this element bodily defilements are cleansed, so he is pleased to wash and purify our souls.
>
> Now then since the Lord Jesus Christ came down to earth, not to diminish the grace of God his Father, but to extend the covenant

---

[36] Ibid., 37.

[37] Ibid., 35.

[38] Hughes Oliphant Old, *The Shaping of the Reformed Baptismal Rite in the Sixteenth Century* (Grand Rapids: Eerdmans, 1992), 207.

[39] Ibid., 207.

of salvation over all the world, instead of confining it as formerly to the Jews, *there is no doubt that our children are heirs of the life* which he has promised to us.[40]

The Reformers expected baptized children to mature as Christians and to take and believe these promises personally as the fruit of their Christian instruction, as evidenced in Calvin's *Institutes*:

> How I wish that we might have kept the custom which, as I have said, existed among the ancient Christians . . . a catechizing, in which children or those near adolescence would give an account of their faith before the church. . . . *A child of ten* would present himself to the church to declare his confession of faith, would be examined in each article, and answer to each; if he were ignorant of anything or insufficiently understood it, he would be taught.
>
> If this discipline were in effect today, it would certainly arouse some slothful parents, who carelessly neglect the instruction of their children as a matter of no concern to them; for then they could not overlook it without public disgrace.[41]

Calvin would have children give an account of their faith and undergo additional instruction if needed. However, this expectation does not equal a guarantee about a child's future faithfulness. If one does not exercise faith and repentance, he is a covenant breaker and will eventually lose his privileged status. Calvin notes concerning the blessing of baptism in the Geneva Catechism that some "by their depravity, make it void to themselves"[42] and the "wicked, so to speak, annihilate the gifts of God offered in the sacraments."[43] Of course, "It is little to have begun, unless you persevere."[44] Faith and repentance are

---

[40] Calvin, "Form of Administering Baptism" in "Form of Administering the Sacraments Composed for the Use of the Church in Geneva," *Treatises,* 114–15. Emphasis mine.

[41] *Institutes of the Christian Religion,* trans. Ford Lewis Battles, ed. J. McNeill (Philadelphia: Westminster, 1960), 1460–1461 (IV.xix.13). Emphasis mine.

[42] Calvin, "Geneva Sacraments," *Treatises,* 87.

[43] Ibid., 85.

[44] Ibid., 83.

required throughout the lives of any covenant member, youth or adult. However, this is not to say that those too young to exercise mature faith are without the benefits of the covenant. He emphatically disagrees with this Anabaptist position while commenting on Matthew 19:13–14:

> To exclude from the grace of redemption those who are of that age would be too cruel. . . . [The Anabaptists] refuse baptism to *infants*, because infants are incapable of understanding that mystery which is denoted by it. We, on the other hand, maintain that . . . it ought not to be denied to *infants*, whom God adopts and washes with the blood of his Son. Their objection, that repentance and newness of life are also denoted by it, is easily answered. *Infants* are renewed by the Spirit of God, according to the capacity of their age. . . . Again, when they argue that there is no other way in which we are reconciled to God, and become heirs of adoption, than by faith, we admit this as to adults, but, with respect to *infants*, this passage demonstrates it to be false. . . . But it is presumption and sacrilege to drive far from the fold of Christ those whom he cherishes in his bosom. . . .[45]

This is the ordinary way that Calvin speaks concerning children born into faithful churches and families. Yes, Calvin does at times make comments, referring to those who were baptized as infants, that God "regenerates in childhood or adolescence, occasionally even in old age."[46] Surely we sometimes see God work at a later age to bring some to mature faith, especially when we fail to nurture their faith properly in the early years. However, he plainly does not hold this to be the expected pattern by which God-fearing parents should raise their children. He writes that the promise to bless a thousand generations of those who fear the Lord "is not vain or fallacious."[47]

---

[45] John Calvin, *Commentary on a Harmony of the Gospels,* trans. William Pringle (Grand Rapids: Baker, 1996), 2:390–391. Emphasis original.

[46] Calvin, "Geneva Sacraments," *Treatises,* 218.

[47] Ibid., 60.

Calvin maintains that children have regeneration. "I then infer that children have need of regeneration. But I maintain that this gift comes to them by promise, and that baptism follows as a seal."[48] He states that he learned this from Augustine. They not only have regeneration, but also the forgiveness of sins, for we should not doubt "whether it is to them a laver of regeneration, nor whether it seals the pardon of their sins."[49] Yet, water baptism is not absolutely necessary to salvation since "we hold, that baptism, instead of regenerating or saving them, only seals the salvation of which they were previously partakers."[50] This is so because

> they are already of the flock of Christ, of the family of God, since the covenant of salvation which God enters into with believers is common also to their children. . . . In one word, unless we choose to overturn all the principles of religion, we shall be obliged to confess that the salvation of an infant does not depend on, but is only sealed by its baptism.[51]

To think otherwise, according to Calvin, is to overthrow all the principles of religion.

Others have come to similar conclusions with respect to the prominent theologians of the sixteenth century. Hughes Oliphant Old, author of *The Shaping of the Reformed Baptismal Rite in the Sixteenth Century,* provides us with an important analysis—even of those who allegedly provide the weakest testimony to the argument thus far presented. While granting that Ulrich Zwingli separated the sign and

---

[48] "Appendix to the Tract on The True Method of Reforming the Church, In Which Calvin Refutes the Censure of an Anonymous Printer on the Sanctification of Infants and Baptism by Women," *Selected Works of John Calvin: Tracts and Letters,* vol. 3, *Tracts Part 3 1554–1558,* ed. Henry Beveridge and Jules Bonnet (Albany, Ore.: AGES Software, 1998), 320.

[49] "True Method," *Selected Works,* 319.

[50] "Concerning the Sacraments, Westphal," *Treatises,* 319, emphasis mine.

[51] "Letter 438 to John Clauberger, Geneva, 24th June 1556," *Selected Works of John Calvin: Tracts and Letters,* vol. 6, *Letters 1554–1558, Part 3,* ed. Henry Beveridge and Jules Bonnet (Albany, Ore.: AGES Software, 1998), 279.

the seal in a more radical way than the other Reformers, Old writes that he eventually came to realize that covenant theology included "a promise of divine grace,"[52] that baptism was the beginning of the Christian life,[53] and that "even in unborn infants God was already at work."[54] With respect to infant baptism, Old notes Zwingli held "that baptism had to do with full and complete forgiveness of all sin . . . that a child is joined to the people of God which is moving from death to life, from a sinful life to a new life."[55] Concerning Martin Bucer, Old writes, "Bucer has doubtlessly drawn too great a distinction between the outward sign and the inward grace," but he goes on to argue, "In coming years Bucer himself would do much to rectify this."[56] Old notes that for John Oecolampadius, the German Reformer and associate of Zwingli known for his patristic scholarship, baptism represents "signs of divine promises to which God will surely be faithful" and "God works where he has promised to work. That was the heart of the theology of the covenant."[57] Therefore, "Oecolampadius is confident that God is working in the hearts even of very young babies."[58] After a review of such sixteenth-century Reformational leaders, Old writes, "The baptism of infants demonstrated very powerfully that our salvation rests not on any knowledge or work or experience or decision of our own, but entirely on the grace of God."[59] *This is the essence of the Reformed faith.*

Of course, we see development in Reformational thought; not every Reformer was as uniform as the aforementioned testimony. However, even men such as Theodore Beza, who made uncertain statements about covenant children at the Colloquy of Montbéliard,[60]

---

[52] Old, *Baptismal Rite,* 124.
[53] Ibid., 131.
[54] Ibid., 133.
[55] Ibid., 247-248.
[56] Ibid., 55.
[57] Ibid., 73.
[58] Ibid., 137.
[59] Ibid., 139.
[60] For instance, see Jill Raitt, *The Colloquy of Montbéliard: Religion and Politics in the Sixteenth Century* (New York: Oxford Univ. Press, 1993), 137–147; or Jeffrey J. Meyers, "The

still considered our children as having the "witness of election" and that "all children born of pious parents are saved, with exception of course for the hidden decree of God."[61]

Jonathan Gerstner has written an excellent study of the Dutch Reformed views on this matter entitled *The Thousand Generation Covenant*. Although personally not in agreement with the Magisterial Reformers at this point, he provides an outstanding overview of the consistent testimony among various sixteenth-century Reformational leaders in the Netherlands. In his catechism, the Reformer John Laski states that our children are "redeemed, washed in Christ's blood, members of Christ's Church."[62] Martin Micron notes, "One can be more sure of the children of believers being in a state of redemption than of adults,"[63] perhaps because although sinful in Adam, they have committed no conscious sins and do not have the mental maturity to apostatize. Gerstner argues that Petrus Datheen "is very typical of the early Reformed in the Netherlands in having an extremely optimistic view of the state of children of believers."[64] In speaking of Gaspar van der Heyden, Gerstner states he held a "strong view of children being redeemed from their mother's womb."[65] This was standard theology in the Netherlands in the sixteenth century. The accepted Dutch Reformed form for baptism teaches, as summarized by Gerstner, "The covenant obligations are entirely thanksgiving for a salvation already possessed."[66]

Writing on the Reformers, Louis Berkhof notes in *The History of Christian Doctrines*, "They had to prove in opposition, especially to the Anabaptists, but also to the Roman Catholics and the Lutherans, that children can be regarded as believers before baptism, and as such

---

Development of the Reformed Doctrine of Baptism" (taped lecture from the 1995 Biblical Horizons Conference, available from Biblical Horizons, P. O. Box 1096, Niceville, FL 32588).

[61] Qtd. in Gerstner, *Thousand Generation Covenant,* 7.

[62] Ibid., 54.

[63] Ibid., 54.

[64] Ibid., 55.

[65] Ibid., 52.

[66] Ibid., 51.

ought to be baptized."[67] The Reformers understood our children as
fully Christian. That is, the children of the covenant did not merely
have certain advantages of being in the covenant or the church, but
they had salvation entire—whether described by forgiveness of sins,
regeneration, being covered by the blood of Christ, justified, sanctified, or members of the kingdom
of heaven. Since this is what they
possessed, they did not need to obtain these blessings for the first time
at some future point. They were

> *The Reformers understood our children as fully Christian.*

members in good standing in Christ's church and were expected to
continue as such through faithful parental training in complete reli-
ance on the work of the Holy Spirit.

Paradigm Transition: The Seventeenth and Eighteenth Centuries

In the two centuries following the Reformation, we find many Reformed leaders continuing to hold to the same "fully covenantal"
perspective in a manner consistent with the Magisterial Reformers.
However, we also observe much change and transition, some of it
revolutionary.

Continuity

It is the tradition of the Continental Reformed Churches to use only
synod-approved sacramental forms. The Synod of Dort (1618–1619)
provided the standard Dutch Reformed infant baptismal form that
is still in use today, with some modifications.[68] Concerning the baptism of infant children, the form states, "Although our children do
not understand these things . . . they are without their knowledge

---

[67] *History of Christian Doctrines* (Grand Rapids: Baker, 1937), 250.

[68] This was itself a modification of the form approved by the 1578 National Synod of
Dort.

partakers of the condemnation in Adam, and so again are received unto grace in Christ."The form ends with a prayer of thanksgiving that includes the following. "Thou hast forgiven us and our children all our sins, through the blood of Thy beloved Son Jesus Christ, and received us through Thy Holy Spirit as members of Thine only be-gotten Son and so adopted us to be Thy children."[69] These very same men who formulated the five points of Calvinism in response to the Arminian controversy also clearly stated that our children are for-given and members of the kingdom of heaven. This is entirely con-sistent with other early Reformed baptismal forms.[70] In commenting on a certain phrase in the Dutch form, Gerstner states,"There cer-tainly is little historical doubt that the phrase was interpreted as speaking of the children of the covenant being internally holy in the early history of the Dutch Reformed Church."[71]

The same Synod composed the following in the Canons of Dort concerning covenant children:

> Since we are to judge of the will of God from His Word, which tes-tifies that the children of believers are holy, not by nature, but in virtue of the covenant of grace, in which they together with their parents are comprehended, godly parents ought not to doubt the election and salvation of their children whom it pleases God to call out of this life in their infancy (Gen. 17:7; Acts 2:39; 1 Cor. 7:14).[72]

Although there has been debate on how to interpret section I.17 of the Canons, the wording is actually quite clear: we should consider

---

[69] *Psalter Hymnal of the Christian Reformed Church* (Grand Rapids: Publication Committee of the Christian Reformed Church, 1959), 87.

[70] For instance, in the French Baptismal Form for infants we read, "Little child, for you Jesus Christ has come, He has fought, He has suffered. For you He entered into the shadows of Gethsemane and the terror of Calvary; For you He uttered the cry 'it is fin-ished.' For you He rose from the dead and ascended into heaven, and there for you He intercedes. For you, even though you do not know it, little child, but in this way the Word of the Gospel is made true, 'We love Him because He first loved us.'"

[71] Gerstner, *Thousand Generation Covenant,* 56.

[72] Canons of Dort, I.17.

our children holy while not doubting their salvation. This view is perfectly consistent with the standard position of Reformed churches at this time. Writing of children who die in infancy, Cornelis Venema of Mid-America Reformed Seminary argues that this section of the Canons teaches "not only that parents should be confident of their children's salvation but also that such children are indeed elect of God."[73]

Regarding the accepted view in the Netherlands in the seventeenth century, C. A. Schouls writes,

> What we see develop in the period after the Synod of Dort is a two track approach in understanding the Covenant of Grace: early on, by far the majority held that all children of believers are internally holy: they are redeemed or, at least, *presumed* to have been born again until they show otherwise later in life.[74]

He asserts that throughout the seventeenth century, "by far" this was the widely held view. This too was the perspective held by the most prominent continental theologians of the century. Arguably the most influential Dutch theologian, Gisbertus Voetius (1589–1676) states that infants "have the Holy Ghost and forgiveness of sins just as much as adults"[75] while Johannes Cocceius (1603–1669) believes in the "internal holiness" of covenant children and that they are "already redeemed."[76] Herman Witsius (1636–1708) defends infant baptism: "It is unjustifiable to exclude from baptism those who are made partakers of the Holy Spirit."[77]

[73] Cornelis Venema, "The Doctrine of the Sacraments and Baptism according to the Reformed Confessions," *Mid-America Journal of Theology* 11 (2000): 63.

[74] C. A. Schouls, *The Covenant of Grace: Its Scriptural Origins and Development in Continental Theology* (Vineland, Ontario: Niagara Ligonier Study Centre, 1996), 29. Emphasis original.

[75] Gerstner, *Thousand Generation Covenant,* 122.

[76] Ibid., 133.

[77] Herman Witsius, *The Economy of the Covenants Between God and Man,* 2 vols., trans. William Crookshank (Escondido, Calif.: The den Dulk Christian Foundation, 1990 [London: R. Baynes, 1822]), 2:441.

Francis Turretin (1623–1687), who exerted significant influence at Princeton Seminary and is a highly respected theologian even to this day in Presbyterian churches, writes:

> Because to infants belongs the kingdom of heaven according to the declaration of Christ. . . . Why should the church not receive into her bosom those whom Christ received into his? . . . Because the children of believers are holy; therefore they ought to be baptized. For since they have the thing signified, they cannot and ought not to be deprived of the sign.[78]

For Turretin, federal holiness did not mean merely external church membership but that our children did in fact—in every respect—belong to the church and were Christians.[79] In fact, the grace of passive regeneration was not to be denied, because "grace operates in infants" even if we cannot understand it.[80] Moreover, similar to the position of those at Dort, holding to such a view in no way weakens the doctrine of perseverance: "The doctrine of perseverance is not at all endangered here, which remains constant with respect to the elect."[81]

His arguments against the Roman sacrament of confirmation are also helpful to note:

> However, we say that in place of this theatrical representation, the sacred custom of the ancient church can rightly be observed (to wit, that the baptized be diligently instructed in catechetical doctrine when they have reached the age of reason and discretion; then that they be presented to the bishop or pastor in order to render an account of their progress and have the promises ratified in their name which were made by their parents and sponsors when they were baptized; that they may be dismissed with the prayers and the blessing

---

[78] Turretin, *Institutes of Elenctic Theology*, 3:417.
[79] See ibid., 417–418.
[80] Ibid., 419–20.
[81] Ibid., 420.

of the bishop and pastor and be admitted to the reception of the
Eucharist with the rest of the adult believers).[82]

Critical to our argument is Turretin's point that this is the "custom
of the ancient church." He complains that the Catholic position be-
littles our children's standing as fully Christian: "It derogates from
baptism because according to the Roman doctrine, it follows that
baptism does not quite make us Christians." Turretin argues that
Christian children have already been "admitted into communion with
Him and by baptism were implanted in Christ."[83] Hence, he sees baptized children of godly parents as fully Christian, without reservation.

Although a detailed analysis of the Westminster Confession of
Faith is beyond the scope of this survey, in the Larger Catechism the
Divines call baptism "a sign and seal of our regeneration and
ingrafting into Christ, *and that even to infants*."[84] The answer to question 167 of the Larger Catechism conspicuously fails to make any al-
lusion to "conversion" (as generally understood today) as a necessary
or normal step in improving our baptism. This is obviously significant since the majority of those baptized in Presbyterian churches are
infants. The Westminster Confession states that a person's baptism
is "a sign and seal of the covenant of grace, of his ingrafting into
Christ, of regeneration, of remission of sins, and of his giving up unto
God, through Jesus Christ, to walk in newness of life."[85] The Confession nowhere distinguishes infant baptism as somehow being less
efficacious.

Matthew Henry's (1662–1714) Catechism for Children states,

Q. 29. What relation do you stand to the Lord Jesus?
A. I am one of his disciples; *for I am a baptized Christian*. . . .
Q. 31. What was the meaning of your being so baptized?

---

[82] Ibid., 549.
[83] Ibid., 549–550.
[84] Westminster Larger Catechism, question and answer 177. Emphasis mine.
[85] Westminster Confession of Faith, 28.1.

A. I was thereby given up in a covenant way, to Father, Son and Holy Ghost."[86]

This is similar to Calvin's catechism and Turretin's arguments for why a covenant youth can consider himself a Christian—on the basis of his baptism. In Henry's catechism for children, although certainly he makes clear the conditions of faith and repentance and the need to take the covenant to oneself personally, nowhere do we see any emphasis or requirement for "conversion" having the modern connotation of the word. It is clear that the views of Calvin and Bullinger, both authors of the standard theological textbooks for the era, were prominent and widely held in the subsequent centuries.

From Covenant to Conversion

At the same time, however, we also see much change during this period. The seventeenth-century Dutch pastor Jacobus Koelman (1632–1695), wrote in 1679 that we should "try to save [our children] with all appropriate means prescribed by God."[87] He elsewhere pleads that we should "pray that [God] may regenerate them."[88] Gerstner comments on Koelman, "He makes very clear that children of believers must be assumed not to be redeemed until they prove otherwise."[89] To underscore Koelman's theological deviation, Gerstner notes that his thought "was before its time. It would not be until the next century"[90] that it was more widely held.

Even though such views would not be common for some time among the Dutch theologians, this was not the case for the Puritans.

---

[86] Matthew Henry, "A Plain Catechism for Children, July 7, 1703," *Concerning Baptism and the Covenant of Grace*, vol. 2 of *The Complete Works of the Rev. Matthew Henry* (Edinburgh, A. Fullarton & Co., n.d.), 260. Emphasis mine.

[87] Jacobus Koelman, *The Duties of Parents*, trans. John Vriend (Grand Rapids: Baker, 2003 [1679]), 30.

[88] Ibid., 41.

[89] Gerstner, *Thousand Generation Covenant*, 130.

[90] Ibid., 132.

Although the Puritans certainly emphasized the covenant and frequently used covenant terminology, we undoubtedly find a devaluing of the blessings assumed to be possessed by covenant children. The well-known and respected Thomas Shepard (1605–1649) argues that our covenant children are rightly members in the church of Christ. However, his understanding of membership varies from the norm of the previous century as he holds that our children are only members of an "outward covenant" and believes that a child lacks grace "till he be converted." Shepard describes two classes of church membership as "they are in external and outward covenant, and therefore outwardly Church members, to whom belong *some outward privileges* of the covenant for their inward and eternal good." He states that covenant children must "repent and be *converted* for [they] are the children of the covenant."[91]

> *In the Puritans we find a devaluing of the blessings assumed to be possessed by covenant children.*

This paradigmatic standard of "conversion," even for covenant infants and young children, becomes normative among the Puritans, especially in America. "Every pious New Englander cherished the experience of conversion,"[92] writes E. Brooks Holifield, and he speaks of the "Puritan notion of genuine conversion as a specifiable experience."[93] David D. Hall notes how the Puritans stressed the "work of grace" or "conversion"[94] in his introduction to Norman Pettit's *The Heart Prepared: Grace and Conversion in Puritan Spiritual Life*. In this work, Pettit outlines the steps of "preparation" to be followed among the Puritans so that one in the covenant might be saved. Cotton Mather (1663–1728) stated, "Alas, man, until your

---

[91] Thomas Shepard, "The Church Membership of Children," in *The Reformation of the Church* (Carlisle, Pa.: Banner of Truth, 1997), 384, 399, 402. Emphasis mine.

[92] E. Brooks Holifield, *The Covenant Sealed* (New Haven: Yale Univ. Press, 1974), 148.

[93] Ibid., 86.

[94] David D. Hall, introduction to Norman Pettit, *The Heart Prepared: Grace and Conversion in Puritan Spiritual Life* (Middletown, Conn.: Wesleyan Univ. Press, 1989), xix.

children become regenerate, you are the father of a fool. Your children are but the wild ass's colt!"[95] William Cooper writes about the duties of parents to covenant children: "They should be often telling them what a miserable and sinful state they are in by nature, the need they stand in of Christ, the necessity of their being born again, and the like."[96] This obviously differs from what has previously been set forth. For instance, note the sixteenth-century post-baptismal prayer in Strasbourg, *for infants*, in which they thanked God "that you have born him again to yourself through your holy baptism, that he has been incorporated into your beloved Son, our only Savior, and is now your child and heir."[97]

In the standard Puritan works on regeneration and conversion,[98] the authors write as though a covenant child's regeneration and conversion would have the same character and appearance as that of an unrepentant adult who is not a member of the church. These authors fail to make any distinction or to note any special, nuanced

> *"Alas, man, until your children become regenerate, you are the father of a fool. Your children are but the wild ass's colt!"*
>
> *—Cotton Mather*

requirements for covenant children and appear not to allow for God's work of grace in a covenant child, which normally allows him to grow up always loving, knowing and trusting in the Lord from his mother's

---

[95] Cotton Mather, *A Family Well-Ordered* (Morgan, Pa.: Soli Deo Gloria, 2001 [Boston: n.p., 1699]), 6.

[96] William Cooper, "God's Concern for a Godly Seed," sermon preached in Boston on March 5, 1723, in Don Kistler, ed., *God's Call to Young People: A Call to the Rising Generation to Know and Serve God While They Are Still Young* (Morgan, Pa.: Soli Deo Gloria, 2001), 26.

[97] Old, *Baptismal Rite,* 167.

[98] See Peter Van Mastricht (1630–1706), *Treaty on Regeneration* (Morgan, Pa.: Soli Deo Gloria, 2002); Joseph Alleine (1634–1668), *Alarm to the Unconverted,* currently published under the title *A Sure Guide to Heaven* (Edinburgh: Banner of Truth, 1989); and Nathaniel Vincent (1644–1697), "Conversion of a Sinner" in *The Puritans On Conversion: Sermons by Samuel Bolton, Nathaniel Vincent and Thomas Watson,* ed. Albert N. Martin (Ligonier, Pa.: Soli Deo Gloria, 1990).

womb. Thomas Vincent (1634–1678) writes of how God works with His Spirit to bring about the "requirement" of conversion:

> Thus the sinner is brought into great distress and perplexity of mind. He looks about him for help, but all succor fails him. He struggles and would fain break the bonds which are upon him, but he finds himself more entangled. . . . So he flies to duties and to ordinances; he prays and hears and reads, and turns from his former ungodly company and practices, and frequents the company of the saints and servants to God, joining with them in all religious observances and exercises. But still he finds (if God works on him effectually) that none of these can remove the guilt of one sin.[99]

Instead of looking to Christ, as symbolized in one's baptism, Holifield writes, "Many of them could recall dramatic experiences of conversion—and memory suggested that the essence of religion consisted in inwardness."[100]

Yet Confidence . . .

Even in light of this shift in thinking, many still had great confidence that God would do a good work in their children and produce generational faith. We do have exceptions to this rule; for example, Edward Lawrence (1623–1695) wrote, "It is ordinary for godly parents to have wicked and ungodly children," and "Let none presume to censure godly parents for their wicked children."[101] However, at this time, his view was not the norm. Edward Morgan writes in *The Puritan Family* about parents' confidence in succession: "If [children]

[99] Thomas Vincent, *The Good Work Begun: A Puritan Pastor Speaks to Teenagers* (Morgan, Pa.: Soli Deo Gloria, 1998), 6–7.

[100] Holifield, *Covenant*, 168.

[101] Edward Lawrence, *Parents' Concerns for Their Unsaved Children* (Morgan, Pa.: Soli Deo Gloria, 2003), originally published as *Parents' Groans Over Their Wicked Children* (London: n.p., 1681), 3, 28. We should note that Lawrence did believe that our children begin their lives as "subjects of the kingdom," but that failed to provide him with confidence regarding covenant succession.

were properly brought up, it was almost certain that the promise would be fulfilled" and he notes they held to "the practical certainty of the desired results."[102] Jacobus Koelman writes, "If you will do this work of rearing children faithfully and successfully . . . you will also have good reason to expect the favor of the Lord upon your work in child rearing," and "A blessing upon its exercise has been promised and is assured."[103] According to Holifield, Thomas Hooker (1586–1647) held that "whenever baptism was lawfully administered, the Spirit would 'go along with it' to assure the faithful of God's fidelity to his covenant promises."[104] Thomas Shepard said that "God gives parents some comfortable hope of their children's salvation"[105] and John Cotton taught that the promise includes "upon the faith of the Parent, salvation to his household" and that God will "sooner or later . . . performe that work in our Children."[106] One could find similar beliefs among later Puritans such as Philip Doddridge (1702–1751), who wrote that godly nurture "may very probably be a means of moving their impressionable hearts,"[107] while Henry Venn (1725–1797) said, "When these things are enforced by a good example accompanied by prayer, there is little doubt but that their children will be greatly blessed and, generally speaking, tread in the steps of their godly and excellent parents."[108]

Although perhaps not as encouraging, another way to see the Puritan commitment to covenant succession is to notice how frequently they lay blame and guilt upon parents for their failure in faithful parenting. Richard Mather (1596–1669) lamented that parents

---

[102] Edward S. Morgan, *The Puritan Family: Religion and Domestic Relations in Seventeenth Century New England* (New York: Harper & Row, 1966 [1944]), 91.

[103] Koelman, *Duties of Parents,* 25, 29.

[104] Holifield, *Covenant,* 156.

[105] Shepard, "Membership of Children," 401.

[106] Holifield, *Covenant,* 157. Original spelling.

[107] Philip Doddridge, "A Plain and Serious Address to the Master of a Family on the Important Subject of Family Religion," in *The Godly Family: Essays on the Duties of Parents and Children* (Pittsburgh, Pa.: Soli Deo Gloria, 1993), 57.

[108] Henry Venn, "The Relative Duties on the Method of Instructing Children," in *The Godly Family,* 139.

"are damned for it,"[109] while Cotton Mather warned, "Thy punishment shall be terrible, in the Day of the Lord's pleading with thee."[110] This became standard fare as George Whitefield (1714–1770) admonished, "Do you not think that the damnation which men must endure for their own sins will be sufficient, that they need to load themselves with the additional guilt of being an accessory to the damnation of others also?"[111] The rebuke of Samuel Davies (1723–1763) is as follows:

> Their souls, sirs, their immortal souls, are entrusted to your care, and you must give a solemn account of your trust; and can you think you faithfully discharge it while you neglect to maintain your religion in your families? Will you not be accessory to their perdition, and in your skirts will there not be found the blood of your poor innocent children? What a dreadful meeting may you expect to have with them at last?[112]

Parents were responsible to discharge their duties and were faithfully warned, in prophetic fashion, concerning the failure to perform these duties.

A Theology of Unbelief

These warnings, promises, and exhortations to confidence, however, oftentimes produced little success in New England. Holifield writes, "In some towns, according to Solomon Stoddard (1643–1729), there were 'scarce five or six' young people who would 'attend the Lord's Supper.'"[113] And although it is well known that churches were composed of multitudes of non-communicant "members" by the time of

---

[109] Richard Mather, "Farewell Exhortation," qtd. in Edward S. Morgan, *The Puritan Family,* 92.

[110] Cotton Mather, *Corderius Americanus,* as quoted in ibid., 92.

[111] George Whitfield, "The Great Duty of Family Religion," in *The Godly Family,* 45.

[112] Samuel Davies, "The Necessity and Excellency of Family Religion," in *The Godly Family,* 15.

[113] Holifield, *Covenant,* 200.

the Great Awakening, the problems clearly began long before the eighteenth century. After the Cambridge Platform of 1648, Morgan notes, "Before two decades had passed, the fact was plain that most children of saints did not receive saving faith by the time they were physically mature."[114] We read in *The Puritan Family*, "In spite of their theological advantages and in spite of all the preaching directed at them, the children did not get converted."[115]

To be sure, their theology often "encouraged" such results in various ways. They told their children to delay faith. Increase Mather (1639–1723) speaks to young and allegedly unsaved covenant members with this advice: "Wait on God in the use of His own means, that He would be merciful to you."[116] Holifield notes that Hooker, Cotton, and Shepard "had not pleaded with the doubtful to advance a claim for the sacrament"[117] while Pettit records, "Seldom in Cotton's thought are the baptized encouraged to anticipate the promises as rightful heirs of the covenant seed."[118] Salvation became intricate and difficult with men like William Perkins speaking of the "ten stages in an individual's acquisition of faith."[119] Pettit writes of Shepard and Hooker "making the standards of grace too high," which is perhaps to be expected since "Shepard's conversion, like Hooker's, was long and painful."[120] An unbalanced emphasis on election and the decrees allowed for accounts such as the following: "Betty Sewall burst into tears when she came to fear that she 'was like Spira, not Elected.'"[121] To wrongly or presumptively

Salvation became intricate and difficult, long and painful.

---

[114] Edmund S. Morgan, *Visible Saint: The History of a Puritan Idea* (Ithaca: Cornell Univ. Press, 1963), 127.

[115] Edmund S. Morgan, *The Puritan Family*, 185.

[116] Increase Mather, "Advice to the Children of Godly Ancestors," sermon given July 9, 1721, in *God's Call to Young People*, 72.

[117] Holifield, *Covenant*, 207.

[118] Norman Pettit, *The Heart Prepared*, 136.

[119] Morgan, *Visible Saints*, 68.

[120] Pettit, *The Heart Prepared*, 88, 107.

[121] Morgan, *Puritan Family*, 93.

partake of the Lord's Supper was to do so at "the risque . . . of Damnation" and the "Seal of their Damnation."[122]

Unquestionably, a theology of doubt took precedence over a theology of faith and belief. Edmund Morgan writes, "The surest earthly sign of a saint was his uncertainty."[123] Hall notes concerning John Cotton and his fellow ministers, "They were dealing with the felt need for an answer to the question, 'Am I saved?' Moreover, they were dealing with a problem that had rarely troubled John Calvin."[124] Matthew Mead (1629–1699), in *The Almost Christian Discovered*, warns that many church members may not be saved (i.e., they may "yet be but almost a Christian"), even though they "maintain a strife and combat against sin," "may have faith," "have great hopes of heaven," "be very zeal-

> *Unquestionably, a theology of doubt took precedence over a theology of faith and belief.*

ous in the matters of religion," and may "obey the commands of God."[125] In other words, instead of looking to God and His mercies in Christ, as confirmed in their baptism, they looked to themselves in doubt, unsure if they were "the visibly good, who understood and believed the doctrines of Christianity and lived accordingly but who lacked the final experience of grace."[126]

By 1662, the perceived problem of "unregenerate" church members had reached such a crisis level that the magistrate called a Synod specifically to address the issue.

> Churchmembers, who were admitted in minority, understanding the Doctrine of Faith, and publicly professing their assent thereto; not scandalous in life, and solemnly owning the Covenant before the Church, wherein they give themselves and their Children to the

---

[122] Holifield, *Covenant,* 203.

[123] Morgan, *Visible Saints,* 70.

[124] David D. Hall, in the introduction to Pettit, *The Heart Prepared,* xviii.

[125] Mathew Mead, *The Almost Christian Discovered, or The False Professor Tried and Cast* (Morgan, Pa.: Soli Deo Gloria, 1993 [1661]) 40, 48, 54, 69, 77.

[126] Morgan, *Visible Saints,* 120.

Lord, and subject themselves to the Government of Christ in the Church, their Children are to be Baptized.[127]

It is noteworthy in this statement that such church members were not considered regenerate, even though they professed "their assent" to the "Doctrine of Faith," lived godly lives, and submitted themselves to the Lord and to the church. It was just such a theological perspective—such a fundamental shift away from covenantal thinking—that gave rise to the "necessity" of the revivals of the eighteenth and nineteenth centuries.

Partial Restoration: The Nineteenth and Twentieth Centuries

The theology and practice of both Great Awakenings did further damage to the doctrine of covenant due to their radical individualism along with an emphasis on the experiential and extraordinary.[128] However, we do find opposing forces in the nineteenth and twentieth centuries that helped counter these sub-Reformed tendencies. Two positive influences in this regard are the Old Princeton Theology and the influence of the Dutch Reformed.

Princeton

The men at Old Princeton Seminary in the nineteenth century were staunch defenders of historic orthodoxy, having the reputation that they never introduced anything theologically original in the history of the seminary. Although we do find some differences between the Magisterial Reformers and the men at Old Princeton,[129] they did

---

[127] Holifield, *Covenant,* 170.

[128] See Charles Hodge, *The Constitutional History of the Presbyterian Church in the United States of America,* or Lewis Bevens Schenck, *The Presbyterian Doctrine of Children in the Covenant,* for a detailed analysis and critique.

[129] For example, contrary to the quotations that follow, Archibald Alexander appears to hold that we must consider our children as unregenerate, and the men at Old

make great efforts to amend the less than fully Reformed perspective that had become so prominent in American churches.

The noted scholars at Princeton did generally grasp the distortion of the covenant among some of the Puritans, as Benjamin B. Warfield (1851–1921) wrote in "The Polemics of Infant Baptism":

> If, on the other hand, we say that [the church's] attitude should be as inclusive as possible, and that it should receive as the children of Christ all whom, in the judgment of charity, it may fairly recognize as such, then we shall naturally widen the circle of the subjects of baptism to far more ample limits. The former represents, broadly speaking, the Puritan idea of the Church, the latter the general Protestant doctrine. It is on the basis of the Puritan conception of the Church that the Baptists are led to exclude infants from baptism. . . . All baptism is inevitably administered on the basis not of knowledge but of presumption.[130]

Hence, according to Warfield, we should consider our young ones as children of Christ in the judgment of charity.

A. A. Hodge (1823–1886) understood the meaning of *nurturing* a young child in faith. He provides a beautiful summary of a primary goal of this entire book:

> When the child is taught and trained under the regimen of his baptism—taught from the first to recognize himself as a child of God, with all its privileges and duties; trained to think, feel, and act as a child of God, to exercise filial love, to render filial obedience—the benefit to the child directly is obvious and immeasurable. He has invaluable birthright privileges, and corresponding obligations and responsibilities.[131]

Princeton would sometimes use language that was consistent with the views of the New England Theology and paradigm they opposed.

[130] Benjamin B. Warfield, "The Polemics of Infant Baptism," *Studies in Theology* (Carlisle, Pa.: Banner of Truth, 1988), 389–390.

[131] A. A. Hodge, "The Sacraments—Baptism," *Evangelical Theology: Lectures on Doctrine* (Carlisle, Pa.: Banner of Truth, 1990), 337.

We see how Hodge stressed that our children were always, from infancy, to think of themselves as fully Christian. He did not see them as aliens or slaves as did some of his southern Presbyterian brethren,[132] but as wholly belonging to God.

No doubt A. A. Hodge received this type of training in his home from his father, Charles Hodge (1797–1878), who correctly perceived the issue of the day:

> So much has this covenanting spirit died out, so little is the relation of our children to God and their interest in his promises regarded or recognized, that we have heard of men who strenuously objected to children being taught the Lord's prayer, for fear they should think God was really their father![133]

And what is the covenanting spirit?

> It is, therefore, a scriptural truth that the children of believers are the children of God, as being within his covenant with their parents, he promises to them his Spirit, he has established a connexion between faithful parental training and the salvation of children.[134]

God's promise is unmistakably qualified and dependent upon the faithful obedience of parents: "Again, it is to be remembered that these promises are conditional. God has never promised to make no distinction between faithful and unfaithful parents."[135] As quoted in the introduction, Hodge takes away every excuse for lethargy when he writes,

> Where is the parent whose children have turned aside from God, whose heart will not rather reproach him, than charge God with forgetting his promise? *Our very want of faith in the promise is one great*

---

[132] For example, compare Hodge's view with Thornwell's (above, p. 61).
[133] Hodge, "Bushnell on Christian Nurture," 514.
[134] Ibid., 507.
[135] Ibid., 505.

reason of our failure. We have forgotten the covenant. We have forgotten that our children belong to God; that he has promised to be their God, if we are faithful to our trust.[136]

We must have faith in the promise to avert continued failure, because there is a real relation between the godliness of parents and God-given fruit in child-rearing: "There is such a divinely constituted relation between the piety of parents and that of their children, as to lay a scriptural foundation for a confident expectation."[137] Seeing faith and faithfulness in our children is not random:

> There is an intimate and divinely established connexion between the faith of parents and the salvation of their children; such a connexion as authorizes them to plead God's promises, and to expect with confidence that through his blessing on their faithful efforts, their children will grow up the children of God.[138]

As stated earlier, *our choice is either covenant or chaos.*

One can scarcely find a more articulate, faithful, consistent, and balanced view of covenant succession than that of Lyman H. Atwater (1813–1883), a colleague of the Hodges at Princeton. His essays sound like Calvin and Turretin: "Baptism, in turn, is a sign and seal of nothing else than of justifying and sanctifying grace, ingrafting into Christ, and union to his body;

> *"All baptism is inevitably administered on the basis not of knowledge but of presumption." —B. B. Warfield*

and so it is the badge of union to his phenomenal body, the visible Church."[139] Opposed to popular revivalism, Atwater analyzes the central problem, which sounds very similar to ours:

---

[136] Ibid., 507. Emphasis mine.

[137] Ibid., 504.

[138] Ibid., 509.

[139] Lyman H. Atwater, "The Children of the Church, and Sealing Ordinances," *The Princeton Review* 29, no. 1 (January 1857): 7.

Consciousness of a radical change within some definite and definable period [and other indications of regeneration became], and have since [Jonathan Edwards] continued to be, in the popular mind, to a great extent, the test of piety; while the value, if not the possibility, of true Christian feeling, inwrought by the Holy Ghost, and developed gradually by Christian nurture, so as sometimes to preclude distinct statements of any time before which it was not, or of the manner and order of its progress in the soul, was then, and with too many, has been since, unduly ignored, and altogether underrated.[140]

Lengthy quotations can be difficult to absorb, but this one deserves careful attention since it so aptly summarizes the thesis of this essay.

Atwater goes on to outline what results we should expect from godly child-rearing, stating that sincere, professing Christians should be accepted at the Lord's Supper

[w]hether they remember the time and manner of the beginning and progressive development of [godly] states of mind and heart, or whether these have ingrained themselves so imperceptibly into the warp and woof of their inner being, that they can mark no distinct epoch, or hinge-point in their career, as the crisis of the new birth. It is enough that they can say, "whereas I was blind, now I see."[141]

And parents must do this with the utmost confidence, since "God will be faithful. If the other parties fulfill the conditions, he will convey the covenant blessings."[142] How are we to understand our failures? "The promise has failed because the condition of it has failed."[143]

In one sense, there is nothing unique about very young children being members of the covenant and church:

It means that the children of believers, by virtue of the divine covenant made with them through their parents, . . . are to be regarded

---

[140] Atwater, "Children of the Church," 14. Emphasis mine.
[141] Ibid., 31.
[142] Ibid., 24.
[143] Ibid., 29.

and dealt with as presumptively one with their parents in their relation to God, his kingdom and salvation; as having in their parents professed Christ, and by baptism put on the seal and badge of such profession; as being, according to their capacities, and in a manner suitable to their years, entitled to all the privileges, and bound to all the duties of Christians, of those to whom God is their God; who, being baptized into Christ, have so far forth presumptively and in appearance put on Christ; and, therefore, are expected to walk, after the manner of childhood, as befits the children of God and followers of Christ.[144]

The child and adult stand in the same place: "He is to be made to understand that the feelings, acts, habits, and manners which Christ enjoins, alone befit his position, as truly as if he were an adult professor."[145] Atwater exhorts, "Do any say that they are too young to exercise faith? Oh dreadful mistake, often made by parents and children!"[146]

Atwater's arguments are not novel but rather are simply expressions of the historic Reformed perspective, as he states, "Our standards surely set forth nothing less than this: they direct that baptized children be taught and trained to believe, feel, act, and live as becomes those who are the Lord's."[147] Our children really belong to the church and to Christ:

The children of believers are members of the visible Church—not *quasi,* but absolutely. . . . But in either case, membership in the visible Church is founded on a *presumptive* membership in the invisible, until its subjects, by acts incompatible therewith, prove the contrary, and thus, to the eye of man, forfeit their standing among God's visible people.[148]

---

[144] Lyman H. Atwater, "The Children of the Covenant, and their 'Part in the Lord,'" *The Princeton Review* 35, no. 4 (October 1863): 634.

[145] Atwater, "Children of the Church," 26.

[146] Atwater, "Children of the Covenant," 643.

[147] Atwater, "Children of the Church," 23.

[148] Ibid., 21–22. Emphasis original.

He quotes the Presbyterian Directory for Worship in which we read that our children are "to be taught to read, and repeat the Catechism, the apostles' creed, and the Lord's prayer"[149] which is to say we are to treat and train them as Christians. The views of the Hodges, Warfield, and Atwater evidenced a returning to the fathers when compared to the views that had become common, even in Reformed circles, during the previous two centuries.

The Dutch Reformed

We find a strong and confident voice for covenant succession in Dutch Reformed circles. Their sense of community alone has helped to inculcate and bring about an atmosphere conducive to covenant succession. Historically, these churches have had a keen consciousness of the antithesis[150] which is vital to pass on the faith, since our children must see themselves as distinct from the world and belonging to the people of God who are at war with the devil—thinking, believing, and acting accordingly. The CRC Church Order requires covenant children to participate in catechism classes, and parents who absented their children were historically subject to censure and discipline. As a people, they identify themselves by teaching their children to love and believe the words of the Heidelberg Catechism, answer to question 1: "I am not my own, but belong body and soul, in life and in death, to my faithful Savior Jesus Christ. He has fully paid for all my sins with his precious blood. . . ." This alone has provided them with a very solid foundation. As noted above, the 1618–1619 baptismal form adopted by the theologians at the Synod of Dort contains strong language concerning the status of the covenant child as a member of the church and as an "heir of the kingdom" with a covenantal obligation to "new obedience." Many such factors have

---

[149] Ibid., 20.

[150] A standard definition of the antithesis taught to many as part of their early training is as follows: "The antithesis is the God-ordained hostility between the seed of the woman and the seed of the serpent, the church and the world, the kingdom of God and the kingdom of the devil, the forces of righteousness and the forces of evil."

helped the Dutch Reformed Churches to be practically mindful of issues relating to covenant succession.

For many in these circles, Christian education of covenant youth is non-negotiable. The Church Order stipulates, "The consistory [elders] shall diligently encourage the members of the congregation to establish and maintain good Christian schools, and shall urge parents to have their covenant children instructed in these schools according to the demands of the covenant."[151] If a covenant child's education is not distinctively Christian, it is "grossly inconsistent," and the parents "are making a big mistake, and are chargeable before God."[152] Y. P. De Jong noted, "We assume that our Covenant children have been adopted into the family of the King of Kings—as such they must be given a princely, a royal education."[153] All this is done in confidence that God will bless obedient efforts, as one publication on Christian education notes: "But if we bring up our children in the fear of the Lord, we may bank on the promise of our Covenant God that in later years they will not depart therefrom (Proverbs 22:6)."[154] What supports this is a robust *and functional* understanding of the covenant and God's promises.

It would be simplistic, however, to state that a uniform theological view of children and covenant succession exists today among those that subscribe to the Continental Reformed confessional standards. Real differences do exist and confessional churches have self-consciously debated the related issues of covenant theology for centuries.[155] In attempting to resolve such differences, the 1905

---

[151] Church Order of the Christian Reformed Church in North America, article 71, based on the original 1618–19 Church Order of Dort.

[152] Idzerd Van Dellen and Martin Monsma, *The Church Order Commentary* (Grand Rapids: Zondervan, 1941), 98.

[153] Y. P. De Jong, *God's Covenant with Man: A Study for Advanced Catechetical Work, Bible Classes, and Societies* (Grand Rapids: n.p., 1939), 40.

[154] "The Cornerstone of Christian Education," qtd. in De Jong, *God's Covenant*, 41.

[155] Although we previously noted consistency in theological approach through much of the seventeenth century in the Netherlands, we cannot say the same for subsequent periods. As in Presbyterian circles, we find a considerable influence of Puritanism, pietism, and other factors bringing about much change in the Dutch Reformed Churches

Synod of Utrecht of the Reformed Churches in the Netherlands (GKN) declared,

> That according to the Confession of our Church the seed of the Covenant by virtue of the promise of God is to be regarded as regenerated and sanctified in Christ, until the contrary is shown in their confession and conduct when they are reaching years of discretion; but that it is less correct to say that Baptism is administered to children of believers on the ground of supposed regeneration, since the ground for Baptism is the command and the promise of God.[156]

The so-called "pacification formula" was an attempt to appeal to the diverse covenantal views within the church. Abraham Kuyper (1837–1920) and Herman Bavinck (1854–1921) were powerful men within this body and the effects of any decisions in the Netherlands had a direct consequence on the North American Dutch Churches. The North American Christian Reformed Church adopted the statement noted above in 1908. D. H. Kromminga summarizes the 1905 synod thus: "Covenant children are to be viewed as regenerate until the contrary appears. Their baptism, however, is not based on their regeneration but on God's command and promise."[157]

To oversimplify one central aspect of the debate, Abraham Kuyper and his followers argued for an unconditional covenant in which God covenanted with the individually elect only. This led to the position that if a child of the covenant apostatized, we should view that individual as never having received a "genuine baptism" or not objectively being in the covenant. Certainly Kuyper was not novel in considering covenant children regenerate, even if we can differentiate his

---

both in the Netherlands and in North America, and some would certainly agree in principle with the Puritan approach noted above. Nevertheless, the "worst" of the Dutch Reformed in this respect are often better than others in the Reformed world for the reasons noted.

[156] W. Heyns, *Manual of Reformed Doctrine* (Grand Rapids: Eerdmans, 1926), 211.

[157] Kromminga, *The Christian Reformed Tradition: From the Reformation to the Present* (Grand Rapids: Wm. B. Eerdmans, 1943), 129.

particular view from that of the Reformers. However, to deny in some way the legitimacy of our children's baptism and the objectivity of their covenant membership was seen as problematic, and tensions over these issues continued in the church.

After Kuyper's passing and when the Synod of 1944 made some of Kuyper's views authoritatively binding on the church, a group led by Klaas Schilder resisted and eventually formed Reformed Churches in the Netherlands (Liberated). Contrary to the Kuyperians, they emphasized the conditionality and objectivity of the covenant. At the same time, they avoided the language of presumptive regeneration and spoke strongly about the promise and call of God in baptism. J. Douma of the Liberated churches argues that our children still must be regenerated and converted after their baptism but yet considers our covenant children "saints," "children of God," "Christian children" and "given the promises of remission of sins and eternal life."[158] And although he is not willing to use the same language as the Magisterial Reformers, he does write that "conversion and faith are daily matters, a calling for us, adults as well as our children,"[159] which is very consistent with the historic Reformed understanding. He also notes that the blessing of God precedes faith.[160] The position statement of the Liberated ministers reads, "To all these children has been given the promise of salvation, belonging to that covenant,"[161] which certainly emphasizes confidence concerning God's work in our children. Thus, although there is much disagreement, we find an emphasis on covenant succession throughout these theological debates.

Even amidst the theological battles, we often still see an underlying confidence that God has promised to do a good work in our children. Berkhof states,

---

[158] J. Douma, *Infant Baptism and Conversion* (London, Ontario: Premier, 1979), 22, 33–35.

[159] Douma, *Infant Baptism,* 35.

[160] Ibid., 29.

[161] Cornelis Van Dam, ed., *The Liberation: Causes and Consequences* (Winnipeg: Premier, 1995), 121.

God undoubtedly desires that the covenant relationship shall issue in a covenant of life. And He Himself guarantees by His promises pertaining to the seed of believers that this will take place, not in the case of every individual but in the seed of the covenant collectively. On the basis of the promises of God we believe that, under a faithful administration of the covenant, the covenant relation will, as a rule, be fully realized in covenant life.[162]

God ensures the fulfillment of His promises and gives the richness of covenant life to our children. De Jong notes,

> Therefore the church must also continually preach and teach that the members of the covenant, that is the believers and their seed, are to be considered and labored with as members of the covenant, unto whom their baptism is a sign and seal of the ingrafting into Christ, of their regeneration, the remission of their sins, and their giving up unto God through Jesus Christ to walk in newness of life.[163]

De Jong argues that we should view and teach our children as belonging to God and as having glorious benefits. Yet we find a balance in that they must give themselves up to walk in newness of life.

Within these circles, a youth makes a profession of faith to signify the taking to himself of the covenant. If one failed to make a profession of faith, it was commonly argued that such a child should be disciplined and, if necessary, placed outside of the church.[164] When a child made a profession of faith, such was not their conversion, gaining them entrance into the kingdom of God, or "joining the church"; rather, such a view is "rightly condemned"[165] in the standard *Church Order Commentary* by Van Dellen and Monsma.

---

[162] Qtd. in De Jong, *God's Covenant*, 21.

[163] Ibid., 28–29.

[164] The Christian Reformed Church stated in 1918, "Those baptized in infancy, having arrived to years of discretion, but that do not make profession of faith, regardless of their walk otherwise, become, as unfaithful baptized members, the objects of church discipline, and if they persist in their sin, are to be excluded from the church."

[165] Van Dellen and Monsma, *Church Order Commentary*, 254.

Although not universally or even consistently the case, we do find at least a partial return to a Reformational view as a result of the Princeton theology of the nineteenth century and the Dutch Reformed influence in both North America and the Netherlands.

Concluding Analysis

Noting historical differences and trends is one thing; evaluating them is quite another. Of course, change is often beneficial—to some, the theological revisions documented here represent progress. This author views the model and approach used by the Magisterial Reformers to be both more biblically sound and more conducive to covenant succession—conducive to seeing the fulfillment of God's glorious promises concerning our covenant children.

Grace is primary in Reformational thought. As Hughes Oliphant Old wrote, "The baptism of infants demonstrated very powerfully that our salvation rests not on any knowledge or work or experience or decision of our own, but entirely on the grace of God."[166] While we do not claim absolute knowledge of God's decree, we entrust ourselves to His promises. Consider this sixteenth-century Strasbourg post-baptismal prayer *for infants*:

> Almighty God, Heavenly Father, we give you eternal praise and thanks, that you have granted and bestowed upon this child your fellowship, that you have born him again to yourself through your holy baptism, that he has been incorporated into your beloved Son, our only Savior, and is now your child and heir. Grant, most loving and faithful Father, that we in the whole course of our lives might prove our thankfulness for your great grace, faithfully bring up this your child through all the situations of life and that we with this child as well, might more and more die unto the world, and joined to the life of your Son, our Lord Jesus, daily grow in grace, that we might ever praise you and be a blessing to our neighbor, through our Lord Jesus Christ. Amen.[167]

---

[166] Old, *Baptismal Rite,* 139.
[167] Qtd. in ibid., 167.

May God answer our prayers today that our children would daily grow in grace and that parents and the church would be faithful in their training.

Ultimately, the difference in approach between the Magisterial Reformers and the Puritans represents a *paradigmatic revolution*. It is not by chance that our Reformed Baptist brothers readily and repeatedly praise the Puritans, for they have similar perspectives. Together, they see children as lacking the fullness of grace. Well before the First Great Awakening, the model of conversion experience replaced the pattern of covenant succession and in some measure established the need for such an ideal, dramatic conversion event. The fact of the matter is that *this expectation of conversion is by far most common today*, even in Reformed and Presbyterian circles.

In appealing to the historic beliefs and practices of the "ancient Christians" and the "ancient church," the normative view among the Reformers was not simply that children had "some covenantal blessings," but that they had redemption, including the forgiveness of sins, as members in good standing in Christ's church. They saw this as being wholly consistent with Reformed soteriology, clearly emphasizing the objectivity of what baptism symbolizes. Based on this, they instructed covenant children to view themselves as

> *The expectation of conversion is by far most common today, even in Reformed and Presbyterian circles.*

full Christians, with all the accompanying privileges, duties, and warnings. They were to live as such, working out their salvation. The Reformers stressed the individual and personal demands of covenant membership and the necessity of demonstrating faith and repentance. They believed that their children would persevere in the faith, because they had the mindset that their posterity should always love the Lord, even from the earliest days of life. Parents were held responsible before God to bring this about by the grace of God.

Hence the Reformers differentiated between the nurturing of a covenant child and the evangelistic approach to an unbaptized pagan.

Failure to do so necessarily results in a baptistic model, is a denial of the essence of covenant, and is inconsistent with historic covenantal theology. *The covenant requires nothing less than charging children, because they have been objectively claimed by God, to be faithful sons and daughters of the King of Kings.* We must do so with eyes of faith, trusting in God's promise and using the means He has given us.

Contrast this with the subsequent idea that covenant children possessed only outward or external privileges of church membership. While our Reformed fathers held that our covenant children are not on the outside looking in, Thornwell viewed our children as "enemies of God," and this is the logical progression of divergent views existing already in the seventeenth century. Despite the continued use of covenantal language, the glory of the covenant was lost and confidence in covenant succession was shattered.

To view, treat, and teach our children as aliens to the church has become a self-fulfilling prophecy. To employ a baptistic approach joined with an unhealthy overemphasis on the subjective element of the covenant, and with a standard often beyond what the Bible requires—either too rationalistic or too experiential—was to ask for failure. Additionally, aside from the excessive infighting that has often consumed evangelical and orthodox churches, we have been rightly combating liberalism, modernism, and humanism, causing us to neglect the issue of covenant succession. Moreover, our loss of the antithesis made humanist child-rearing approaches as acceptable as those of Moses and Paul, and our contempt for the law of God as the biblical means of training children certainly contributed to our modern-day disaster. Our loss of covenant—a covenant word, a covenant antithesis, and a covenant paradigm—has resulted in covenant chaos and a loss of confidence in the promises of God concerning His generational work.

> *To view, treat, and teach our children as aliens has become a self-fulfilling prophecy.*

We should stress that adhering to the right paradigm certainly does not guarantee success. There is no substitute for faith. While trusting in the blood of Christ and the work of the Spirit, there is no substitute for faithful obedience. However, we should not minimize these theological differences. To be captivated by this covenantal call will affect all aspects of child-training. Further, as Calvin warned, to deny these essentials of covenantal thinking is to "overturn all the principles of religion." Undoubtedly, we have overturned many principles of religion since that time. Theology has consequences.

However, even amidst the chaos of our day, there is hope. God is gracious and His promises are still true. Many among us recognize our deficiencies and are committed to seek the Lord's blessing in raising our children. May we strive ever more to honor the Lord, to whom our children belong, as our God and the God of our precious little ones, in the cultivation of our covenant seed.

II
Implications

Covenant Succession and Church Leadership: Believing and Obedient Children in 1 Timothy 3:4–5 and Titus 1:6

David G. Hagopian

From Genesis to Revelation, God promises not only to be our God, but also the God of our children: "For the promise is to *you* and *your children*" (Acts 2:39, emphasis added).[1] Just as He calls us to have faith that He will fulfill His promises to *us*, so also He calls us to have faith that *He* will fulfill His promises to *our children*.

The salvation of our children, however, is no more automatic than was the salvation of the Pharisees merely because they were "sons of Israel": "For they are not all Israel [the church] who are descended from Israel [the blood line]" (Rom. 9:6). No one is saved by blood, only by faith.

But how is such faith awakened in those who are saved? Ordinarily, God uses means to accomplish His divinely ordained ends. In particular, He uses the faithful preaching of the Word (evangelism) to awaken saving faith in those born to unbelieving parents. For those born to at least one believing parent, however, He ordinarily uses not only faithful preaching of the Word at church, but also faithful parental nurturing in the Word and prayer at home.

Saying that God ordinarily uses means to accomplish His divinely ordained ends does not reduce salvation to works. Those gently led,

---

[1] Unless otherwise noted, all quotations are taken from the New American Standard Bible (La Habra, Calif.: The Lockman Foundation, 1977).

by God's grace, to saving faith through faithful parental nurture in the Word and prayer are no more saved by "works" than are those who, by God's grace, are led to saving faith through the faithful preaching of the Word. Paul could not have been more explicit about the connection between divinely ordained means and ends when he wrote,

> "Whoever will call on the name of the LORD will be saved." How then will they call on Him in whom they have not believed? How will they believe in Him whom they have not heard? And how will they hear without a preacher? How will they preach unless they are sent? (Rom. 10:13–15)

In this passage, Paul holds forth an *end* or promise regarding the salvation of unbelievers ("Whoever will call upon the name of the LORD will be saved"). He then traces out in reverse order the *means* necessary to accomplish that divinely ordained end (belief, hearing, preaching, and missions). The whole point of the passage is that *the church* is the divinely ordained means to herald the gospel to those who have never heard of Him. The church is the means God has ordained to accomplish the end of saving those He has promised to save—those who call on Him. And we know that God's Word does not go out void. It will accomplish its divine purpose and hence fulfill the divine promise. The same is true of faithful parental nurture in the Word and prayer. It will accomplish its divine purpose in fulfillment of the divine promise to save the children of believers who also benefit from the preaching of the Word at church. And while God is free to work above and beyond means, He ordinarily uses faithful parental nurture in the Word and prayer as the means of awakening saving faith in the children of believing parents.

While this book explores different facets of the promises God has made to the children of believing parents—parents who believe that they are saved by grace alone, through faith alone, because of the finished work of Christ alone—this chapter turns to two passages that some tend to overlook in discussions of those promises: 1 Timothy

3:4–5 and Titus 1:6. In these passages, Paul, under inspiration of the Spirit, sets forth a number of qualifications for men who serve or aspire to serve the church as pastors or elders. Among those qualifications, Paul requires that such men manage their households well, keeping their children under control with all dignity (1 Tim. 3:4–5) and that they raise believing children who are not accused of dissipation or rebellion (Tit. 1:6).

As we shall see, these passages gloriously confirm the doctrine of covenant succession by teaching that pastors and elders are responsible for, and prove themselves to be examples in, the way that they raise their children. In particular, the children of pastors and elders are to "believe" (*pistos*) in Christ and be "well-behaved" (*hupotage*). These passages, then, unmistakably teach that fathers bear responsibility before God for the state of their children with respect to both their *spiritual* and *civil righteous-*

Only those who faithfully prove themselves effective with their first flock at home are fit to serve the broader flock of the church.

ness,[2] and that only those who faithfully prove themselves effective with their first "flock" at home are fit to serve the broader flock of the church. *By God's grace, pastors and elders must raise children of faith who demonstrate the obedience of faith.* In the pages to follow, we will (1) explain what these passages mean in more detail, (2) explore their most important implications for the life and leadership of the church, and (3) respond to some common objections, all with the

---

[2] By *civil righteousness,* the Reformers meant conforming one's conduct to the outward requirements of God's Law—e.g., not stealing from a neighbor. In a sense, this distinction between spiritual righteousness and civil righteousness breaks down because any supposed righteousness that does not flow from saving faith is pharisaical—pure ethical formalism—holding to a form of godliness but denying its power. Put differently, there is ultimately no true righteousness apart from God, in Christ, empowered by the Spirit. Subject to this caveat, I still will use the distinction between spiritual and civil righteousness in this chapter because those who oppose the interpretation I am advancing here wrongly assume that some form of civil righteousness is the only thing Paul has in view in 1 Timothy 3:4–5 and Titus 1:6, and then mistakenly read that meaning into the text when that meaning makes no sense in context.

intent to see how these texts encourage all believers by ensuring that those who oversee them as their spiritual leaders at church first demonstrate that they are fit to serve as examples in the way that they have cared for their own children.

Explaining the Texts

Paul articulates objective standards for those who aspire to lead His church. Among other things, Paul requires that a pastor or elder "must be one who manages his own household well, keeping his children under control with all dignity (but if a man does not know how to manage his own household, how will he take care of the church of God?)" (1 Tim. 3:4–5). He also requires that pastors and elders "have children who believe, not accused of dissipation or rebellion" (Tit. 1:6).

Everyone agrees that 1 Timothy 3:4–5 objectively requires pastors and elders to manage, control, direct, rule, govern, or preside over their households well. But that interpretation is where the agreement sometimes ends. The text, however, sheds light on exactly what this requirement means. While pastors and elders must have well-ordered lives, from top to bottom, Paul's particular focus in this passage is on *their children*. He explains exactly what "managing his household" means by immediately adding the clarifying phrase "keeping his children under control." Whatever else the requirement to manage one's household means, it especially means that pastors and elders are to raise self-controlled children. But raising self-controlled children is not all Paul requires. An elder is to keep his children under control "with all dignity" or reverence. He is to raise them in such a way that they are known for their well-ordered lives. He is to do his job in a dignified or reverential way and is to raise dignified or reverential children, not children who lack self-control or who have been exasperated or provoked to wrath because of undue harshness (Eph. 6:4; Col. 3:21).

Notice the connection Paul makes between *how* a father disciplines and *the way his children act*. Christian fathers are required to have self-control in the way they discipline their children not only because harsh discipline is wrong in itself but also because such behavior ordinarily will show up in their children. Likewise, the dignity and reverence with which children have been disciplined will be seen in them as well. Pastors and elders are to treat their children with the dignity and self-control that should adorn the gospel they profess, and their children are to demonstrate the same kind of dignity and self-control in their own lives. Well-raised children are no accident.

But why are pastors and elders required to raise self-controlled children? Fortunately, Paul answers this crucial question for us: "If a man does not know how to manage his own household, how will he take care of the church of God?" By asking this rhetorical question, Paul gently leads his readers to conclude that if a man does not raise self-controlled children, he cannot be entrusted with the even broader responsibility of managing the church.[3] One who does not manage himself or his first flock well cannot be entrusted with the responsibility of managing the broader flock of Christ's church. If a man does not prove himself a fit ruler in his family by raising children who rule themselves well, then *he* is unfit to rule the church. The family is a man's training ground; it is where he proves himself, at least in part, fit for office. With typical succinctness, Calvin notes "that a man who does not know how to rule his own family is unsuited to govern in the Church of God."[4]

In Titus 1, Paul parallels many of the general requirements he sets forth in 1 Timothy 3. He also parallels the particular requirement in view here by mandating that pastors and elders "have children who believe, not accused of dissipation or rebellion." So important is the behavior of leaders' children that Paul does not even want them to

---

[3] Indeed, the phrase "managing his own household" appears at both ends of this requirement, and sandwiched in between that phrase is the explanation of what it means—raising self-controlled children.

[4] *The Second Epistle of Paul the Apostle to the Corinthians, and the Epistles to Timothy, Titus and Philemon*, vol. 10 of *Calvin's New Testament Commentaries*, trans. T. A. Smail, ed. David W. Torrance and Thomas F. Torrance (Grand Rapids: Eerdmans, 1964), 226.

be *accused* of dissipation or rebellion. Chrysostom concurs when, in a homily on this passage, he comments, "And [Paul] has not only said, 'not riotous,' but not even 'accused of riot.' There must not be an ill report, or such an opinion of them."[5]

As important as it is for a pastor's children not to be accused of riot, this is not the only requirement Paul sets forth in Titus 1:6. A man is not fit for office simply because no one accuses his children of ransacking the village. Paul is not exclusively concerned about what the Reformers and their heirs sometimes refer to as *civil righteousness*. He also is concerned about *true, spiritual righteousness*. More accurately, we can say that Paul is concerned about *faith and the obedience of faith*. Pastors and elders are to raise children who believe and whose behavior reflects their belief, or more succinctly, children who believe and act like it. Calvin agrees:

> But here his first requirement is that the children should be believers, that it may be obvious that they have been nurtured in the sound teaching of godliness and in the fear of the Lord. . . . [T]hey must not be *unruly* for he who cannot obtain any reverence or submission from his children could scarcely restrain [other] people [in the church] by the bridle of his discipline.[6]

When Titus 1:6 requires pastors and elders to father "believing children," the word translated "believing" is the adjective *pista* (from *pistos*). Because *pistos* is sometimes rendered as "faithful" or "trustworthy" in other contexts as opposed to being rendered as "believing" or "trusting," some translators and commentators render it as "faithful" or "trustworthy" in this specific context.[7] Several considerations,

---

[5] Chrysostom, *Homilies on Galatians, Ephesians, Philippians, Colossians, Thessalonians, Timothy, Titus, and Philemon,* vol. 13 of *Nicene and Post-Nicene Fathers* (Peabody, Mass.: Hendrickson, 1994), 525. Emphasis added.

[6] Calvin, *Commentaries,* 359.

[7] While the KJV and NKJV render this passage as "having faithful children," most other translations render it as requiring an elder to raise believing children: NASB ("having children who believe"), NIV ("whose children believe"), ASV ("having children that believe"), ESV ("his children are believers"), CEV ("Their children must be followers of

however, convincingly argue in favor of rendering *pista* as "believing" in Titus 1:6.

First, while *pistos* admittedly has other meanings in the New Testament, those meanings have no bearing on the translation of Titus 1:6. When *pistos* is used to refer to God or Christ, for example, it means that God is faithful, trustworthy, or reliable, that He is the One in whom we can place our full trust and confidence because He will do what He has promised us as His people (1 Cor. 1:9, 10:13; 2 Cor. 1:18; 1 Thes. 5:24; 2 Thes. 3:3; 2 Tim. 2:13; Heb. 10:23, 11:11; 1 Pet. 4:19; 1 Jn. 1:9). Obviously, in these contexts, the word cannot mean "believing" since God cannot believe in Himself. Because He is the One who alone is worthy of all of our faith or trust, these passages simply teach that God is completely faithful or trustworthy. These passages uniquely refer to God and thus provide no justification for construing *pistos* as "faithful" or "trustworthy" in Titus 1:6. We can say the same thing about how *pistos* is used to describe the reliability of certain sayings in the New Testament. Paul often writes that certain sayings are faithful, reliable, or trustworthy: "faithful is the saying" or "trustworthy is the saying" (e.g., 1 Tim. 1:15, 3:1, 4:9; Tit. 3:8). John does so as well on at least one occasion (Rev. 21:5). Because these passages are contextually unique, referring to God or to particular sayings, they have no bearing on the proper interpretation of Titus 1:6.

Second, *pistos* and related words refer specifically to believers in numerous New Testament passages (e.g., Acts 16:1–2, 15; 2 Cor. 6:15; Eph. 1:1; Col. 1:2; 1 Tim. 4:3, 10, 12; 5:16; 6:2; 1 Pet. 1:21).[8]

---

the Lord"), AMP ("whose children are [well trained and are] believers"), NLT ("his children must be believers"). See also the RSV and NEB.

[8] Citing Titus 1:6 along with these other passages, Walter Bauer observes that "The abs. πιστός also means believing (in Christ), a (Christian) believer and is used both as adj. and as subst" (*A Greek-English Lexicon of the New Testament and Other Early Christian Literature*, trans. William F. Arndt and F. Wilbur Gingrich, rev. F. Wilbur Gingrich and Federick W. Danker, 2nd ed. [Chicago: Univ. of Chicago Press, 1979], 665). See also Rudolf Bultmann, s.v. "πιστεύω," *Theological Dictionary of the New Testament*, 10 vols., ed. Gerhard Kittel and Gerhard Friedrich, trans. Geoffrey W. Bromiley (Grand Rapids: Eerdmans, 1988 [1968]), 6:215, note 311 ("The adj. πιστός simply means 'Christian.'").

Thus Paul's use of *pistos* in 2 Corinthians 6:15 should inform our understanding of Titus 1:6, because the main thrust of 2 Corinthians 6:14–18 is that believers ought to separate themselves from unbelievers. In this specific context, Paul tells us that we ought not to be "unequally yoked" with unbelievers. He then draws a clear line between that which belongs to God and that which does not—a demarcation of righteousness versus lawlessness, light versus darkness, and the temple of God versus that of idols. In the midst of drawing this boundary, Paul asks rhetorically, "Or what harmony has Christ with Belial, or what has a *believer* in common with an *unbeliever?*" (emphasis added). Here he uses *pistos* and *apistos* as words of contrast, unmistakably indicating that in his mind *pistos* refers to believers and *apistos* to unbelievers.

Third, just as in 2 Corinthians 6:15, Paul uses *apistos* elsewhere in the New Testament almost exclusively to refer to unbelievers in contrast to believers. In 1 Corinthians 6:6, for example, he says that he has heard about Christian brothers suing fellow brothers "and that before unbelievers," thereby explicitly contrasting believers (brothers) and unbelievers. Believers ought not to drag each other into court before the *apistoi* (unbelievers). A few verses later in 7:12–15, he addresses believing husbands who

> *Paul teaches that pastors and elders are to raise believing children, not children who are pagans, or characteristically act like them, or are accused of acting like them.*

have unbelieving wives and vice versa, once again reinforcing the contrast between *apistos* and *pistos*. Still later in the same letter, Paul refers to various sign gifts and how unbelievers respond to them in clear contrast to how believers do so (1 Cor. 14:22–24). Elsewhere, he says that "[t]he god of this world has blinded the minds of the unbelieving" (2 Cor. 4:4). And he tells believers that if they fail to provide for their own households, they have denied the faith and are "worse than unbelievers."

Outside of Paul's epistles, Christ Himself challenged Thomas to touch His resurrected body so that he would "be not unbelieving, but believing" (Jn. 20:27), using *apistos* in contrast to *pistos*. And Christ elsewhere tells His followers that those who claim to belong to Him but are not ready for His return will be assigned a place in judgment with unbelievers, again tracing out the implications of belief and unbelief (Lk. 12:46). We should not be surprised, then, to find Paul using *apistos* this same way in Titus 1:15, where, in the local context of the passage in question, he explicitly contrasts the pure (and hence, believing) with "those who are defiled and unbelieving." Thus, in the local context, Paul contrasts *apistoi* (unbelievers) with believers, thereby strongly suggesting that *pista* in verse 6 should consistently be construed as *believing*.

Fourth, although believers by sinning act like unbelievers, believers ought not to be *characterized* by these same sins. A believing child may rebel by not meeting his curfew a few times, but that is far different from being characteristically rebellious. In Titus 1:6, Paul intentionally contrasts believing children on the one hand with those accused of dissipation and rebellion on the other hand. We cannot separate hearts from lives at this crucial juncture. Good trees bring forth good fruit (Mt. 7:16–20, 12:33–37). Pastors and elders are to raise believing children who act like they believe, in contrast to pagan children who are accused of "dissipation" and "rebellion." Significantly, the words *dissipation* and *rebellion* describe unbelieving conduct specifically in Titus 1 (vv. 6, 10–16), and elsewhere in the New Testament (1 Pet. 4:4; 1 Tim. 1:9). *Dissipation* and *rebellion* also describe unbelieving conduct or the conduct of professing believers who act like unbelievers (Eph. 5:18). In 1 Timothy 1:9–10, for instance, the term *rebellion* keeps company with other unflattering words such as *lawless*, *ungodly*, *sinners*, *unholy*, and *profane*. Paul also includes disobedience to parents in his list of vices characterizing incorrigible pagans (Rom. 1:30) and commands Christian children to exhibit the corresponding virtue by obeying their parents in the Lord (Eph. 6:1; Col. 3:20). Christian youth should not be accused of acting like pagans, and this takes us to the heart of the matter. Rebellious children are rebelling against their parents, but they also are rebelling against the God of their parents. On the other side of the coin, a child does not truly obey his parents unless he does so *in the Lord*. Characteristically disobedient and rebellious children, like those Paul describes in Titus 1:6, not only have a problem with their fathers on earth but also with their Father in heaven. By contrasting the children of pastors and elders with such pagan children, Paul teaches us that pastors and elders are to raise *believing* children, not children who are pagans, who characteristically act like them, or who are even accused of acting like them.

Fifth, the rendering of *pistos* as "believing" is the only one that makes sense. The office of elder is first and foremost a *spiritual* office. Requiring that pastors and elders raise children who refrain from robbing banks is not all that Paul has in view, because *any strict pagan can raise that kind of child*. External obedience is not the goal of Christian parenting. The ultimate goal of Christian parenting is to raise sons and daughters of heaven who are not accused of unrighteous living. The children of pastors and elders are to demonstrate both true spiritual righteousness and civil righteousness. The requirement is *both/and*, not *either/or*. Christians are to raise believing children—not children who just *say* that they believe, but children who *live* like they believe. As one commentator puts it, "The children of a bishop should show in their conduct that they believe what their father preaches."[9] Those who attempt to limit this passage to matters of civil righteousness drive an artificial wedge between true spiritual righteousness and civil righteousness and undermine the Pauline rationale for the requirement. The underlying rationale of this passage is that if a man cannot rule his first flock at home by raising believing and well-behaved children, then he is not fit to rule the broader flock of the church. But what kind of rule is in view? Is it just a rule of decorum or a rule of civil righteousness? Is it merely required that

---

[9] George Stoeckhardt, *Exegetical Lectures on the Epistle of Paul to Titus*, trans. H. W. Denger (St. Charles, Mo.: Holy Cross Lutheran Press, n.d.), 13.

a son takes out the trash when it is full? Hardly. The rule that is in view encompasses everything, both spiritual and civil righteous-ness—or more accurately, *faith and the obedience of faith.* Pastors and elders are to raise children who believe and who live like they believe.

Sixth, even if we were convinced that *pista* should be rendered as "faithful" or "trustworthy," we would not escape the force of the pas-sage; we would simply move the analysis back one step. Even grant-ing this alternative translation of *pista*, we still must ask *faithful in what and faithful to whom? Trustworthy in what and to whom?* Should an elder's daughter obey her father when he commands her to clean her room, but not when he commands her to cast herself upon Christ as her only hope in this life and

> *If Scripture gives the expectation of covenant succession for all Christian parents, all the more should it be ex-pected for leaders in the Church.*

the life to come? How could such a man ever be an ex-ample to his flock? How could he ever say, "Follow me; do as I have done. Let me show you how, by God's grace, you can raise sons and daughters of God Almighty"? Moreover, passages like Acts 16:21 and Ephesians 1:1 should lay the concern over this alter-native interpretation to rest once for all. In Acts 16:21, we read that Lydia and her household were baptized when she, as the head of her home, came to faith in Christ. In this passage, she describes herself as "faithful to the Lord"—that is, full of faith in the Lord. In a simi-lar vein, Paul describes the saints at Ephesus in Ephesians 1:1 as those "who are faithful in Christ Jesus." So even if Titus 1:6 should be con-strued literally as "faithful," Paul obviously means that the children of pastors and elders should be full of faith in Christ. They should be believers.

The rest of this volume has taken great pains to prove that Scrip-ture gives every faithful believer the godly expectation of believing children. If the rest of Scripture gives this expectation for *all* Chris-tian parents, then all the more should it be certain for those who function as leaders and examples in the church. In other words, we must interpret Titus 1:6 not only by looking at its local context, but also by looking at the general context of Scripture as a whole (the analogy of faith). Taken as a whole, Scripture teaches us that a relationship exists between one's ability to rule his family and his ability to rule the church, and that pastors and elders are to be examples to the flock in this regard. A man who raises unbelieving or rebellious children is not a good example and, according to Paul, is unfit for office notwithstanding how nice he may be, how many people come to hear him, how much money he has in his retirement plan, or how well-liked he may be in the congregation or the community at large.

When the very same passages teach that pastors and elders are not to be addicted to wine, we understand that an addiction to wine demonstrates a lack of self-control, thus making a man unfit for office. His inability to control himself ought not to be set before the congregation as an example to follow. But this requirement is not limited to pastors and elders; it also applies to *every* believer too. In the same way, the requirement to manage one's house well and raise believing children applies not only to pastors and elders, but also through them, to *all* heads of households. The only difference is that it applies *especially* to pastors and elders. Just as a habitual drunk is unfit for office, so is a man with unbelieving or habitually rebellious children. With these requirements, these passages assume that pastors and elders are examples to the flock and that they are responsible for the faith and conduct of their children.[10]

---

[10] Interestingly, some commentators who attempt to construe *pista* as "faithful" or "trustworthy" in Titus 1:6 do so explicitly in order to avoid the obvious implication that there is a relationship between an elder's parental nurture and the faith and obedience of his children. For example, evangelical commentator Walter L. Liefeld, in *1 and 2 Timothy and Titus*, part of the NIV Application Commentary (Grand Rapids: Zondervan, 1999), observes: "Here the elder's children are to 'believe,' as well as not be open to the charge of being 'wild and disobedient.' This seems to make the parent responsible for the child's salvation, and, by extension, would make the church leadership dependent upon the elders' children" (99). Liefeld understands the relationship between an elder's nurture and his child's faith and obedience; his non-covenantal categories, however, appear to preclude him from grasping the real force of this passage. Other evangelical

Exploring Some Implications

Having examined the meaning of 1 Timothy 3:4–5 and Titus 1:6, we also must explore the significant implications of these passages for the life and leadership of the church.

Where the Buck Stops. If a pastor's children do not believe or if they live unruly lives, he is responsible before God for his children and is unfit to serve as an example to the flock. On this point, no one has put it better than Chrysostom, who noted in the fourth century A.D.,

> We should observe what care he bestows upon children. For he who cannot be the instructor of his own children, how should he be the Teacher of others? If he cannot keep in order those whom he has had with him from the beginning, whom he has brought up, and without? For if the incompetency of the father had not been great, he would not have allowed those to become bad whom from the first he had under his power. For it is not possible, indeed it is not, that one should turn out ill who is brought up with much care, and has received great attention. Sins are not so prevalent by nature, as to overcome so much previous care. But if, occupied in the pursuit of wealth, he has made his children a secondary concern, and not bestowed much care upon them, even so he is unworthy. For if when nature prompted, he was so void of affection or so senseless, that he thought more of his wealth than of his children, how should he be raised to the Episcopal throne, and so great rule? For if he was unable to restrain them it is a great proof of his weakness; and if he was unconcerned, his want of affection is much to be blamed. He then that neglects his own children, how shall he take care of other men's?

commentators understand and affirm the relationship between parental nurture and their children's faith and obedience without any hint of placing it in the context of the doctrine of covenant succession. Lea and Griffin, for example, correctly note, "This additional requirement that the elder be capable of influencing his own children to become Christians demonstrates Paul's conviction that effective spiritual leadership in the home suggests the probability of effective spiritual leadership in the church. Not only is the elder to be a good father as reflected in his children's behavior, but he is also to be a spiritual father as reflected in the spiritual commitment of his children" (*1, 2 Timothy, Titus*, New American Commentary [Nashville: Broadman and Holman, 1992], 282).

And he has not only said, "not riotous," but not even "accused of riot."
There must not be an ill report, or such an opinion of them.[11]

By their incompetence, unbiblical priorities, lack of affection, failure
to discipline, or absence of concern, fathers can raise children who
disown the faith or who profess belief but are really rebels. Such men
are not fit to rule the church, and moreover must give an account
to their Father in heaven for their failure of stewardship regarding
their children on earth.

But we live in an era when many refuse to accept their God-given
responsibilities and look all around for anyone and anything to blame.
Instead of taking responsibility for the mind-numbing "entertainment" to which we expose our children, for example, we blame the
entertainment industry. Instead of taking responsibility for the god-
less propaganda that is pumped into children's minds in the public
school classroom, we blame the educational system. We even spiritualize our blame-shifting by castigating the father who spends too
much time at home slumped in his La-Z-Boy with remote control
in hand to the exclusion of his wife and children, while at the same
time we fail to see that the father who spends too much time with a
systematic theology vol-
ume in hand to the ex-
clusion of his wife and
children is no better. In
Chrysostom's words, if
we make our children "a
secondary concern," we

> *We castigate the father who spends too much time in his La-Z-Boy with remote in hand, but not the one who spends too much time with a theology volume in hand.*

have no one to blame but ourselves. In the recent movie *Gladiator*,
the character of the pagan Marcus Aurelius understands this important truth in a telling and memorable line. Upon informing his own
son that he would not become the next emperor of Rome because
of his lack of virtue, Aurelius nevertheless accepts full responsibil-

[11] Chrysostom, *Homilies*, 525.

ity by saying in a tear-filled scene, "Your fault as a son is my failure as a father." Christian fathers, do you have the humility to accept such responsibility? The buck stops with you.

Missing in Action. If our churches were to take 1 Timothy 3:4–5 and Titus 1:6 seriously, we would see men rightly choose not to serve as pastors and elders, and we would see still others step down immediately from serving in this capacity because their children are unbelievers or live rebellious lives. Becoming an elder is not a *right* belonging to every believer, but a *privilege* and *responsibility* belonging only to a few who, by God's grace, are qualified to serve as required by Scripture. The pastorate and eldership are sobering, and we should not take them lightly. If a man does not have believing children, he has no more right to serve than does a drunkard. We are duty-bound to obey our Lord, regardless of the consequences, and should be heard shouting at the top of our lungs, "Let God be found true!" *Instead of lowering the divine standard to meet a man, we must always ask every man to meet the standard.*

When believers respond with a "parade of horrors" ("What will happen to the church if we take these passages seriously?"), we patiently need to remind them that we should obey God at all costs and trust Him with the consequences. We should not underestimate the requirements for office that God has established in His Word. The church is God's, and consequently, He alone has the right and prerogative to determine who is and is not fit to rule *His* church. The requirements are not up for grabs. We have no right to decide which requirements are binding and which ones we can throw overboard. Just as we should not underestimate God's requirements for office, we also should not overstate the contributions of those who serve the church. If an elder works hard for his church, but his son is a con man by day or a drug dealer by night, the church will find someone else

> The church has impaired the credibility of the gospel by allowing the term "preacher's kid" to become synonymous with "rabble-rouser."

to do his work after he steps down from office. God assures us that He always will provide for His church, and He does not "need" anyone who fails to satisfy the qualifications He has articulated for governing His church. God promises to provide for His people, and He always keeps His promises. Do we trust Him?

Who knows what blessedness would attend our faith if we were to stand firm on God's Word? Instead, I fear that the church has impaired the credibility of the gospel by allowing the term "preacher's kid" to become synonymous with "rabble-rouser"—the exact opposite of what Scripture requires. And we wonder why some people want nothing to do with our tepid gospel.[12]

Veteran Leadership. Taking 1 Timothy 3:4–5 and Titus 1:6 at face value *appears* to generally argue in favor of older men serving as pastors and elders since we do not have to speculate about whether they meet the qualifications for office.

However, age is not the issue as much as maturity. Because maturity can be somewhat difficult to determine, it seems our priorities have shifted so that we have come to care more about a man's *doctrine* than his *life*. In fact, in some denominations, the soundness of a man's doctrine is formally tested, and that is fine as far as it goes—but it

---

[12] While this volume addresses the doctrine of covenant succession more fully, we must pause to note that there may be some mitigating circumstances for men who come to faith later in life. This essay is directed primarily to pastors and elders who fathered their children as Christians. If, however, a man lived and raised his children as an unbeliever before becoming a pastor, some mitigating circumstances may apply if his children are not believers. On the one hand, he is responsible before God for the consequences of not coming to faith sooner. But, on the other hand, Paul seems to suggest at least some mitigating circumstances for marriage (1 Cor. 7:10–16) that may apply by analogy to the family for our purposes here. Admittedly, these cases are difficult because, in context, Paul is not addressing a man's fitness for office in 1 Corinthians 7. In other words, just because a man is free to remarry, he still may not be a "one-woman man" or meet the other qualifications for office, such as raising believing and obedient children. While Paul never instructs polygamists who converted to divorce all but one of their spouses, they were not fit for office either under the requirements of 1 Timothy 3 or Titus 1. It is one thing to be a believer in good standing in the local church and quite another to be qualified to serve as an example to the flock. This area is difficult and requires great sensitivity and further study, but it is beyond the focal point of this essay.

simply does not go far enough. Sadly, some of these same churches fail to pay the same kind of exacting attention to a man's life, marriage, and family. A man may be examined for hours regarding his views on certain biblical issues (and rightly so), but why isn't he examined with the same kind of vigor regarding the state of his soul, marriage, and family? Both right doctrine (*orthodoxy*) and right living (*orthopraxis*) are crucial for pastors and elders, and we must stop pretending that a man whose life, marriage, or family is a wreck nevertheless can continue in office because of the supposed soundness of his confession. How a man lives shows what he *really* believes, and what a man really believes will show up in his life, wife, and children. It may not appear right away, but it will eventually. Some things take time to reveal themselves, and the more time we have to observe them, the better.

But younger men are not necessarily disqualified from serving as pastors and elders, especially in light of Paul's injunction to Timothy that he should not let anyone look down on him because of his youthfulness. But in the same breath, Paul tells Timothy to prove himself an example in his speech, conduct, love, faith, and purity (1 Tim. 4:12), and this passage comes right

> *We must stop pretending that a man whose life, marriage, or family is a wreck nevertheless can continue in office because of the supposed soundness of his confession.*

on the heels of the qualifications for office a chapter earlier. Younger men can serve the church, but as with all pastors and elders, they must realize that the door *into* office is also the door *out* of office. If they have a child who rebels, they should consider stepping down, if not for a season to restore that wayward child, then permanently, depending upon the nature and severity of the rebellion.

The Circle of Responsibility. A rebellious child is responsible for his own conduct. But as we have shown elsewhere in this book, the child's parents are also responsible, and his father in particular is responsible as the covenant head of his home. As the covenant head, the father's responsibility multiplies and expands with his family. When unmarried, he is responsible for himself. When he takes a wife, he becomes responsible for her. When he has children, he becomes responsible for them too. The responsibility for a child's misconduct ascends upward toward the father, and the consequences of the father's sin may flow downward to the child. A child who steals is his father's responsibility, and an angry father provokes his children to wrath. As Mark Sumpter demonstrates elswhere in this volume, the church also bears some responsibility when a covenant child seriously strays from the faith. But a father who also is a pastor or elder bears even more responsibility before God for the behavior of his child in particular, both as a pastor or elder and as a father.

The Bright Line. Many want to qualify 1 Timothy 3:4–5 and Titus 1:6 by reading some kind of age of majority into them in an attempt to limit their application to the time when a child is still at home or when he is still a certain age. Several problems plague this attempt to qualify the texts. From the outset, these attempts seem to evade the force of the texts. They seem to be a classical example of *eisegesis* (e.g., reading an Anglo-American legal understanding of the age of majority into the text), as opposed to *exegesis* (drawing the true meaning out of the text in accordance with its Hebraic, covenantal context). Eli, an Old Testament priest, was held accountable for the fornication and idolatry of his *grown* sons (1 Sam. 2).[13] Much the same could be said about King David and his rebellious son, Adonijah, since Scripture tells us that Adonijah turned out that way as an adult because David never properly disciplined him as a child (1 Kgs. 1:6).

Additionally, if we were to allow the age of majority qualification to guide our interpretation of 1 Timothy 3:4–5 or Titus 1:6, the exception would end up swallowing the rule. An elder could raise a number of children, all of whom turn out to be reprobates, but all of whom were over the age of eighteen and out of the house before they made their rebellion official. While a biblical mitigating factor

---

[13] Incidentally, the word translated as "dissipation" in Titus 1:6 is used in the Septuagint to describe Eli's sons in 1 Samuel 10:27.

may exist for children who rebel after they are married, at which time Scripture teaches that a young man becomes head of his own home and a young woman is given to the headship of her husband, the age of majority rationale still appears to stand the explicit logic of the texts on their head. If an elder does not faithfully do his job with his own family, he proves himself unfit to rule the broader household of God. If he has not demonstrated himself faithful in exercising his headship with his first flock, then he cannot be entrusted with the responsibility of exercising it with respect to the broader flock of the church.

But when ought we to remove pastors and elders from office? While this area calls for special sensitivity, it seems that pastors and elders should step down whenever their children prove their father to be disqualified from office. But if that standard appears to be too vague, pastors and elders should consider stepping down or be removed no later than when their children are excommunicated (Mt. 18:15–17). Churches that do not practice formal discipline ought to begin to do so patiently and lovingly, but in the meantime, pastors and elders in such churches have another litmus test that they can use: *the point in time at which a child abandons the faith.* At that point, the child has made his rebellion official, and his father ought to bear responsibility for the unbelief and rebellion of his child, thereby protecting the integrity of his office. He also ought to devote himself anew to restoring his wayward child and leave the work of the church to others. This may only be for a time until he gets his family back in order, but his child needs his undivided attention; the church needs to see the pastoral heart of a father-elder for his child in action. Think of the message that stepping down or aside would send to his child: *My father cared enough about me to do that! He really must love me!*

A Good Start. Despite the clear biblical requirement for pastors and elders to raise believing and well-behaved children, we would do well to have the church at least start by admitting that, at a minimum, men who do not raise well-behaved children should be removed from office. At that point, half the battle would be won. If a pastor or elder with children *accused of* dissipation and rebellion, much less those given to actual dissipation and rebellion, were asked to resign or were asked to refrain from assuming office, our work would not be done, but at least it would be well underway. Our house still would not be completely clean and in order, but we have to start somewhere.

The problem is that many churches sadly ignore Scripture at this point, thinking that they know better than God who is fit to serve *His* church. Our problem is that we don't take Scripture seriously. Like Marcion, the early church heretic who excised God's law from the Old and New Testaments to produce his own "version" of the Bible, we too have taken scissors to Scripture and cut out the portions with which we disagree because they offend our modern sensibilities. And it shows. We wonder aloud why the church has declined in its influence as salt and light, and we need look no further than our own front doors. We have men occupying office who are disqualified according to Scripture, but we marshal all kinds of exegetical wit to excuse our disobedience.

Caution and Common Sense. If a pastor's child breaks curfew once, the pastor is not automatically unfit for office. There is something qualitatively different about a child who may go through a temporary but short-lived streak of rebellion and a child who is living for a protracted period of time in active rebellion against his parents and the God of his parents. But even in some instances of short-term rebellion, it would be far more prudent for an elder to be a true man and take a leave of absence, invest himself in his child, and if the situation is fully resolved, return to office.

> *Many churches sadly ignore Scripture, thinking that they know better than God who is fit to serve His church.*

Such prudence would be an example to the church and may give the elder the time he needs to be used by God to reclaim and restore his wayward child. Handling problems this way will protect the honor of the office and may very well help the child in his time of need.

Responding to Common Objections

Having set forth the meaning of 1 Timothy 3:4–5 and Titus 1:6, as well as having explored some of the implications of these passages for the life and leadership of the church, we will now respond to the most common objections raised by those who oppose the doctrine of covenant succession as it is brought to bear on the life and leadership of the church.

"Because no one is a perfect head of household, an unbelieving or unruly child cannot disqualify a man from office." The premise of this objection is true enough: none of us is perfect on this side of glory. But the conclusion does not follow from the premise. Although none of us can lay claim to *perfect* parenting, not all failures are *equally heinous.* There is a difference between a child who fails to clean his room when asked one morning and a child who is a drug dealer. We also need to be comforted with the fact that God calls us to faithful parenting, and part of faithful parenting is recognizing when we have failed, confessing our sins, and seeking reconciliation with those against whom we have sinned. In the end, this objection also assumes that a man cannot disqualify himself from office. But if no one can be *disqualified* from office, then this objection proves too much, because no one would be *qualified* for office either! Yet we know that some are called by God and so are qualified for office. The very standards that we use to determine whether a pastor or elder is qualified are also the same standards that we should use to determine whether he has disqualified himself from office. The door *in* is also the door *out.* Just because a man becomes an elder does not necessarily mean that he will serve as an elder for life. *Appointment for life* (in churches that practice it) should not be confused with *life tenure.* A man can, by his life or doctrine, forfeit the privilege of serving the church as a pastor or elder. The ministry is not an *entitlement.* It is a *privilege* with corresponding responsibilities.

"If a pastor or elder genuinely repents, he should be restored to office." While we rejoice any time a fallen saint has been restored to full fellowship, that fact alone does not qualify a man for office.

Ultimately, this objection does not properly distinguish between *forgiveness* and *the consequences of sin*. Children may repent after disobedience, but that does not relieve their parents of the duty to discipline them appropriately. A murderer may truly repent, but he nevertheless must be punished for his crime. A man can get drunk on a bottle of wine or overdose on drugs and then repent, but the physical consequences of the latter will be far more devastating and lasting than the former. So it is with the sins of unbelief and habitual rebellion in the children of pastors and elders. The consequences are grave, and one of them is that the father is unfit for office. Just as this objection fails to distinguish forgiveness from the consequences of sin, so it also fails to see that repentance is a *necessary* requirement for office, but it is not in itself *sufficient* for office. 1 Timothy 3 and Titus 1 require far more of a man than mere repentance.

"What about King David?" Those who argue that forgiveness necessarily entails restoration to office object that even though King David sinned miserably, he was used mightily of God thereafter. Indeed, God did use him mightily. But the life of King David is not a pattern for those aspiring to the office of elder. David principally was a statesman—a civil ruler. He was not a pastor or elder. Thus, we cannot assume that what was true of David is normative for pastors and elders today. In addition, while King David was a picture of the Eternal King, at this particular point in his life he was a warped, distorted picture. Moreover, those who make this objection often appeal selectively to the life of David and paint an unbiblically rosy picture of the aftermath of his sin. *Even though David was forgiven, God told him that the sword would never depart from his house.* His baby died; his daughter, Tamar, was raped by her half-brother Amnon, who, in turn, was murdered by Tamar's full brother, Absalom; Absalom died rebelling against his father; another undisciplined son, Adonijah, attempted to usurp David's throne and eventually was executed by Solomon. David was a failed father who raised a rapist and two treasonous rebels, both of whom died attempting to usurp their father's throne. What gross immorality and unimaginable wickedness! What dissipation and rebellion! What unbelief! Even limiting 1 Timothy 3:4–5 and Titus 1:6 to civil righteousness, at least three of David's children were civilly, if not criminally, corrupt to the core. Put bluntly, *David was not qualified for the office of elder in Christ's church.* Those who would look to him for support of the opposite position must look elsewhere.

"*Scripture does not speak explicitly to this issue.*" This objection begs the question at issue—whether 1 Timothy 3:4–5 and Titus 1:6 explicitly require pastors and elders to have believing and well-behaved children. Even setting aside the requirements set forth in these two passages, because the rest of Scripture teaches covenant succession, we expect that those who occupy church office would live as examples to the rest of the flock in this regard. In the end, the objector's problem is not really that Scripture fails to speak explicitly to this issue but rather that it speaks to it all too clearly.

"*Imposing this requirement constitutes a double standard.*" The only response to this objection is to say that there is only one biblical standard for right and holy living before the Lord, but pastors and elders are held more strictly accountable to that standard because of the office they hold. No one should become a drunkard, but a layman can do so (with repentance) and still be a layman. Not so for a pastor or elder. Not everyone is qualified to occupy church office. And not everyone who serves the church this way is qualified to continue to do so. The standard imposed on pastors and elders is not a different standard, but the accountability to that standard more strictly applies to them. This is Paul's point in warning that becoming a teacher is not God's call on every man because teachers incur a greater judgment (1 Tim. 3:2–7; Tit. 1:6–9; see also Jas. 3:1). Another way of saying this is that to whom much is given, much is required (Lk. 12:48).

"*Removing men from office because of their children's behavior is legalistic.*" This objection is a cause of real concern. However, while some might turn the apostle's requirements into a legalistic code, pointing out such potential or actual abuse does not constitute an argument against legitimate use. Taking the qualifications for office seriously is not legalistic; it is biblical. Would it be legalistic to tell a polygamist that he cannot become a pastor or elder? Of course not! But why? Because polygamy unequivocally disqualifies a man—even an otherwise decent man—from office. So it is with a man who has raised an unbelieving or rebellious child. The church is God's, and He has a right to rule it as He sees fit. If the Word of God commands a particular response, we are not legalists if, by His grace, we respond as He has commanded. While we always have to guard against the sin of legalism, we also have to be wary of the sin of antinomianism. We would most all agree that to allow a polygamist to assume office would be clear disobedience to God's Word. So why do the charges of legalism start flying when it comes to this particular requirement for office?

"Determining whether a child believes is a hopelessly subjective matter." Some think that while determining whether a man is a polygamist is an objective matter (you can simply go down to court and pull a file), determining whether a child believes is a hopelessly subjective matter. Admittedly, some cases are more difficult than others, but if a teenager says he doesn't believe, chances are he doesn't believe. And God does not leave us in the dark. While we should presume that our children are believers until they prove otherwise, God gave the keys of the kingdom to the church, and, in particular, to the elders of the church. One of the most important tasks the church performs is to hear professions of faith and to admit those who make a credible profession to membership, along with their children. Confessionally Reformed churches have discharged this responsibility for literally hundreds of years. So this is not a hopelessly subjective enterprise (and whatever subjectivity exists has been responsibly dealt with by godly men for centuries). Thus, this objection mistakenly assumes that determining the belief of a child is hopelessly subjective, when it is not a subjective process at all. But even if this determination is subjective, so is a determination of habitual drunkenness—there's not necessarily a court file you can pull

for that offense either—but we don't allow such men to serve as pastors or elders. God wants His church to be ruled by those who father believing and orderly children. The real question is whether we hear His voice. Is His voice unclear?

"The requirements only apply to pastors, not to elders." Good biblical scholars disagree about whether the qualifications enumerated by Paul in 1 Timothy 3:2–7 and Titus 1:6–9 apply only to pastors or to pastors and elders. Of course, this disagreement emanates from the age-old debate about whether Scripture teaches that there are two church offices (elder and deacon) or three church offices (pastor, ruling elder, and deacon). The two-office view posits that the requirements set forth in 1 Timothy 3:2–7 and Titus 1:6–9 apply both to pastors and elders since the New Testament uses the terms *bishop* and *elder* interchangeably in many passages. What is true of one is true of the other, since ultimately they bear the same office with different functions. The three-office view, by contrast, holds that the office of minister is distinct from the office of elder and that the requirements set forth in 1 Timothy 3 and Titus 1 apply only to ministers.

While this debate is important, it is beyond the scope of this chapter, and fortunately we do not need to resolve it in order to apply the requirements at hand. If you subscribe to the two-office view, then *ipso facto* the requirement to manage one's household well and to have believing children applies both to pastors and elders. But even if you subscribe to the three-office view, you only need to supply one additional premise to complete the argument—that the requirement for an elder to raise believing and well-behaved children runs to the very heart of what it means to rule the church. Paul removes all doubt by telling us that a man who cannot rule himself or his family is unfit to rule the church (1 Tim. 3:5).

If a pastor cannot be addicted to wine, then an elder cannot imbibe to his heart's content with impunity. If a pastor must manage his marriage and family well, then an elder cannot make shipwreck of his marriage and raise hellions and still be qualified for office. Clearly,

1 Timothy 3 and Titus 1 apply to pastors. One is unfit to be a pastor if he has children who have abandoned the faith and who live habitually rebellious lives. Even if you subscribe to the three-office view, consistency and integrity demand the same answer for elders so long as we supply the additional Pauline premise that a failure to manage one's household well runs to the heart of a man's ability to rule the church.

"The requirements are fulfilled by Christ who is our sufficiency." Many dismiss the requirements set forth for office—and indeed the imperatives of Scripture—by arguing that they are part of God's law and have been fulfilled by Christ. Indeed, Christ has fulfilled every dictate of God's holy law for us, died for every infraction of that law we will ever commit, been raised for our justification, and ascended to glory to judge the living and the dead. But the finished work of Christ does not excuse our disobedience or prove that the requirements for office no longer bind the church. Remember that Paul issued these requirements after the life, death, resurrection, and ascension of Christ.

We end up with teetotalers who sire sons of hell, and we hold them up before the congregation as examples to follow. God be merciful to us!

I am concerned that this objection fails to take God's law seriously and, if unchecked, results in antinomianism. Its "reading" cuts the requirements for office right out of the Bible. Based on this reasoning, everyone would be qualified to serve as a pastor or elder since the law is not the law; it only amounts to a few *suggestions* we are free to reject because Christ already fulfilled them for us. In the end, Christ's church is left without true pastors and elders who, by His grace, satisfy the qualifications for office. This objection lacks merit and flows from a misunderstanding of grace and a misunderstanding of the role of God's law as the standard of the good works that are to flow from the sanctification Christ bestows upon us as His beloved.

Conclusion

More and more, it seems, the church is tempted to impose standards that the Bible doesn't impose, and to ignore the standards that the Bible itself imposes. We speak when Scripture is silent, and we remain silent when Scripture speaks. How often have we heard teachers assert without any biblical support that pastors and elders cannot drink alcohol, when the *only* biblical standard is that pastors and elders cannot be addicted to wine? Then we turn a blind eye to pastors and elders who fail to manage their own lives, much less the lives of their wives and children. So we end up with teetotalers who sire sons of hell, and we hold them up before the congregation as examples to follow. God be merciful to us!

May we have the strength and courage to do what our Lord requires of us. May we rely solely upon the One who is without spot or blemish, the One who is our true and perfect Father in heaven who, by His grace, has adopted us into His family. May we, as His servants, strive to be like Him, and may we embrace the twin truths that in us dwells no good thing and that all of our righteousness is as filthy rags in His sight. May we believe that our sole sufficiency is Christ, that He is our all in all, and that we have no hope in this life or the life to come apart from Him. May we turn to our Father in heaven, trusting that He has promised to be not only our God, but also the God of our children. And may we, by His grace, guided by His Word, and empowered by His Spirit, raise sons and daughters who faithfully love and adore Him, from generation to generation.

Covenant Succession and the Emasculation of the Church

Timothy Bayly

Abraham will surely become a great and mighty nation, and in him all the nations of the earth will be blessed. For I have chosen him, so that he may command his children and his household after him to keep the way of the LORD by doing righteousness and justice, so that the LORD may bring upon Abraham what He has spoken about him. (Gen. 18:18–19)

When the Lord entered into a covenant with Abraham, He was pleased for that covenant's fulfillment to be dependent upon Abraham "command[ing] his children and his household . . . to keep the way of the Lord." Still today it pleases God to use means to accomplish His will, and He has declared the church should be built up, instructed, and guarded by men—not angels. Where those men are missing or their work is soft and effeminate, the church has suffered the removal of its vital manhood; it has been emasculated.[1]

When we speak of the emasculation of the church, though, we are not saying she has been robbed of her Bridegroom or that her adoptive Father has cast her out of His household. Christ is "faithful over God's house as a son" (Hebrews 3:6 RSV),[2] and we have His promise

---

[1] Since the church is the bride of Christ, it seems counterintuitive to speak of "her" emasculation. Yet God has been pleased to tie the growth, purity, and protection of His Household to the faithful performance of their duty by male officers. It is these men, called to represent Christ the Bridegroom, who are the focus of this chapter.

[2] Unless otherwise indicated, Scripture is from the New American Standard Bible, Updated Edition (La Habra, Calif.: The Lockman Foundation, 1995).

that the gates of hell shall not prevail against her. So then, the church can never be emasculated in any definitive sense, even though her officers may be characterized by an effeminate softness and sentimentality.

Such, though, is the church of our time. About twenty years ago I heard Elisabeth Elliot Gren say, "The problem with the church today is that it's filled with emasculated men who don't know how to say 'no' to a woman." At the time, I was floored by her audacity, but now I realize she was guilty of understatement. Christian men today have a problem saying "no" to almost anyone—not just women. Preachers, elders, and Sunday school teachers place an overwhelming emphasis on the positive and have an almost insurmountable aversion to the negative.

In the mid-eighties, my father was asked to represent the pro-life side at a campus-wide dialogue on abortion held at the Stupe, Wheaton College's student union. He began his presentation with the statement, "I am not here to represent the pro-life, but the anti-abortion, side of this issue. Evangelicals always want to speak positively, but imagine the abolitionist referring to himself as 'pro-slave.'"

Preachers place an overwhelming emphasis on the positive and have an almost insurmountable aversion to the negative.

Speaking negatively, saying God's "no" as well as His "yes," is almost a definition of faithful eldership, but what was true two decades ago has accelerated to the point where we are surrounded by men who, though called to guard God's truth and Bride, have little or no courage—that trait essential to masculinity which our Lord singles out when describing true shepherds: "The good shepherd lays down his life for the sheep." And the false shepherd? "They have healed the brokenness of My people superficially, saying, 'Peace, peace,' but there is no peace" (Jer. 6:14).

Preaching

Likely the most public example of the effeminacy of the leadership of church officers is in the proclamation of God's Word. Regularly I hear Christian men lament the softness of the preaching they and their wives and children sit under. One of them, a lawyer who serves as a ruling elder in the PCA, put it this way: "Along with the indicative, can't we please have God's imperative?" Pastors, though, know the risk of applying the Word of God to the lives of their sheep, so they decline to alter their pulpit ministry in order to address the will and heart as well as the mind.

Indicative of the balance struck by apostolic preaching is this summary by the apostle Paul: "We proclaim Him, admonishing every man and teaching every man with all wisdom, so that we may present every man complete in Christ" (Col. 1:28). Whereas "teaching" (*didaskontes*) is the imparting of knowledge, "admonishing" (*nouthetountes*) aims for the will and heart. Such heart-appeals are noticeably absent from many of our pulpits.

We have excuses: one thinks he follows a redemptive-historical hermeneutic and preaches every verse of Scripture as if it were John 3:16; another is attuned to the feminization of discourse and approaches the pulpit with a deathly fear of making any claim of authority which might cast him as insensitive or arrogant; a third believes grace to be the key

> *Believers are increasingly characterizing preachers and sermons as "preaching McLite" or "a nice thought for the week."*

doctrine of Scripture and demonstrates impatience with fellow pastors who preach the grace of the law and the lordship of Christ; a fourth tools through poems and humorous anecdotes, all warmly appreciated by the audience; and a fifth sidesteps the matter neatly with the pious claim, "It's not the preacher's job to convict—that's the work of the Holy Spirit."

Regardless of our high principles aimed to produce an acquittal by our peers, few would say we live in a golden age of preaching. With increasing frequency, believers may be heard characterizing preachers and sermons as "preaching McLite," or "a nice thought for the week." In such a climate, consider this warning Martin Luther gave to the men sent out to evaluate parish pastors:

> In regard to doctrine we observe especially this defect that. . . . many now talk only about the forgiveness of sins and say little or nothing about repentance. There neither is forgiveness of sins without repentance nor can forgiveness of sins be understood without repentance. It follows that if we preach the forgiveness of sins without repentance that the people imagine that they have already obtained the forgiveness of sins, becoming thereby secure and without compunction of conscience. This would be a greater error and sin than all the errors hitherto prevailing. Surely we need to be concerned lest, as Christ says in Matthew 12[:45], the last state becomes worse than the first.
>
> Therefore we have instructed and admonished pastors that it is their duty to preach the whole gospel and not one portion without the other.[3]

Preaching is both content and delivery, though, and the method of delivery employed by pastors today is also deficient. Some years back, Rob Suggs drew a cartoon showing a mousy pastor behind a large desk, glancing back over his shoulder at a chart on the wall that graphed a severe decline in worship attendance over the past few years. Standing to the side of the chart with a pointer directed towards the downward spiral was another man who said, "I'm no expert in these things, but I do wonder whether it might not help if you didn't end each sermon with, 'But then again, what do I know, anyhow?'"

One of the more insidious attacks upon the proclamation of the gospel in our time is the *feminization of discourse* permeating our culture,

---

[3] Martin Luther, "Instructions for the Visitors of Parish Pastors" *Church and Ministry II*, vol. 40 of *Luther's Works*, ed. Conrad Bergendoff (Philadelphia: Muhlenberg Press, 1958), 274–75.

yet this attack which saps preaching of its authority is rarely noticed. What is meant by the "feminization of discourse?"

Soon after Communism's fall, Aleksandr Solzhenitsyn was free to return to his beloved homeland. Just prior to his departure, a *New Yorker* correspondent visited him in his Vermont farmhouse:

> Back in the study, I asked Solzhenitsyn about his relations with the West. He knew that things had gone wrong, but had no intention of making any apologies. "Instead of secluding myself here and writing *The Red Wheel*, I suppose I could have spent time making myself likable to the West," he said. "The only problem is that I would have had to drop my way of life and my work. And, yes, it is true, when I fought the dragon of Communist power I fought it at the highest pitch of expression. The people in the West were not accustomed to this tone of voice. In the West, one must have a balanced, calm, soft voice; one ought to make sure to doubt oneself, to suggest that one may, of course, be completely wrong. But I didn't have the time to busy myself with this. This was not my main goal."[4]

Pastors do busy themselves with this; making ourselves "likable" is close to our hearts so we voice our sermons "balanced, calm, [and] soft." Although called to be heralds of Christ, we appear to believe we have arrived at a time when the proclamation of the gospel no longer requires that the faithful messenger resign himself to being "condemned to death . . . a spectacle to the world" (1 Cor. 4:9). Yes, we observe our culture's growing hostility toward God's moral law and the gospel of Jesus Christ, but we reassure ourselves that our United States Constitution still guarantees us free exercise of religion and it's quite unlikely the moral decadence surrounding us will give birth to suffering and persecution in our own time—particularly if we guard our lips and tactfully orchestrate the occasional strategic retreat required in order to keep the peace.[5]

---

[4] David Remnick, "The Exile Returns," *The New Yorker* (February 14, 1994), 74.

[5] Calvin, commenting on Acts 28:29, says, "To enjoy peace with God, it is necessary for us to wage war with those who treat Him with contempt" (*Acts of the Apostles*, vol. 7

Meanwhile, the show must go on:

> We all know what it is to play warfare in mock battle, that it means
> to imitate everything just as it is in war. The troops are drawn up,
> they march into the field, seriousness is evident in every eye, but also
> courage and enthusiasm, the orderlies rush back and forth intrep-
> idly, the commander's voice is heard, the signals, the battle cry, the
> volley of musketry, the thunder of cannon—everything exactly as
> it is in war, lacking only one thing . . . the danger.
>
> So also it is with playing Christianity, that is, imitating Christian
> preaching in such a way that everything, absolutely everything is
> included in as deceptive a form as possible—only one thing is lack-
> ing . . . the danger.[6]

Thus, congregations expect from their pastor nothing more than a
finely-tuned, intimate "sharing of the journey," with clever illustrations demonstrating that he lives in the real world and is hip to the
decadence of their house-
holds' cultural consump-
tion and its resultant ennui.

*Preachers have allowed themselves to be
cast as pleasant companions, chaplains
looking spiffy in their dress whites.*

Lest he break the mood, he
must avoid any "Thus saith
the Lord" histrionics—ex-
cept, that is, in his authoritative proclamation of the sovereignty of
God and the grace and eternal security He bestows on His covenant
people—we are Reformed, after all.

So preachers have allowed themselves to be cast as pleasant companions for the journey, chaplains looking spiffy in their dress whites.
If the concept of manhood still holds some residual attraction, we can
always experience that courage vicariously, watching *Terminator 3*,
reading the dashing exploits of Horatio Hornblower, or remembering the glory days of the past through the pen of our own Iain Murray.

---

of *Calvin's New Testament Commentaries*, trans. John W. Fraser, ed. David W. Torrance and
Thomas F. Torrance [Grand Rapids: Eerdmans, 1965], 314).

[6] Soren Kierkegaard, *Attack Upon "Christendom" 1854–1855*, trans. Walter Lowrie (Boston: Beacon, 1956), 258.

Church Discipline

The pool of blame widens when we begin to discuss the emasculation of the church in the matter of church discipline. Here even the
faithful pastor who sounds crystal-clear notes from the pulpit and
desires to lead his session to be faithful shepherds will find his hands
full as, each month, he faces elders intent upon protecting the congregation from their well-meaning but overzealous shepherd. Such
elders, resistant to the terrible drain of time and emotional energy
intrinsic to faithful shepherding, feel no compunction in relegating
such dirty work to men they refer to as "our staff."

Church discipline, then, is quite rare. When the overlooking of a
particularly flagrant sin would cause an outcry within the congregation (particularly the women), the session may be led to see the wisdom of rebuke and censure—or even excommunication. Still, this
is the exception to the rule; normally, neither teaching nor ruling
elders have the heart for discipline and shame is the only goad sufficiently painful to drive them to its use.

As with those who practice soft preaching, those who practice soft
pastoral care cloak themselves in principle. Some, for instance, deny
that discipline is the third mark of the church. There are not three,
but two marks, they argue—the right preaching of the Word and the
right administration of the Sacraments.

Is it possible, though, that the sort of preaching that lacks personal
application can be considered "the right preaching of the Word of
God?" Richard Baxter answers:

> [People] will give you leave to preach against their sins, and to talk
> as much as you will for godliness in the pulpit, if you will but let
> them alone afterwards, and be friendly and merry with them when
> you have done, and talk as they do, and live as they, and be indiffer-
> ent with them in your conversation. For they take the pulpit to be
> but a stage; a place where preachers must show themselves, and play
> their parts; where you have liberty for an hour to say what you [de-
> sire]; and what you say they regard not, if you show them not, by

saying it personally to their faces, that you were in good earnest, and did indeed mean them.[7]

Similarly, is the unrestrained marking of non-covenantal children by the sign of the covenant, and the unrestrained distribution of the Lord's Supper to souls with no ecclesiastical affiliation requiring their submission to officers of the visible church, in any sense "the right administration of the Sacraments"? No, it's hard to deny this declaration of the Scots Confession:

> The notes of the true Kirk, therefore, we believe, confess, and avow to be: first, the true preaching of the Word of God, in which God has revealed himself to us, as the writings of the prophets and apostles declare; secondly, the right administration of the sacraments of Christ Jesus, with which must be associated the Word and promise of God to seal and confirm them in our hearts; and lastly, ecclesiastical discipline uprightly ministered, as God's Word prescribes, whereby vice is repressed and virtue nourished.[8]

The absence of a loving application of church discipline to those souls under a session's care is a betrayal of the Lord who purchased those sheep with His own blood, and it indicates there isn't much that has changed since, centuries ago, Richard Baxter wrote,

> Sure I am, if it were well understood how much of the pastoral authority and work consisteth in church guidance, it would be also discerned, that to be against discipline, is near to being against the ministry; and to be against the ministry is near to being absolutely against the Church; and to be against the Church, is near to being absolutely against Christ. Blame not the harshness of the inference, till you can avoid it, and free yourselves from the charge of it before the Lord.[9]

---

[7] Baxter, *The Reformed Pastor* (Carlisle, Penn.: Banner of Truth, 1974), 85.
[8] The Scots Confession, chapter 18.
[9] Baxter, *Reformed Pastor*, 111.

Few then would deny this to be the general state of today's church—
shepherds are not manly. Rather, panting after success, we refuse to
do the work of loving and guarding God's truth and flock. And while
it is true that the most vulgar expressions of the "health and wealth
gospel" are normally outside the Reformed theological community,
Reformed pastors and elders also worship success. Listen to conversations at presbytery or synod
meetings and count the seconds
that elapse before that all-impor-
tant question, "What's your average attendance?" is asked. Read
conference speakers' bios, glance
at the handsome faces gracing

> *Shepherds are not manly. Rather,
> panting after success, we refuse to
> do the work of loving and guard-
> ing God's truth and flock.*

glossy dust jackets, feel the sultry vibes of the latest CCM offerings,
and it becomes apparent that the normal business of the church is just
that—business—not instruction and discipline.

The orders our Lord left prior to His Assumption were to "make
disciples," "baptizing" and "teaching them," but simply making con-
sumers appears to be more in line with our priorities. As my father
used to say about church leaders, "Everyone's out to build his own
kingdom."

And if, in one of our more transparent moments, we were asked
why pastors avoid preaching repentance and practicing church discipline, we might well sputter, "It's the numbers, stupid!" The modern pastor is a suave entrepreneur, charged by his denominational
expansion board or search committee with meeting certain membership projections, and only a fool would think he could grow a congregation by preaching to unfelt needs or spending valuable session
time in admonishment, rebuke, or censure. Furthermore, who's
going to stick around to be disciplined? The very week a member
receives a summons to appear before the board of elders, he'll be out
church-shopping.

Covenant Succession and the Discipline of Covenant Children

It's when we turn to the neglect of the discipline of children of the covenant—particularly those in their teens and early twenties—that an organic connection between the emasculation of the church and the decline of the doctrine of covenant succession begins to emerge. Officers of the church who operate more from fear than faith are unlikely to apply to their children the tools God has ordained as the means for the accomplishment of covenant succession, particularly discipline. In turn, covenant children robbed of this divinely ordained care are unlikely to make a good confession themselves or demonstrate courage in their own leadership when their generation takes over the mantle of leadership.

Proverbs frequently warns against partiality in judgment, so it should be no surprise that church officers find it difficult to discipline their peers. For this reason the apostle Paul wrote concerning the discipline of elders, "I solemnly charge you in the presence of God and of Christ Jesus and of His chosen angels, to maintain these principles without bias, doing nothing in a spirit of partiality" (1 Tim. 5:21). Add to the temptation of partiality our culture's sentimental view of childhood, and it's not hard to guess that the children of the church—particularly officers' children—are chronically neglected by those called to guard their souls.

Eli is the quintessential example of the man to whom God had delegated authority for the protection and nurture of His people, yet who was unwilling to use that authority to bring his own sons into subjection first. Because of Eli's failure, God declared to him, "[You] honor your sons above Me" (1 Sam. 2:29), and pronounced this judgment: "I am about to judge his house forever for the iniquity which he knew, because his sons brought a curse on themselves and he did not rebuke them" (1 Sam. 3:13).

As a loving Father, God shows His own partiality toward His children by disciplining them faithfully. Thus His judgment and discipline begin with His own household, the church (1 Pet. 4:17); and within that household, with the leaders and their children. Pastors and elders, though, are slow to believe that following this same pattern with their own children will produce good fruit, so they are hesitant to discipline their children—and tenaciously resistant to allowing others to do so.

When warning younger men of the risks involved in caring for the youth of a church, I remind them of the hornet's nest of opposition that Jonathan Edwards stirred up in his Northampton congregation when he tried to discipline some covenant children for their indecent perusal of a "midwives' manual" that was widely regarded as pornography. True, part of the opposition was a result of the infelicitous method of communication that Edwards used to address

> *The instruction of covenant children is hazardous work, and many pastors and elders have conveniently concluded that avoiding it is not weakness but principle.*

the problem on a particular Lord's Day, but there are few pastors, elders, youth leaders, or Sunday school teachers who last long without learning the parental proverb, "Touch my children and you've touched me." The instruction and care of covenant children is hazardous work, and many pastors and elders have conveniently concluded that avoiding this risk is not weakness but principle.

So, for instance, whether covenant children ought properly to be the subjects of church discipline was one of the questions addressed by the Committee of Revision of the *Book of Discipline* appointed by the 1857 General Assembly of the Presbyterian Church in the United States of America. Reporting on its work two years later to the 1859 General Assembly in Indianapolis, the committee's divergent viewpoints were represented by two of its members, Princeton's Charles Hodge and Columbia Theological Seminary's J. H. Thornwell.

Hodge argued that the church's baptized children were truly members of the church by virtue not of their own confession of faith but the covenant promises of God, and therefore ought rightly to be extended the privileges of membership including, particularly, ecclesiastical discipline. This was not to say these children were known to be regenerate; on the contrary, all involved in the debate agreed that, regardless of baptism, the state of the souls of both adults and children is known only to God.[10] Hodge put it this way:

> When, therefore, we assert the church membership of the infants of believing parents, we do not assert their regeneration, or that they are true members of Christ's body; we only assert that they belong to the class of persons whom we are bound to regard and treat as members of Christ's Church. *This is the only sense in which even adults are members of the Church, so far as men are concerned.*"[11]

Opposite Hodge, Thornwell believed that baptized children ought to be considered guilty until proven innocent:

> Are they not the slaves of sin and the Devil? . . . Should they not, then, be carefully instructed on the one hand, and on the other be treated according to their true character as slaves? [Until their profession of faith they are] to be dealt with as the Church deals with all the enemies of God. She turns the key upon them and leaves them without."[12]

Thornwell was, then, opposed to the application of ecclesiastical discipline to covenant children.

The debate of the Indianapolis General Assembly led to the mat-

---

[10] "The presumption of election is not founded on their baptism, but their baptism is founded on this presumption; just as the presumption that Jewish children would take Jehovah to be their God was not founded on their circumcision, but their circumcision was founded on that presumption" (qtd. in Lewis Bevens Schenck, *The Presbyterian Doctrine of Children in the Covenant* [New Haven: Yale Univ. Press, 1940], 135).

[11] Ibid., 129, 130.

[12] J. H. Thornwell, "A Few More Words on the Revised Book of Discipline," in *The Southern Presbyterian Review* 13, no. 1 (1861): 6 (qtd. in Schenck, *Children in the Covenant*, 94–95). Although not responding to this historical debate, Vern Poythress cogently addressed the same error recently: "Others may be tempted to rigorism. They view baptized children as members of the church only 'formally,' while in practice they think of

ter being recommitted to the Committee of Revision. Reporting back one year later, in 1860, the committee's work continued to be the center of such a storm of controversy that the question was again recommitted, this time with the addition of six members to the Committee of Revision. The debate raged in Presbyterian publications right up to the Civil War, at which time the Northern and Southern Presbyterian churches went their separate ways.

In 1863 the Northern Presbyterian Church in the United States of America adopted a revised *Book of Discipline* adhering to the historic Reformed view, held by Hodge and others, that baptized but non-communicant children of the covenant were fully members of the church and properly subject to her instruction and discipline.

The Southern Presbyterian Church in the United States took the path of innovation advocated by Thornwell and R. L. Dabney, affirming two distinct categories of church membership and denying children the privilege of ecclesiastical discipline. In the southern church, then, the historic 1736 *Book of Discipline's* statement, "Inasmuch as all baptized persons are members of the Church, they are under its care, and subject to its government and discipline," was changed to reflect Thornwell's 1859 proposal in which baptized members were no longer "subject to [the Church's] government and discipline," but "under [the Church's] government and training." And this explanatory note was added: "Only those, however, who have made a profession of faith in Christ are proper subjects of [discipline]."[13]

Indicative of the concern at the heart of this debate was this lament by Princeton's Samuel Miller:

---

them as sub-Christian until they reach teenage years and go through the rite of confirmation. In many instances paedobaptists describe confirmation as 'joining the church' or 'becoming a member of the church,' when in actual fact the people about to be presented in a confirmation ceremony have already joined the church and are already members, for they have been baptized as infants. The thinking that they are not yet members of the church seems to reveal a subtle form of rigorism" ("Indifferentism and Rigorism in the Church with Implications for Baptizing Small Children," *Westminster Theological Journal* 59, no. 1 [1997]: 13–29).

[13] Schenck, *Children in the Covenant*, 90.

That baptized children should be treated by the Church and her officers just as other children are treated: that they should receive the seal of a covenant relation to God and his people, and then be left to negligence and sin, without official inspection, and without discipline, precisely as those are left who bear no relation to the Church, is, it must be confessed, altogether inconsistent with the nature and design of the ordinance, and in a high degree unfriendly to the best interests of the Church of God.[14]

Recently, Vern Poythress worked to open the eyes of church officers and parents—both credo- and paedobaptists—to the inconsistent treatment of children in our churches. He described two seemingly opposite but sometimes, in practice, interwoven errors in the shepherding of covenant children, errors he labeled "indifferentism" and "rigorism." Chiding both sides of

> *Where covenant succession is not believed, parents are inclined to wait for a crisis conversion experience.*

the baptism debate for failing to deal with children as souls with the capacity and spiritual duty to repent, believe, and obey, he wrote,

We ought not to shunt smaller children over into a backwater, merely waiting indifferently until they grow old enough to be like us [but] to treat both adult church members and their children as Christians, with all the love and encouragement, the discipline and rebuke, the hopes and the warnings that we owe to Christians.[15]

But where covenant succession is not understood or believed, parents are inclined to adopt a hands-off posture toward the rearing of their children, waiting for the work of the Holy Spirit through

---

[14] Samuel Miller, *Infant Baptism Scriptural and Reasonable and Baptism by Sprinkling or Affusion the Most Suitable and Edifying Mode* (Philadelphia: n.p., 1835), 47 (qtd. in Schenck, *Children in the Covenant*, 83).

[15] Vern Sheridan Poythress, "Linking Small Children with Infants in the Theology of Baptizing," *Westminster Theological Journal*, 59, no. 2 (1997): 143–158.

Vacation Bible School, summer camp, youth retreats, or other extraordinary moments—all of which are expected to produce a crisis conversion experience. Then and only then may they consider applying covenant expectations and discipline to that child.

What has led to such a weak understanding and application of the covenant promises of God that our children are being raised bereft of the very discipline and instruction that proves they are legitimate and loved children? If, as Hebrews 12:6–8 says,[16] discipline is one of the principal ways God demonstrates His love to us, how have we come to the point where we believe He no longer finds secondary means necessary or even useful? Do we expect any negative consequences for our own children or the church as a result of our refusal to make use of the power of the keys and every lesser but related tool God has appointed for their building up and protection?

God has ordained that the children of believers grow up in homes and churches where instruction and discipline are understood to be a key part of their patrimony and applied faithfully in the belief that it is by such means God fulfills His covenant promises. Still, an objective examination of our behavior leads to the conclusion that many of us think we have found a better way to assure covenant succession than this way ordained by God.

Having grown up in the ecclesiastical wasteland of evangelicalism, I was led by Calvin to a new view of the church's glory:

> Let us learn even from the simple title 'mother' how useful, indeed how necessary, it is that we should know [the visible church]. For there is no other way to enter into life unless this mother conceive us in her womb, give us birth, nourish us at her breast, and lastly, unless she keep us under her care and guidance until, putting off mortal flesh, we become like angels.[17]

---

[16] "For those whom the Lord loves He disciplines, and He scourges every son whom He receives. . . . But if you are without discipline, of which all have become partakers, then you are illegitimate children and not sons."

[17] *Institutes of the Christian Religion*, trans. Ford Lewis Battles, ed. John T. McNeill, Library of Christian Classics (Philadelphia: Westminster, 1960), 2:1016.

And again, "into [the church's] bosom God is pleased to gather his
sons, not only that they may be nourished by her help and ministry
as long as they are infants and children, but also that they may be
guided by her motherly care until they mature and at last reach the
goal of faith."[18]

Herman Witsius makes an equally tender statement of God's loving care for each of His little ones, likening their baptism to being
transferred from their mother's bosom into the arms of God:

> Here certainly appears the extraordinary love of our God, in that
> as soon as we are born, and just as we come from our mother, he
> hath commanded us to be solemnly brought from her bosom, as it
> were, into his own arms, that he should bestow upon us, in the very
> cradle, the tokens of our dignity and future kingdom. . . .[19]

When, with Calvin, we speak of the children of God being "continually preserved under [the church's] care and government" or,
with Witsius, of covenant children being brought "from [their
mother's] bosom . . . into [God's] arms," we are acknowledging the
solemn duties of the church and her officers to those children. Note
well that these duties are in addition to all those God has delegated
to the children's natural sovereigns, their father and mother.

A great irony of parts of the home schooling movement is that,
despite their commitment to recover the biblical obligation of fathers
in the home to instruct and train their offspring, these same fathers
seem so often to view the household of faith and her fathers (pastors
and elders) with disdain. Instead of teaching their wives and children
to love the church, and to honor and respect her leaders, too often
the church is viewed as a threat to the household's spiritual welfare—
or more likely, to its self-protective insularity. Those seeking a restoration of biblical patriarchy among the people of God would do

---

[18] Ibid., 1012. Note 3 on the same page cites Cyprian: "You cannot have God for your
Father unless you have the church for your Mother."

[19] *The Economy of the Covenants* (qtd. in Schenck, *Children in the Covenant*, 148).

well to study the constancy of household language in the New Testament in reference to the church's members, officers, and work, and to meditate on the significance of that language for the love we owe Christ's bride, and the honor and deference due those whose calling it is to exercise the Father's authority within His household (a church's failures notwithstanding).

But to return to our theme, there is a symbiotic relationship between the decline of the doctrine and practice of covenant succession and the emasculation of the church. As the church's officers have lost their manhood, doctrinally and practically, they have failed in their covenant duties to the children of the church, and those children in turn have shown the fruits of that absence of manly shepherding and leadership.

> *The absence of vital male leadership and the absence of discipline feed off one another.*

Church discipline takes courage, especially the discipline of one's own children or the children of fellow elders, but the kind of vital male leadership capable of such courage cannot be grown without discipline. Thus these two pathologies—the absence of vital male leadership and the absence of discipline—feed off one another.

To clarify the big picture, the church has neglected or forgotten God's promises throughout Scripture to keep His covenant with our children. Consequently, the children of believers have come to be considered outside the covenant even as they grow up within the church. They are denied covenant blessings reserved for church members, including particularly the blessing of church discipline. And, failing to provide her children discipline, the church's manhood is lost as fathers are disqualified from holding office because their households are not in order. Finally, sons of the church are not able to take over the shepherding of God's flock because they have not been raised and disciplined to that end.

But let us also look at the mirror image. Where God's covenant promises are claimed and acted upon in faith, the children of believers are granted their rightful patrimony—namely, the covenant blessings of instruction and discipline at home and within the body of believers. Further, by instruction and discipline they are trained to love God's covenant promises and persuaded and enabled to embrace them themselves as the Holy Spirit works in them the graces He promised. Now the fathers of the home and church have created a true *seminary*—a "seedbed"—where sons of the covenant are equipped and prepared to assume the yoke of leadership when, through the congregation, the Holy Spirit extends the call.

Over my lifetime, I've noticed a decline in the usage of certain terms and phrases, one of which is "son of the church." Twenty to thirty years ago, this phrase was commonly used in session and presbytery meetings to refer to a young man who had grown up in the church and was now under care, testing a call to the ministry of the Word and Sacrament. With some pride, he was called a "son of the church," meaning that his church was not failing to raise up shepherds from her midst. And so it has always been the expectation that a vital congregation will raise her sons with an eye to providing for her future well-being, calling out from among them those who have been given gifts for the building up of the church. The healthy church looks to her sons for future leadership, but an emasculated church is impotent in this regard.

Faith of Our Fathers Living Still

As I read to the end of Joshua this morning, I was reminded of Joshua's last words to Israel just before he died: "But as for me and my house, we will serve the Lord" (Josh. 24:15). And thinking on his words, I thought back to my own father. Dad loved his children, but he found it easier to bring discipline to bear on the larger evangelical world through, for instance, his monthly column in *Eternity* magazine, than to discipline his own children. This is not to say we weren't disciplined; as Dad's wonderful helpmate, Mud (our family's pet name for her) filled in many of the gaps left by our father—both those which were the result of his constant travels and those simply the products of his temperament—and I praise God that He gave me a tough mother who fought for my soul, disciplining me through my teenage years. But as distasteful as he found it, Dad himself also disciplined us. I want to tell of a particular act of discipline which I view as the supreme act of love I ever received from my father, but to fully communicate its significance, I must open my father's heart to you a little more.

Dad grew up in Philadelphia and New York City. He was urbane and fastidious—a gentleman. Had John Henry Newman been speaking of Dad, he would have had it right: "it is almost a definition of a gentleman to say he is one who never inflicts pain."[20] But this aversion to inflicting pain on others—particularly his own family—wasn't the whole reason Dad avoided disciplining his children. During our childhood, three of my siblings died, at different times: Danny, the third born, of leukemia when he was five; Johnny, the fifth born, of cystic fibrosis when he was two weeks; and then the heartbreaker—my father's firstborn, his eldest son, died after a Christmas night sledding accident. Joseph Tate Bayly V was a full-ride National Merit Scholar in his sophomore year at Swarthmore College, preparing for the Lord's service, when it pleased the Lord to call him home. As you might imagine, it was hard for Dad and Mud to recover from that blow—or any of us, for that matter—and after Joe's death, the heart of our home was missing for a number of years.

Of course, I don't mean to imply that Dad and Mud stopped loving one another, nor that our home lacked affection between parents and children and husband and wife. But it was clearly hard work, particularly at Christmas. And it's my own belief that the severity of this blow was one part of my father's inability to invest himself fully in the rest of his children, particularly his two eldest whose time of greatest emotional need was immediately following this third death. (My two youngest brothers were barely out of the toddler stage at

---

[20] John Henry Newman, *The Idea of a University Defined and Illustrated* (NewYork: American Press, 1941), 227.

the time, so when they hit the years of greater emotional need, Dad had regained some of his emotional equilibrium.)

Skip ahead, then, a few years. I had graduated from high school and, after a year at Columbia Bible College, I was living at home while holding down a job packing books for a Christian publisher in Wheaton. Although not flagrantly so, I was a covenant-breaker and my presence in the home caused Dad and Mud, as well as my two younger brothers, some degree of turmoil. As usual, though, Mud caught the brunt of it—not Dad; while she tended the home-fires, he was out fulfilling his speaking engagements.

Then came the day he showed me the full extent of his love. It was a Saturday morning and I had been on my way upstairs to my bedroom. Dad stood on the brick floor of the entryway looking up at me and asked me to stop a moment. He had something he needed to say to me.

"Tim, you are not honoring the Lord and you may no longer live in our house."

There were no raised voices: just Dad's plain speaking and my silent acceptance. Packing my bags, I was awed by the weight of Dad's action—not at all as I bore it, but as my father bore it himself.[21] By then I was his eldest son but I held my life cheap, taking a solo backpacking trip into the San Jacinto Wilderness of eastern California without water, hitch-hiking cross country in cars driven by drug- and alcohol-addled freaks, driving my own Volkswagen Beetle buzzed to the max—I was a fool and remained a living and breathing soul only by God's mercy.

Most of this Dad knew, but he refused to allow fear to rule his relationship with his son. Or, to put it another way, he chose the fear

---

[21] "As a father, when he turns out of his house a contumacious son and deprives him of his presence and the testimonies of paternal favor, still not as yet on that account does he wholly disinherit him or divest himself of all fatherly affection towards him; nay, then using this remedy to bring him to repentance, even by this deed exercises his love towards him although not acknowledging it then, will afterwards acknowledge it, when by true conversion he shall have returned into favor with his father" (Francis Turretin, *Institutes of Elenctic Theology*, 3 vols. [Phillipsburg, N.J.: Presbyterian and Reformed, 1994], 3:295).

of God over the fear of the loss of a son's friendship or even his life. And for this I am eternally grateful, seeing how pivotal this day was in the work of God in my life ever since.

In fact, this act of love is what sticks in my mind as I carry on the baton of leadership as a husband, father, and pastor. It is this memory of my father's courage that God has used innumerable times to strengthen me when, sitting in a session meeting, I feel faint of heart and wish to avoid using the tool of

> *Dad refused to allow fear to rule; or rather, he chose the fear of God over the fear of the loss of a son's friendship, or even his life.*

discipline that God has appointed for the restoration of wayward souls and for the protection of His name and bride. It is this loving discipline I received as a son that gives me courage when I find myself recoiling from giving a needed rebuke to one of my own children, fearing that he will resent me for it and there will be a breach in our relationship. It is this concrete and painful application of God's Word by my father to his son that I remember when I find myself inclined to flinch in the application of a sermon text to the lives within my congregation.

Conclusion

When God promised to establish His covenant and to be God to Abraham and his descendants, He said, "I will establish My covenant between Me and you and your descendants after you, throughout their generations for an everlasting covenant, to be God to you and to your descendants after you" (Gen. 17:7).

How was Abraham to do this? Enabled by God, he was to "command his children and his household after him to keep the way of the Lord by doing righteousness and justice" (Gen. 18:19). In other words, the means of bringing about what the Lord had promised Abraham was manly and faithful instruction in God's Word and application of it to the lives of his children and his children's children.

God is pleased to carry on the covenant through the faithfulness of men—fathers in the home and church.[22]

Jesus came to do the work of His Father: "Whatever the Father does, these things the Son also does in like manner" (Jn. 5:19). If ever there was a man who ought to have been able to grow into His Father's work without the necessity of discipline, it was Jesus. Yet we read, "Although He was a Son, He learned obedience from the things which He suffered" (Heb. 5:8).

If we pastors and elders understand our duty to assure a succession of leadership in the church, we will strive with all our might to pass our work on to the sons God has blessed us with, loving and disciplining them as God loved and disciplined His own Son.

[22] This is not in any way meant to neglect or treat dismissively the godly work of women—for instance, Timothy's grandmother and mother, Lois and Eunice, and Augustine's mother, Monica—but only to focus our attention, particularly, on fathers and sons.

Picking up the Pieces

Randy Booth

It was the best of times, it was the worst of times, it was the age of wisdom, it was the age of foolishness, it was the epoch of belief, it was the epoch of incredulity, it was the season of Light, it was the season of Darkness, it was the spring of hope, it was the winter of despair, we had everything before us, we had nothing before us, we were all going direct to Heaven, we were all going direct the other way. . . .

The above passage is not only the famous introduction to a famous Dickens novel; it is also not a bad description of child-rearing in many households. Those cute, sweet little bundles of joy will grow up, and sometimes they break our hearts. The disappointment and pain of a wayward child can be overwhelming. Few if any pains can compare to the loss of a child, physically or spiritually, and our hearts will always go out in sympathy and pity to those who feel that stinging grief or disappointment. As part of the covenant community, we are especially sad as we "weep with those who weep" and in some cases even share the responsibility for failures. Parental sins and corporate sins often contribute to these situations and so we must look to ourselves and our covenant communities as we seek remedies from God's Word and rely on the powerful work of the Holy Spirit.

God's Word raises such high standards that we, in our weakness, might be tempted to become discouraged rather than encouraged.

There is not one parent who has not failed at various points. Some of the failures are relatively minor, while others are major and even catastrophic. Regardless of our level of understanding when we begin our households, the one thing we are guaranteed is that we will fail to some degree. It is also certain, regardless of where we start, that we will learn many things during the lifetime of our household. Failing will be a big part of that learning process. *The ultimate failure, however, is failure to learn from our failures*. It is not so much a question of where we are today in our quest for the faithful covenant household. Rather, in which direction are we headed?

No matter how well we begin, no matter how much we know, it is impossible to raise a child for twenty years and not learn a good deal. Who would not change some things if they could start over? Our improved theology, experience, and wisdom would surely enable us to do a better job. Often, by the time

> *The ultimate failure is the failure to learn from our failures.*

a serious problem becomes evident, it seems too late to do much about it. Perhaps others saw it coming or the parents had some kind of warning, but frequently parents feel blindsided by their child's bad attitude, unruly behavior, or lack of faith.

Sermons, lessons, or books about covenant succession can add to the heartache of parents who are not experiencing such covenant blessings. As a result, many pastors are reluctant to speak out on these issues for fear of further injury to their suffering sheep. Yet a different perspective might be helpful for both pastors and the parents who are dealing with such problems.

Parents who are suffering should desire the message of covenant succession—"If only someone had warned and helped us sooner!" I remember a particular couple that was deeply grieved over their adult unbelieving children. I felt great concern and compassion for them as I prepared to preach on the Christian household. They came to me after one particularly difficult message on covenant succession and said to me, "Thank you. We wish we had been taught these things when we were raising our children. We are so glad that these young couples will be better equipped than we were."

Many failures come on a daily basis and are common to every Christian parent. With these kinds of failures we have the opportunity to receive forgiveness, correct the mistakes, and move on. This is one of the blessings of having such a long time period for raising our children. However, other failures are more systemic in the household and become habitual. This kind of perpetual covenant irresponsibility, due to ignorance and/or rebellion by parents, produces far more serious and long-lasting problems in the home.

Since it is certain that we all fall short of God's standards for the covenant household, how do we handle the failures? How do we deal with the past? How do we respond in the present? How do we prepare for the future? Will we learn from our failures, or will they destroy us? Is there hope for those who have failed in the past, or is all lost? Let us consider a biblical response.

Suffering and the Covenant Community

The church, the community of the saints and household of God, bears several responsibilities toward her members. These important responsibilities are both proactive, with prevention through covenant nurture, as well as retroactive, in repair and redemption for those whose children have rejected the faith. The church must proclaim the word of God as it applies to families and the rearing of children, teaching its standards and promises. We must not fail to lovingly lead our members to do what God required of our father Abraham: "For I have known him, in order that he may command his children and his household after him, that they keep the way of the LORD, to do righteousness and justice, that the LORD may bring to Abraham what He has spoken to him" (Gen. 18:19).

Yet even the church that is faithful in this duty must still be prepared to serve its members in another way. People come to the church in various conditions, with a wide variety of needs. Many of these needs will be manifest in families that are in need of special help. The author of Hebrews reminds the Christian to "strengthen the hands which hang down, and the feeble knees, and make straight paths for your.feet, so that what is lame may not be dislocated, but rather be healed" (12:12–13).

Chief among the evidences of a true church of Jesus Christ is love. Jesus said, "By this all will know that you are My disciples, if you have love for one another" (Jn. 13:35). The apostle John sets love for the brethren as one of the essential proofs of genuine saving faith: "We know that we have passed from death to life, because we love the brethren. He who does not love his brother abides in death" (1 Jn. 3:14).

When problems arise, many people (even friends) are prone to withdraw, while others judge, criticize, gossip, and advance their own causes.

Biblical love is fervent, compassionate, persistent, and honest. Love covers a multitude of sins without covering up sin. Nevertheless, for those who are suffering the pain of a family wreck, binding their wounds must come before correcting their mistakes. Life is complicated and we must not presume that we can unscramble an egg.

One of the ways that love is tested is when one of our member households suffers failure or disappointment with a child. This is an opportunity to put love into action—to show friendship, compassion, and affection. Unfortunately, when personal problems arise, many people (even friends) are prone to retreat and withdraw while others find it the perfect occasion to judge, criticize, gossip, and advance their own causes.

When our children fall into sin, they and their parents are in need of help and encouragement. Pastors, elders, deacons, and the congregation all have special obligations to serve families with wayward children: "Now we exhort you, brethren, warn those who are unruly, comfort the fainthearted, uphold the weak, be patient with all. See that no one renders evil for evil to anyone, but always pursue what is good both for yourselves and for all" (1 Thes. 5:14–15). The goal is complete recovery. This will require wisdom, love, hope and patience. This is not the time to say, "I saw this coming" or "I told you so." Now is the time to "weep with those who weep." The covenant community must come together to lend support to the suffering family and help them through the storm.

Selfishness frequently tempts us to avoid unfamiliar and uncomfortable situations. Therefore we often simply do nothing. "I didn't know what to say or do" becomes our refuge. Christian maturity, however, sets aside such excuses and owns its responsibility by embracing those who suffer and sacrificing for them. Simply being there and offering hopeful and comforting words—showing friendship and affection—is what every hurting soul desires and needs.

Job's friends offered little comfort with their speculative counsels concerning matters too complicated for them to evaluate honestly. Godly counsel is humble, wise, and compassionate, being careful to achieve the objectives of genuine assistance and restoration: "Brethren, if a man is overtaken in any trespass, you who are spiritual restore such a one in a spirit of gentleness, considering yourself lest you also be tempted. Bear one another's burdens, and so fulfill the law of Christ" (Gal. 6:1–2). This kind of environment—the loving, active covenant community—provides the greatest possibility for redemption when a family crisis arises.

Owning Our Responsibility

Despite all the comfort friends can give, when our children stumble or fall we still ask ourselves questions such as "Why? What went wrong? What could I have done differently?" Some parents will be too hard on themselves, while others will find a way to shift the blame and excuse themselves of any responsibility. There is no shortage of well-intentioned fellow Christians who will assist in either errant direction. Some pile guilt on the parents while others exonerate them, in case they need the exemption for themselves later. And then there are those many well-meaning, sympathetic people who feel the pain of their suffering friends and simply want to give them comfort and relief. Nevertheless, if we are to grow in the midst of these trials, an honest assessment of the situation is called for—honest in light of the biblical standard.

So we must examine ourselves, not as an act of morbid introspection, but rather to provide to the greatest extent possible a true assessment of what went wrong. This is part of our own sanctification. God gives children to parents who in turn are given the authority and responsibility for raising those children to the glory of God (Mal. 3). The Bible teaches that children are both a reflection *of* their parents as well as a reflection *on* their parents. Wise and godly children are a joy to their parents and reflect honor upon them, which is exactly what children are commanded to do toward their parents. Foolish and ungodly children bring sadness and shame to their parents. This is the nature of the covenantal relationship between parents and their children. The sooner we own this responsibility and accept the covenantal connection, the sooner we can get on with recovering from our failures and repairing the broken relationships.

> *Children are both a reflection of their parents as well as a reflection on their parents.*

Keep in mind that the Bible teaches that our children bear the guilt for their own sins. They have their own sinful nature. Moreover, there are many other people and things that influence and tempt them. God makes it clear that they will be held personally accountable for their own sins (Ezek. 18). Nevertheless, parents are still responsible for what their children are taught, who and what influence them, and other forms of temptation they may be exposed to. This is exactly what God charges parents to do (Gen 18:19). Parental sins and the sins of the child are distinct but connected.

Before we can begin to fix what is broken, parents need to acknowledge their responsibility before God. We must stop making excuses for our children and ourselves and stop shifting the blame to others. The buck stops with us parents. There is a relief and even a joy that comes only by agreeing with God that these children are our responsibility. Now we can honestly evaluate, repent, confess, confront, forgive, and redeem.

Special Circumstances

Life is complex and there are as many special circumstances as there are unique households (e.g., divorce, adoption, illness, or financial burdens). As a pastor my heart has gone out to many who have suffered the burdens of family crisis, especially when it involves a child. While these special circumstances can make parenting more difficult, and while we can sympathize with those difficulties, nevertheless they cannot relieve us of our parental duties toward God nor our responsibilities toward our children. They may offer explanations for the problems, but they never provide a legitimate excuse for disobedience.

Failures of the church and the influence of the culture contribute to our problems in raising godly children. Unbelieving, unsupportive, or irresponsible spouses remind us of why it is so important to marry only in the Lord and to marry godly husbands or wives. Likewise, divorce is devastating to the entire household, and especially to children. Single parents face many special circumstances. We acknowledge all of these as genuine obstacles and feel sincere compassion for those who face these challenges. We must love these families and help them overcome their particular challenges, but the responsibility for children remains where God put it—with their parents.

Evaluation

Failure in various aspects of child-rearing is usually due to ignorance, negligence, laziness, rebellion, or a combination of these. Many of our sins are due to ignorance—no one ever taught us any better. Nevertheless, they are still sins and still produce bad results. God looks on sins of ignorance differently than sins of rebellion (Lev. 5). Some of our sins, however, are sins of willful rebellion. We know better but we do not want to obey God, so we are often sloppy and careless with His commands. God looks on these sins more seriously.

We must begin by considering which sins have been sins of ignorance and which have been willful rebellion, making an *honest* evaluation of our performance. For example, if we make an unwise financial decision, it is helpful for us to acknowledge our mistake and to accept the consequences of our sin. We will still have to pay our debt, but hopefully we will have learned from our mistake and will be able to avoid it in the future, and furthermore help others avoid similar mistakes. This will require us to swallow our pride and ask for help from family, friends, and our church.

> *Parents need to initiate reconciliation by first dealing with their own sins and accepting responsibility for their disobedient children.*

When it comes to the problem of a rebellious or unbelieving child, or simply a child who committed a particular sin, parents are often very defensive. There is no shortage of excuses and justifications. But the fact remains that "a wise son makes a glad father, but a foolish son is the grief of his mother" (Prov. 10:1); and again, "He who gathers in summer is a wise son; he who sleeps in harvest is a son who causes shame" (Prov. 10:5). The connection between the behavior of a child and his parents is unavoidable. The sooner we acknowledge this, the sooner we can deal with the problem.

Parents are sinners. Parents need the grace of repentance, forgiveness, and redemption. Children are sinners. Children need the grace of repentance, forgiveness, and redemption. There is a lot of room for love and ministry here, for all parties involved. If there is to be any hope of repair, however, we must start with ourselves. Parents need to initiate reconciliation by first dealing with their own sins and accepting responsibility for their disobedient children.

Sins of Presumption

Presumptuous sins are a frequent cause of household failures. We presume that the rules do not apply to us the way they do to others. As unbelievers, some parents never thought the Word of God applied to them at all. Many Christian parents falsely presume that because they are Christians, God will bail them out regardless of their conduct. After all, He has promised to forgive us, so we operate on the edge. Having been presumptuous we eventually fall. "Be sure, your sins will find you out" (Num. 32:23). "Do not be deceived, you reap what you sow" (Gal. 6:7). Such falls are, at best, painful and humiliating.

We must distinguish, however, between biblical presumption (called faith), which rightly believes what God has promised, and the *sin* of presumptuousness, which wrongly assumes God's blessings are automatic. The former, taking God at His word, employs the means God has ordained for raising godly children—"faith working through love" (Gal. 5:6). It takes seriously the duty to "train up children in the fear and admonition of the Lord" and to "diligently" teach them the Scriptures (cf. Deut. 6:6–7; 2 Tim. 3:15). The latter ignores God's ordained means and expects the benefits anyway—"The rules may apply to everyone else but they don't apply to me." We expect covenant blessings while being covenant-breakers. These are presumptuous sins.

We see the flipside of this in overzealous parenting—parents who are determined to raise perfect children. Parental pride at this point can crush the spirit of the child. Some parents allow their lambs to wander from the fold; others drive them away. Sin is doing *less* than what God commands and it is doing *more* than He commands. A man can fall off a horse on the left or the right side (Josh. 23:6). Both licentious parenting and legalistic parenting can produce rebellious children. Even children who have been educated in a Christian school—and yes, even home-schooled children—can be rebellious products of such presumptuous parenting. Any time we assume that something can take the place of loving, godly, diligent, disciplined parenting, we risk a bad outcome. God's covenant blessings are conditional promises.

The Bible offers many prominent examples of sinful parental presumption: Eli and his corrupt sons Hophni and Phinehas, Isaac and his famously opposed sons Jacob and Esau, David and his rebellious sons, and so on. Likewise, many Christian parents have raised children who have grown up to deny the faith. Why is this? Is God not keeping His promises? We must remember that He promises both blessings (i.e., happiness) and curses (i.e., misery). Like the Pharisees, we often offer up the excuse that we were busy with many godly pursuits—our jobs, our ministries, church work, etc. But Jesus reminded them and us: "Woe to you, scribes and Pharisees, hypocrites! For you pay tithe of mint and anise and cumin, and have neglected the weightier matters of the law: justice and mercy and faith. These you ought to have done, without leaving the others undone" (Mt. 23:23). There are consequences to persistent disobedience in regard to our children, intended or otherwise.

Sins of Abdication

Having committed sins of presumption, Christian parents often wind up in the ditch (or canyon) of failure. We are then tempted to another kind of failure—abdicating our responsibilities, shifting the blame, or simply giving up. Perhaps the children are out of control and it seems too late or too hard to rein them in. Or perhaps they are grown up and it seems that all is lost. Sins of abdication are manifested in quitting or giving up, crawling into a hole, failing even in our failures. This abdication of our responsibilities denies the power of God to strengthen and change lives, to repair the ruins. "What's the use? It's too late. The damage has been done. We cannot make up for our past sins." Abdication says that failure is all there is, and there remains no hope for future success.

Repentance and Confession

The despairing belief that failure cannot be repaired is simply not true. With God, all things are possible for them that believe (Mk. 9:23). The solution to any failure begins by turning away from the things that caused the failure. As we honestly evaluate our own sins and failures, care should be given not to assume our children's guilt as well. We should, however, assume *all* the parental responsibility. There is a time and place for dealing with the real sins of others, including the sins of our children, but only after we have removed the beam from our own eye. My sins do not excuse the sins of my children and my children's sins do not excuse mine.

Men, as covenant heads, are especially given the responsibility for their families. Godly men eagerly own up to their sins. They humble themselves before God and before men, and this includes their families. They set an example for others by accepting the responsibility for their households (including its failures) and by demonstrating true repentance, graciously seeking reconciliation and repairing relationships.

We must remember, though, that sorrow and regret are not repentance. We may feel sorrow and regret for many things and still fall short of repentance. Sorrow and regret might lead us to repentance, but it is possible to have the former and still fall short of the latter. True repentance begins with the honest acknowledgment of our sins. To repent, or turn from our sins, is to change the way we *think* and the way we *live*. The Bible teaches us that God's mercy awaits those who repent of their sins. "Let the wicked forsake his way, and the unrighteous man his thoughts; let him return to the Lord, and He will have mercy on him; and to our God, for He will abundantly pardon. 'For My thoughts are not your thoughts, nor are your ways My ways,' says the Lord" (Is. 55:7–8). Repentance gives us a new perspective that enables us to look away from ourselves and look to Christ, and in Christ there is always hope. It enables us to seek first the kingdom of God and His righteousness (Mt. 6:33). Making excuses, rationalizing, and blaming others is the opposite of repentance.

We need the grace of repentance to enable us to have an unqualified turning away from our own sins.

Confession is agreeing with God that He has been faithful and true and that what He says about us and our situation is true. Confession flows from repentance to an outward expression of our sins. With our words we humbly admit to the offended parties that we were wrong. Having honestly evaluated ourselves in the light of God's Word, we now need to bow before Him and say: "I was not as diligent and faithful as I should have been in training my children in the ways of the Lord." On our knees before God is the place where remedy and healing begin. It is here that we ask the Holy Spirit to deal with us and to comfort and help us. In addition, confession to our children, spouses, or other offended parties may be necessary. Our confession needs to be as broad as our sin. The necessary groundwork has now been laid for forgiveness.

Not all relationships will be repaired, but all can be improved.

Confrontation

Having listened to God's Word and responded by going to Him in repentance and confession of our own sins, we now face some remaining obstacles. Wisdom is necessary as we move to repair damaged covenantal relationships. Repentance toward our children often requires much humility, especially when our children might have been horribly offensive and sinful toward others and us. Admitting our own failures is not an approval of their sins. Moreover, we can love our wayward child without approving of his or her sinful behavior.

Pastoral counsel is recommended before initiating such a confrontation; we want to be sure not to make the situation worse. Guidance in what should be said and done is needful. A face-to-face conversation or a well-thought-out letter might be a good place to start. Some situations may seem hopeless, but we must remember the words of our Lord: "With men this is impossible, but with God all things are possible" (Mt. 19:26), and again, "If you can believe, all things are possible to him who believes" (Mk. 9:23). Not all relationships will be repaired, but all can be improved, some marvelously so.

Godly confrontation need not be hostile. Our approach should be gentle in manner while remaining resolute in purpose. The apostle Paul admonishes us,

> Let no corrupt word proceed out of your mouth, but what is good for necessary edification, that it may impart grace to the hearers. And do not grieve the Holy Spirit of God, by whom you were sealed for the day of redemption. Let all bitterness, wrath, anger, clamor, and evil speaking be put away from you, with all malice. And be kind to one another, tenderhearted, forgiving one another, just as God in Christ forgave you. (Eph. 4:29–32)

God's Word remains the standard for godly relationships; our desire to remove any possible tension must not be allowed to reduce the standard. Nevertheless, the goal is to make true repentance and reconciliation as easy as possible. Clear, calm, and humble communication that lays out biblical expectations for all the parties involved provides the only solid foundation for restoration. Establishing new trust will likely be a slow process. We probably cannot deal with every issue at once, so setting priorities is important.

Forgiveness

Sin always inflicts damage to ourselves and to others—it hurts. Biblical love provides the only environment for dealing with the damage. It does not ignore the sinner or his sin: "But God demonstrates His own love toward us, in that while we were still sinners, Christ died for us" (Rom. 5:8). God loves *us* even though He is the offended party. Despite the offense, He provides a way for reconciliation: "And you, who once were alienated and enemies in your mind by wicked works, yet now He has reconciled us in the body of His flesh through death, to present you holy, and blameless, and above reproach in His sight" (Col. 1:21–22). The Bible lays out the way, telling us, "If we will confess our sins, He is faithful and just to forgive us our sins and to cleanse us from all unrighteousness" (1 Jn. 2:9). God may not take away the consequences of our sin, but He will take away the guilt of our sin along with its shame. Forgiveness clears the ground of past offense so that a new relationship may be built in its place. Reconciliation is the goal.

Redemption

Mending will not begin by nurturing animosity but rather by creating an atmosphere for redemption. Paul admonishes the church regarding a repentant sinner, "On the contrary, you ought rather to forgive and comfort him, lest perhaps such a one be swallowed up with too much sorrow. Therefore I urge you to reaffirm your love to him" (2 Cor. 2:7–8). There must be hope. Most of us have done plenty of sinful and stupid things in our past, and we owe a debt of love and gratitude to those who have not perpetually held them against us but rather helped us to stand again.

As we move ahead to accomplish reconciliation and redemption, we must leave behind any remaining bitterness in ourselves and seek the good of our children. There is always hope in Christ. Since salvation and sanctification are gracious, undeserved works of God, healing and hope can come to any situation. Sinners are converted. By the power of the Holy Spirit, husbands and wives can change. Broken lives can be put back together. Lost children, by the grace of God, sometimes come to their senses and embrace the faith of their parents. And like our Savior, we earnestly seek after our lost sheep.

The Proverbs teach us that "the way of the transgressor is hard" (13:15). The consequences of sin often bring enough pain that the sinner is humbled, making a return possible. Without compromising God's standards, we must facilitate this possibility by providing an environment in which such a return is safe. We long for humble repentance on the part of the sinner, but this is not accomplished by an attempt to humiliate. We do not want repentance to be any more difficult than necessary.

The parable of the prodigal son provides a model of redemption between a foolish son and loving father. There are few pictures more profoundly moving than that painted by this verse: "And he arose and came to his father. But when he was still a great way off, his father saw him and had compas-

Just as our parental failings were instrumental in our children's unbelief, so God can and will use our humble and faithful efforts to regain our children.

sion, and ran and fell on his neck and kissed him" (Lk. 15:20). This captures the heart of the gospel of redemption. As John the Baptist prepared the way for the Lord, the effect of his message was to "turn the hearts of the fathers to the children, and the hearts of the children to their fathers" (Mal. 4:6; Lk. 1:17). This is one of the powerful effects of the work of Christ; without it there is no hope of redemption.

Conclusion

Salvation is always by grace—we are saved in spite of who and what we are. Success in child-rearing is therefore not cause for pride but rather humility. We cannot save ourselves by our works and neither can we save our children by our works. As long as there is breath, it is never too late for grace to conquer even in the worst of situations. As long as there is life, it is never too late for the prodigal to come home.

Often, these trials with our children turn out to be bad chapters in otherwise good books. God's severe mercy proves His love for us: "And you have forgotten the exhortation which speaks to you as to sons: My son, do not despise the chastening of the Lord, nor be discouraged when you are rebuked by Him; for whom the Lord loves

He chastens, and scourges every son whom He receives" (Heb. 12:5–6). Just as our parental failings were instrumental in our children's unbelief, so God can and will use our humble and faithful reclamation efforts to regain our children. Let us renew our efforts, pick up the pieces, and seek the Lord. "Now no chastening seems to be joyful for the present, but painful; nevertheless, afterward it yields the peaceable fruit of righteousness to those who have been trained by it" (Heb. 12:11).

Will My Child Go to Heaven?

Charles A. McIlhenny

This chapter focuses on the comfort Scripture can give to grieving Christian parents after the death of their infant. In particular, what can pastors utilize to console grieving parents during this most trying time? The answer lies in understanding what theologians call the Covenant of Grace, which is a special relationship established by God between Himself and the believer and his seed.

What could a pastor possibly say to parents who lost an infant to sickness, disease, or even greater tragedy? No greater human hurt can be endured than this. Where was God at that moment? And especially what does one say to Christian parents who trust their loving Heavenly Father's promise to take care of the widows and *orphans?* Thankfully the Bible has the answer. The surest hope for grieving parents is found in what theologians have called "the promise of the covenant." Let me build the case that the child of a believing parent belongs to Christ in the fullest sense, thus giving parents the greatest of comfort and confidence about the blessed state of their beloved child.

Reformed theology finds its distinctiveness not so much in the five points of Calvinism or even the concept of the sovereignty of God (as true and awesome as these doctrines are) as it does in the concept of the covenant as revealed in Scripture. This doctrine is what distinguishes Reformed theology from other Protestant theologies (Lutheran, Baptist, Independent, and broadly evangelical).

The Discomfort of Dispensational Theology

In order to clarify a concept it is sometimes helpful to contrast it with its opposite. This can be seen in the difference between covenant theology and dispensationalism. This comparison posits a sharp contrast between God's covenant promise to the church and the dispensational view that the biblical covenants belong only to Jews. Thus, dispensationalism gives no covenantal ground of comfort in the personal lives of members of the church.[1]

Covenant theology, by contrast, holds that the Old Testament covenant promise is applicable to the church in the New Testament because the New fulfills the Old.[2] The promise gives a practical hope, which is fulfilled in the children of believers just as in the Old Testament households.[3] It is no abstract theological concept, nor a mere analogical, spiritualized application, but a prophetically promised hope, which finds definitive, organic fulfillment in the church today—a promise of hope for the households of the church in this age.

According to dispensationalism, the Old Testament covenants did emphasize family relations ("you and your household"),[4] but that was only because these covenants were ethnically Jewish and thus household-oriented. It follows, according to dispensationalism, that when we get to the New Testament all mention of the "new covenant" in the founding of the New Testament church is devoid of the familial-organic connection which existed in all the previous covenants. The New Testament "new covenant" is somehow structured differently—unwelcoming to the infant seed of believers (i.e., disallowing the organic spiritual connection of the believing parent with the child). The child is effectively "cut off" from the covenant promise of eternal life

[1] This is the case in terms of their theology, though thankfully in practice many self-conscious proponents of dispensationalism are not consistent with that theology.

[2] This is Paul's argument that the Abrahamic covenant finds fulfillment in the church, which is the heir of the Abrahamic covenant—by faith in Jesus Christ, the true seed of Abraham.

[3] Deut. 30:6; Is. 44:3; Jer. 31:31 ff.; Joel 2:28 ff.; Lk. 19:9; Acts 2:38, 29; 1 Cor. 7:14.

[4] Josh. 24:15; Gen. 17:7 ff.; Deut. 30:6; Jer. 31:1–3.

due to a shift in covenants from the Old to the New.[5] Yet no other historically revealed covenant behaved that way previously.

The Comfort of Covenant Theology

Covenant theology recognizes just one "people of God" and the organic relation between dispensation and dispensation, age and age, and Old and New Testaments, culminating in the New Testament people of God. What now is called the Christian church is essentially the same "people of God" as Israel in the Old Testament. So covenant theology broadens the meaning of the national/political theocracy of the ethnic stock of Jacob to include now other ethnic stock in the circle defined by the same faith in the God of Abraham, Isaac, and Jacob through the real (i.e., fulfilled) Seed of Abraham, Jesus Christ.

Covenant theology, founded on the absolute sovereignty of God and the faithfulness of His Word, constructs and organizes the whole of our theological pursuit, as well as the structure and membership make-up of the church. The covenant in Scripture informs us that the family as God created it (mother, father, and children) is not torn apart by salvation, but rather restored together in salvation.[6] Covenant theology teaches that the promise of salvation is given "to you and your children, and those afar off" in the way of faith (Acts 2:39).

The Hope of the Covenant Child

The Word of the covenant from Genesis to Revelation is the Word that includes our children in the hope of eternal life. So when "the

---

[5] Dispensationalists, Baptists, and Presbyterians all agree that the structure of "believer and child" belonging together was essential to the Old Testament promises—regardless of the covenant. The child is included by virtue of the way God includes "the seed" along with the parents. The Presbyterian's question is, How and why is the seed "cut off/cut out" of the covenant structure in the New Testament? By what proof of Scripture does "the seed" (i.e., the covenant child) lose its standing in the New Covenant? The covenant theologian sees no New Testament evidence of such an "automatic" disallowing of the promise to the children of believers.

[6] See Acts 16:15, 31: "you and your house."

rubber hits the road" we can say to grieving Christian parents, "Your child is with the Father in Heaven." This is no pragmatic platitude to salve tender sentiments, nor a speculation about God's general disposition of common grace toward children, but a specific covenant promise made to such parents.[7] They have objective covenant confidence that their child is in heaven. Such a holy child (1 Cor. 7:14) is as much saved as one's godly, dear, departed grandmother. You can give pastoral comfort and assurance that their child is resting with his and your Savior. The infant's salvation is not due to the fact that God is generally loving and merciful, though that is true, but due to His covenant word of promise that includes children of believers. The promise is not to believers *if* perhaps someday these little ones too will believe. The covenant states that the promise is to believers and their seed—*together at the same time*. They lawfully can say the promise is theirs. It does not belong just to those who publicly express that it belongs to them; it belongs to the "professionless" child as much as the confessing parent.

> *The covenant states that the promise is to believers and their seed—together at the same time.*

The covenant does more than promise salvation to believers and their children; it promises the same salvation at the same time. It is not consecutively promised; it is not given when the parent believes and later on, when and if ever, the children believe too. When God promised His redemptive blessing to Abraham, it was addressed to him and his seed together at the same time. The wording of the covenant includes children along *with* the believing parent. That word of promise—the covenant promise—is the word of salvation, not a promise of a promise that one's child may later on be included in His saving work.

---

[7] The "age of accountability" concept, however, *is* such a platitude, not based on Scripture but speculation. The covenant concept gives historic and concrete hope to believing parents—not a speculation on accountability, but a promise of God's covenant embrace of "believers and their seed."

Two things are important in the history of the covenant establish-ments. First, the covenant structure is always family-oriented. God makes His covenant with "you and your seed." Second, the promise is redemptive. This covenant word is the word of saving grace me-diated by Christ through the working of the Holy Spirit.

The genius of the divine covenant is that it is God's sovereign ini-tiative and not man's response that brings it to pass. Our salvation rests first and foremost on what God does and what God says. His promise comes before the obedience that He requires. The command of the covenant rests embedded in the promise.

The promise God historically gave to Abraham and his seed (Gen. 17:7–8), as the New Testament clearly describes it (Gal. 3:6 ff.), was not a future prospect that God's people hoped would possibly come to pass, sometime later. Rather, the promise belonged to the seed then as well as to future generations. In other words, it was not that the children in the covenant have a blessed future if they, too, even-tually believe (i.e., make a public profession of faith)! What hope is that for grieving parents who have lost their little one before such a profession? None at all.[8] The Bible does not exclude covenant chil-dren—not in the Old Testament or in the New Testament—despite their inability to make public their profession.[9] Thus we can say with the Synod of Dort (from which the five points of Calvinism origi-nated),

> Since we are to judge of the will of God from the Word, which tes-tifies that the children of believers are holy, not by nature, but in virtue of the covenant of grace, in which they together with their

---

[8] Certain Presbyterian theologians do exclude the infant seed of believers from the covenant promise. J. H. Thornwell, for example, defines the infant seed as a "covenant child" but until that child makes his own profession of faith, we (according to this ar-gument) ought to think of that child as spiritually united with the ungodly (*Ecclesiasti-cal Writings*, vol. 4 of *The Collected Writings of J. H. Thornwell* [Carlisle, Pa.: Banner of Truth, 1974], 340–341).

[9] Of course, what makes the "public profession of faith" any surer an indicator of the child's sincere belief? It is the promise of the covenant that makes all the difference.

parents, are comprehended, godly parents ought not to doubt the
election and salvation of their children whom it pleases God to call
out of this life in their infancy. (I.17)[10]

The only time covenant blessings and covenant curses can be split
apart in their application to the household is when the covenant parents repudiate the faith. Both parents, in that case, would have to
reject the Christian faith in order for their covenant child to also be
subject to the curse of the covenant. It's not enough that one parent
repudiates the faith while one remains faithful—this only occurs in
the tragic event that both do so (1 Cor. 7:14).

According to Romans 11, a covenant member can be cut out of
the olive tree through unbelief.[11] Paul's discussion about the reinclusion of Israel is based on the covenant promise God originally made
in Abraham. He argues for the old Israel's reinclusion in its own olive tree by means of faith, and goes on to say, "If the root is holy, so
are the branches" (Rom. 11:16).

Romans 9–11 is suffused with covenant language and covenant
imagery as illustrated by the olive tree paradigm. (The Old Testament
uses such imagery to describe the covenant people.[12]) Here in Romans 11, Paul argues that what was promised to the fathers (the
root) is also for the seed (the branches). Though not every branch
will show itself to be a true part to the "olive tree" by faith, the seed
is already included in the promise, for the covenant embraces "you
and your seed."

In Romans 11:26–27, Paul quotes the Scripture, "The Deliverer
will come from Zion. . . . For this is my covenant unto them, when

---

[10] Qtd. in Peter Y. DeJong, ed., *Crisis in the Reformed Churches* (Grand Rapids: Reformed
Fellowship, 1968), 235.

[11] If it takes unbelief to be excised from the covenant, how should we apply this to
covenant infants, since they can neither believe nor disbelieve? How can these little ones
be automatically excluded from the New Covenant promise—as some Calvinistic Baptist theologians say?

[12] The "vine" image is used often in the Old Testament for Israel's relationship to the
Lord, e.g., Is. 24:13, 65:22; Hos. 14:6.

I shall take away their sins." Here Paul is referencing the whole household/covenantal structure of believers and their seed which we find in Isaiah 59 and Jeremiah 31. The restoration of Israel to the church—now the New Testament church—does not exclude the infant seed.

Peter's message at Pentecost discusses baptism in relation to the children of believers.[13] The promise of the Holy Spirit, which the Father gives along with the promise of the covenant (Lk. 24:49), belongs to "you and your children and all that are afar off." The Holy Spirit and His attending gifts are theirs by faith (repentance and baptism included). The baptism required by the apostle is not applied based upon some spiritual "revelatory insight" into the hearts of believers and their children. The requirement to apply the water of baptism comes from the word of the covenant, not from a minister's special insight into the candidates. To make the inner working of the Holy Spirit the objective measure that determines who receives the covenant sign would, in effect, preclude everybody—even adults—from receiving the rite of baptism; since you cannot tell of the inner spiritual worth of an adult any more than that of a child.

> *The requirement to apply baptism comes from the word of the covenant, not from a minister's special revelatory insight into the candidates.*

Though regeneration, described as a sovereign, secret working of the Holy Spirit, must take place at the pleasure of the Holy Spirit, it is never the *basis* for the human administration of the sacrament.[14] God never requires ministers to apply baptism to those whom they *perceive* as *secretly* regenerate. So in order to count the number of believers and their seed, one must count those who fulfill the *observable* covenant requirement.

---

[13] Isaiah 44:3 promises believers and their seed the effusion of the Spirit, as does Acts 2:38–39.

[14] Baptism is the "sign and seal" of regeneration, but only insofar as regeneration is perceptible to fallible ministers of the church.

In Stephen's defense of the faith before the Sanhedrin, he also sets forth the covenant purpose and structure in his review of Israel's history: "And God gave [Abraham] no inheritance in it, not even enough to set his foot on. He promised to give it to him for a possession and to his seed after him" (Acts 7:5). We see the same covenant structure mentioned here as was mentioned by Peter in Acts 2. Notice the same pattern in Acts 2:39: "The promise . . . is to you and your children." Also, this same covenant arrangement is further manifested in Paul's first apology in Acts 13:32–33: "And we declare to you glad tidings—that promise which was made to the fathers. God has fulfilled this for us their children, in that He has raised up Jesus." Paul, in summarizing the fulfillment of this prophecy, reaffirms that the familial character of the covenant is still intact: the fathers were given the promise and we, their children, are included in the fulfillment.

The one who receives the ceremony of baptism is designated by what the sign ascribes to him. Baptism *means* salvation, but baptism does not *cause* salvation. Baptism is the sign and seal of regeneration; regeneration is not the ground of baptism. Thus those that receive it are to be sincerely considered saved. Applying this to infants, it means they belong to Christ in the same spiritual sense as their believing parents. Their baptism cannot imply a truncated salvation that is complete only when they express their faith. That is not the meaning of the sign. Some Reformed theologians argue that infant baptism can only mean that we may look for a future salvation if and when the child professes faith. For them it is the promise of a promise—a hope of a possible ("on average, more than likely") salvation experience to come if the child eventually believes. That explanation fails to grasp the full significance of the covenant understanding of baptism—nothing less than salvation.

Others have an inward-regeneration perspective on baptism, not in the sense that baptism regenerates, but that baptism can only be given to those whom we determine are in fact regenerate. Those who hold this view understand regeneration purely in relation to the "secret will of God." Since we cannot discern whether the infant is "really" regenerate, baptism cannot be applied to them, say the Baptists. But credobaptists fail to acknowledge that regeneration must be seen from the perspective of the "revealed will of God," or rather, from the covenant perspective. Regeneration, like election, is itself a sovereign, secret, invisible act of God to bring the dead to life, whether adult or infant. If we judge a person's regeneration from the perspective of God's secret, sovereign work, we can never know, even in the case of an adult, whether he is saved. Since we're not given knowledge from God's secret invisible workings, our perspective can only be from the covenant promise. We can "see" these secret workings of God through the "eyeglasses" of the fulfillment of the covenant promise.

This seeing or knowing is not by special miraculous revelation, but rather by a very ordinary means. As John says, "These things I have written [a covenant document] to you who believe [assuming regeneration already accomplished] in the name of the Son of God [that's what is required in the covenant document], that you may *know* that you have eternal life" (1 Jn. 5:13). Here we are told that we can truly know about our current salvation status, not by some special revelatory act of God, but by what He has written concerning the revealed gospel.

In Ephesians 6:1–4, Paul gives us an indication of how he views the children of the church. Leading up to that, in chapter 5, Paul specifically addresses the husbands in the Ephesian church and then the wives. He's not addressing husbands as such, nor wives as such, but church-member husbands and church-member wives. This text cannot be universalized as teaching about husbands in general. The context of the exhortation addresses the church members and their offspring, which is a crucial hermeneutic consideration for the text.[15] In chapter 6, Paul addresses the children of the parents. Again, this

---

[15] John MacArthur, in his book on infant salvation *Safe in the Arms of God*, misses the point of the text that he uses to prove all children—apart from any covenant considerations—go to heaven. He universalizes the texts on covenant children to apply to all children.

is not an abstract, general address to the church about what God wants children to do. Paul addresses the children of the church, telling them directly to "obey their parents." He addresses the children as a real Christian group, as real as the Christian church-member husbands and Christian church-member wives he addressed earlier. After addressing the children, he similarly addresses the church-member slaves and masters. Again, this is not a matter of what slaves ought to do, but what Christian church-member slaves ought to do, along with their Christian masters.

In conformity to the context, Paul admonishes the children from the perspective of their ecclesiastical state. The instruction is not that they should repent and accept Jesus as their Savior and then obey the commandments. He does not warn them that they cannot please God unless they first become Christians. Granted, they must be Christians for such acts of obedience to be acceptable to the Lord, but that is not what Paul exhorts. Paul's exhortation calls the children of the church at Ephesus to obey their parents "in the Lord." The phrase "in the Lord" does not refer to the "parents in the Lord" that is, it does not mean that obedience is only to *believing* parents. The children's obedience is in the sphere of their redeeming Lord. He commands the children of the church to obey "in the Lord," which is tantamount to calling these children of the church to obey in faith, in the realm of the Lord. The children of the church need not first self-consciously repent of their sins before they are treated as God's children, liable to His commands. They are responsible to obey from the very start of their lives.

Further, this exhortation is rooted in the Fifth Commandment: "Honor your father and your mother, which is the first commandment with promise." This comes right out of the covenant relationship between the Lord—the Redeemer of Israel—and His people. The Ten Commandments begin by mentioning God's past act of redemption from bondage, then exhorting His people to obedience. The order of redemption followed by obedience evidences Israel's redeemed status, as already the people of God. The commandment presupposes a redeemed relationship: "You are redeemed, therefore obey . . . in the Lord." The obedience-laden commandment does not establish this saving relationship; it presupposes it in the command to the child.

This commandment is the first with promise that "you may live long on the earth." Its primacy is due to the fact that Adam was God's child in the most literal sense.[16] He had no father other than the Lord God by direct creation; hence, the first human relationship was one of union and communion with God as Father as well as Creator. What other re-

> *The children of the church need not first self-consciously repent of their sins before they are treated as God's children, liable to His commands.*

sponse should such a "son" have towards his father but that of love and devotion (i.e., honoring his father and his mother)?

God's command, whether addressed to Adam, His first covenantal human son, or to the children of the church at Ephesus, presupposes the addressees are in union and communion with the Lord, members of Christ in the fullest sense—that is, saved. No need to parse this "saved" as legal versus experiential. The legal and experiential are enveloped, if you will, by the covenant relationship.

Paul exhorts the fathers of such children—not a general exhortation to any fathers of any children, but fathers of these "churched" children—not to provoke them to wrath through either neglect or imposed hardship. Instead he orders fathers to "train them in the nurture and admonition of the Lord." Only believing fathers can do that. The construction of this sentence as contrasting clauses reminds us of how the Proverbs were written. An example of contrasting clauses is "A prudent man foresees evil . . . but the simple pass on." The same pattern of "don't do this, but instead do such and such" is present in Ephesians 6:4. The contrast helps to define the meaning of what fathers ought not to do to their covenant children, and what they ought

---

[16] Luke 3:38: "Adam, the son of God."

to do—bring them up[17] in the nurture and admonition of the Lord. These children, again, are considered to be in the care of the covenant community, not just in some natural, familial way. Such covenant children are to be trained in the admonition of the Lord.

We are told that the Lord loves those whom He admonishes. Hebrews 12:5 says, "My son, do not despise the chastening (admonition) of the Lord. . . ." The writer of Hebrews argues from Proverbs 3:11 that if you endure chastening (admonition), then God deals with you as with *sons*, "for what son is there whom a father does not chasten?" Hence, the assurance is that these children of the church are instructed as the Lord would instruct His own—as children who are also sons and daughters of the covenant.

> *We can say with covenant confidence that our departed children are under the protection of God's salvation.*

Concerning what comfort to give grieving Christian parents, here is the word of the promise for such children, whether living or dead: *they equally belong to the Lord,* belong to the church, and belong to God's saving work. Especially in the case of infant children who have no "voice," the covenant indicates their favored position with Christ. They are reckoned with their parents as believers and members of Christ's body by the covenant.

We can say with covenant confidence that our departed children are under the protection of His salvation even as are older believers when they pass away. The promise of the covenant extends to the living members as well as the departed sons and daughters who die in the covenant.

Paul further argues in 1 Corinthians 7:14 that the children of one believing parent are holy: "For the unbelieving husband is sanctified by the wife, and the unbelieving wife is sanctified by the husband, else were your children unclean; but now are they holy." The fact that Paul included this remark about the place of the children of a mixed mar-

---

[17] The word may also be translated as "educate."

riage indicates that the covenant structure, as it was in the Abrahamic covenant thousands of years earlier, is still in force under the New Covenant.

The believing parent sanctifies the unbelieving parent, but that does not mean the unbelieving spouse is saved. It also does not articulate that it is the believing parent who "sanctifies the child," supposedly calling the child "holy." The holiness of the child depends not on the believing parent but on Christ who sanctifies; that's how the epistle opens. When Paul addresses the church at Corinth as those sanctified in Christ Jesus, called "holy," this is exactly the same word that is used to describe the children of a confessing parent. Here the covenant structure, though implied, is still maintained. It is being in Christ that constitutes a child as holy. That's how the covenant has always worked and continues to do so.

The Normal Covenant Life

Covenant sons and daughters are called to express their faith precisely because they are covenant members and the promise belongs to them. It is not because they are unsaved, but because this is their covenant heritage and responsibility (Acts 3:25–26).

How did Paul describe Timothy's early childhood experience? "But you must continue in the things which you have learned and been assured of, knowing from whom you have learned them, and that from childhood [*brephos*, 'infant, unborn, babe'] you have known the Holy Scriptures, which are able to make you wise for salvation through faith which is in Christ Jesus" (2 Tim. 3:14).

It seems that the apostle assumed the existence of his faith from infancy—as a babe—due to his mother's and grandmother's faith and training (2 Tim. 1:5), even though his father was apparently an unbeliever. The covenant child is considered "holy" (as in 1 Cor. 7:14) with no hesitancy on Paul's part about Timothy's long-time spiritual condition. The apostle was persuaded that the faith of his covenant parent existed in him also. There was no exhorting him to be converted in addition to his covenant training. Of course, the case of Timothy could be construed by some as unusual. Apart from the covenant structure and promise, it would be perceived as unusual to have such an early spiritual experience. But the fact is, in the way of the covenant, this is what normally happens. Covenant sons and daughters are assumed to be believers and are called to make *public* their inward heart attitudes. This assumption (not a brute presumption) can be legitimately made of covenant children, even as infants (*brephos*).[18] Such an assumption is based upon the covenant promise, not upon speculations or rational deductions from God's generous attributes of mercy and grace.

That's not to say that the regenerating work of the Spirit is not needed in the life of every covenant child. Nor is it to conclude that there is no need for repentance and faith in the life of the growing child. Nor is it to say he does not need to commit him or herself personally to Christ. It is to say that the "normal Christian life" is one of union and communion with the covenant Seed. By virtue of the covenant promise, the child is expected to be one of Christ's own lambs—which He may choose to take away in the beginning stage of life. We should expect our covenant children, as they grow up in the faith, to follow through with owning up to the promise and the responsibility of covenant membership. We should expect, though not presumptuously, that the blessings of the covenant will follow the child throughout the rest of his life.[19] Such an expectation expresses itself by the faithful prayers and diligent nurturing of the believing parent or parents.

> *Covenant sons and daughters are assumed to be believers and are called to make public their inward heart attitudes.*

---

[18] Luke 18:15, "bringing infants to Him."

[19] "When he is old he will not depart from it" (Prov. 22:6). Proverbs teaches us what the "normal covenant life" is all about—not naturally normal but spiritually normal.

The Psalmist Praises the Covenant Condition

David's psalms also manifest this covenant language. In one passage he describes his own spiritual condition:

> But You are He who took me out of the womb;
> You made me trust while on my mother's breasts.
> I was cast upon You from birth.
> From my mother's womb
> You have been my God. (22:9–10)

Here David describes the covenantal condition of his conception and birth. God, his covenant Lord, took him out of the womb, symbolizing his redemption from the "depths of the earth," the darkest place on earth.

The psalmist "trust[s] while on [his] mother's breasts." This is the physical condition of the newborn as he rests secure on his mother, but it is more than just physical imagery. An infant upon his mother's breast images the spiritual condition of the covenant son who "hopes, trusts and finds confidence" physically. The spiritual condition of the child is depicted most tenderly at that time of birth, especially as the child is place in the arms of the mother. The child is the reward from the Lord (Ps. 127:3).

Is this a description of the extraordinary life of King David or does this song express what the covenant people normally experience in belonging to the covenant community? No extraordinary reason is included in the text as to why the psalmist would have such spiritual assurance. That is, there is no appeal to the miraculous, even though its prophetic antitype is the life of Christ. (The fact that Christ did not resort to miracles in order to sustain His own life until the resurrection meant He lived an ordinary life—the experience of the average Israelite. Jesus Himself was the very embodiment of Israel. Though His conception was a miracle, His birth was not.) The psalmist's description of covenant infancy provides great hope and comfort to all covenant children and parents.

Comforting Words

1. The Orthodox Presbyterian Church's definition of the sacrament of baptism states,

> Baptism is a sacrament . . . a sign and seal of the *inclusion of the per-*
> *son who is baptized in the covenant of grace.* . . . It witnesses and *seals*
> *unto us the remission of sins* and the bestowal of all the gifts of salva-
> tion through union with Christ. . . . [It] signifies and seals cleansing
> from sin by the blood and Spirit of Christ . . . who is pleased to *claim*
> *us as his very own*; we are baptized into the name of the Father, and
> of the Son and of the Holy Ghost.[20]

(1) Here the candidate for baptism is included in the covenant of grace before receiving the sign of baptism. So until the parent has reason to believe the contrary (apostasy, excommunicating discipline of the church), the child is to be received as included in Christ—not temporarily included or possibly not included. (2) The baptism ritual means "remission of sins and the bestowal of all the gifts of salvation" and nothing less. The sign means that the child has remission of sins, as much as is promised to the adult receiver. (3) "Claimed as His own," in this context, refers to the candidate truly belonging to Christ until evidence to the contrary contradicts the sign. The can-didate, no matter what his age, is baptized because he is a member of Christ. He or she is not baptized so that he or she would *become* a member of Christ. A sincere assumption is made on the basis of God's covenant made with Abraham and his seed.

This is the comfort of baptism as the Christ-mandated signature of ownership, which the church, even though fallible, has a warrant to bestow. One must take this ritual to heart and be assured that "whatever you bind on earth will be bound in heaven, and whatever you loose on earth will be loosed in heaven" (Mt. 16:19). The actions of the church reassure us of who belongs to Christ.

---

[20] *OPC Directory of Worship* (year 2000 edition), 144. Emphasis mine.

2. Know that the infant's inability to confess Christ does not keep you from giving comfort to the parent. You must direct the parent to the covenant of Abraham in order to understand Christ's ownership of the children of the kingdom. "Suffer the children to come unto Me . . . for of such is the kingdom of God" (Mt. 19:14). Very few dispute that Christ included the newborns—and unborns—in the saving work of the kingdom of God. Their lack of ability to communicate maturely is no detriment to their inclusion in the kingdom and thus is of great encouragement for the believing parent. God has supernaturally and covenantally included them with the believing parent.

Frankly, the Bible gives no uncertain or hesitant word to believing parents and their seed, but rather teaches salvation for both believing parents and their children. We as pastors can confidently assure those under our charge to take heart. The child whom God in His wisdom took to be with Him has been promised a place at the great banquet hall of heaven, where he or she will sit with Him who has secured redemption, "even for the least of these my brethren" (Mt. 25:40). King David, who relied on the covenant promise even independently of its stipulated sign (circumcision), confessed that he and his child would share the same resting place (2 Sam. 12:23).

> *The covenant child whom God in His wisdom took to be with Him has been promised a place at the great banquet hall of heaven.*

Comfort the covenant parent in their most dreadful experience—that of losing a child—with the greatest of comforts: the word of promise given to Abraham. As Hebrews 6:17–18 says,

> Thus God, determining to show more abundantly to the heirs of promise the immutability of His counsel, confirmed it by an oath, that by two immutable things, in which it was impossible for God to lie, we might have a strong consolation, who have fled for refuge to lay hold upon the hope set before us.

III

Covenant Nurture

Covenant Nurture: Faith at Work through Godly Parenting

Douglas Wilson

The question of the relationship between faith in God's covenant promises and our responsibilities to bring our children up in the nurture and admonition of the Lord is really, at bottom, the same question as the perennial one about faith and works. And because the question of faith and works is much vexed, it is not surprising that we have trouble when we come to apply our understanding (or lack of it) to the tumultuous world of child-rearing. In the hurly-burly of the average Christian home, we sometimes forget about what we think are the theological niceties. But the Word of God is our *life*; it does not belong in a museum case. The relationship of saving faith to *any* aspect of our lives has to be understood as a living relationship. Consequently, the first task undertaken in this essay is to describe briefly the right relationship of faith and works. Secondly, we need to take note of the promises of God, the particular promises that we are to have faith in. Lastly, the bulk of the essay will be dedicated to a discussion of what might be considered the "three legs" of covenantal nurture.

Most confusion about faith and works is the result of a category mistake. Faith is thought to be one kind of a thing and works another. The two of them are thought to be like two billiard balls that cannot occupy the same space at the same time; one necessarily displaces the other. In the contemporary evangelical version of this, faith is the first billiard ball and then along comes works to displace it and finish the job. But this is to fall rather dramatically into the Galatian error. How can we begin by faith and then finish by our own efforts? Paul dismisses that notion immediately and somewhat impatiently (Gal. 3:3).

But if faith is a fundamental demeanor of submission to God, and works are the actions that proceed naturally and readily from that demeanor, then the problem disappears. When God first gives the gift of faith (Eph. 2:8–10), the first thing that faith does in the individual is receive the imputed righteousness of Jesus Christ. But saving faith is not like those animals in the natural world that give birth only to die. Saving faith is extremely long-lived and fertile and has *many* more children. In the wonderful words of the Westminster Confession, the "principal acts of saving faith are accepting, receiving, and resting upon Christ alone for justification, sanctification, and eternal life, by virtue of the covenant of grace" (XIV.ii). In other words, it is not true that a man is given saving faith only to have that faith immediately die right after his justification, leaving him in the position of having to come up with some other means or instrument of advancing the works of sanctification. Rather, *all* the work of his sanctification is brought about by the instrumentality of saving faith. Note also that the Confession wisely states that saving faith has Christ for its object, and not the abstract transactions of justification or sanctification. Like Peter walking on water, we can do it as long as we are looking at Christ. But as soon as we begin to look at ourselves walking on water, we find that we are looking at ourselves *not* walking on water.

> *Faith and works are mistakenly thought to be like two billiard balls that cannot occupy the same space at the same time.*

We tend to slip off this point, not because it is too complicated, but because we are spiritually dense. Sovereign grace is always offensive to the flesh, and so the flesh doesn't really want to "get it." But for the one who has been given true saving faith, these remaining difficulties with the flesh are overcome in the process of sanctification. When God gives a new heart, that heart is now capable of believing what God says. It is now possible to *believe* His promises. Before that time, the serpent's whisper of "Hath God said?" was the sinful heart's constant refrain. The carnal heart does not and cannot believe God. But the new heart does and will persevere in it. When God gives the gift of a new heart, that heart believes God for justification, sanctification, and eternal life. Saving faith believes God initially to justification. The next moment *that same saving faith* believes God's promises concerning sanctification, and the life-long process starts. The process culminates when we enter into glory, receiving our inheritance of eternal life. We are saved by faith, through faith, to faith, and under faith. Ironically, because of this emphasis on faith I have been accused in the past of seeking to undermine the historic Protestant doctrine of *sola fide*. (Confused? I didn't really understand it either.) But in all cases, a faith that *remains fruitful* is the instrument we were given in order to respond to the promises of God.

This is relevant to our questions about covenant nurture because bringing up our children is an important part of our sanctification. Bringing up children before the Lord is one of the most important things we do. In the midst of this task, we must never labor apart from a reference to the promises of God in what we are doing. When we look to the promises concerning our children, we must remember that this really means looking to *Christ*, the one in whom all the promises of God are "yea" and "Amen." The promises are not understood rightly if we understand them in separation from the person of Christ. We look to Christ because the Scripture tells us that in Him "all the promises of God in him are yea, and in him Amen, unto the glory of God by us" (2 Cor. 1:20). The importance of this should become obvious when we consider the details of covenant nurture below. But for the present, if we treat our covenant relationship with the person of

> *Bringing up our children is an important part of our sanctification.*

Christ as impersonal, this will necessarily corrupt our application of the covenant relationship we have with our children. This is how covenant nurture deteriorates from following Christ into following the instructions on child-rearing paint-by-numbers kit. Simply "following the procedures" is not covenantal faithfulness.

Faith in God's Promises

So we look to Christ in the promises. But what is the content of these promises of God with regard to our children? God's promises to parents are ably discussed elsewhere in this volume, and so I will limit my references to them to just this paragraph. God promises that the children of His servants will continue (Ps. 102:28). He says He will show mercy to thousands of generations of those who fear Him (Deut. 5:9–10). Our God keeps covenanted mercy over the course of thousands of generations (Deut. 7:9). God promised that in the days of the Messiah He would bless us, our children, and our grandchildren forever (Ezek. 37:24–26). According to Isaiah, we will no longer bring forth children for trouble (Is. 65:23). And our Lord's mother knew that the Son she bore was not to be the one in whom all generational blessings cease, but rather the one in whom all generational promises are fulfilled (Lk. 1:48–50).

These promises are important to mention because we face the constant temptation to have faith in our faith instead of having faith in the God who promises Christ to us and our children.

These promises are important to mention here because we face the constant temptation to have faith in our faith instead of having faith in the God who promises Christ to us and to our children. In theological terms, we tend to make faith the ground of what we receive instead of the instrument by which we receive what is promised, through the one who promised.

In Scripture, we see faith described in just this way:

Now faith is the substance of things hoped for, the evidence of things
not seen. (Heb. 11.1)

But without faith it is impossible to please him: for he that cometh
to God must believe that he is, and that he is a rewarder of them that
diligently seek him. (v. 6)

Through faith also Sara herself received strength to conceive seed,
and was delivered of a child when she was past age, because she
judged him faithful who had promised. (v. 11)

Faith is the substance of what is hoped for, but it is not hoped for on
the strength of personal whims. It is the *evidence* of things not seen—
in other words, there is reason for the hope. That reason is simply that
God is the one who has promised. The man who comes to God must
believe two things about Him. First, he must believe that God exists, and secondly, that God rewards those who seek Him. He rewards them because to do so is
keeping His word, keeping His
promise to Abraham. And bringing it down to the precise point at
issue, Sara appropriated the bless-

> Faith is the natural response to
> the perceived faithfulness of God.

ing of the promise through faith. Her faith consisted precisely of
this—"she judged him faithful who had promised." So this then is
faith; faith is the natural response to *the perceived faithfulness of God.*
Faith is "judging Him faithful." God makes promises throughout His
Word. When we see what He has said, and we understand that He
is faithful, this demeanor of ours is what the Bible calls faith. We are
sustained by the faithfulness of the object in which we trust, and
never by the quality of our trust. A man with wobbly faith can get
on an airliner but his wobbly faith won't make the plane crash. And
a man with great faith can strap on a couple of wings and jump off
the barn but his faith can't make him fly. Sound faith is what places
us in the care of a faithful object.

The "Three Legs" of Parenting

The "three legs" of covenant nurture, which I mentioned earlier, are prayer, personal example, and instruction/discipline. If we have understood what has been argued in the first part of this essay, these three things must be understood as *faith* resulting in prayer, *faith* resulting in personal example, and *faith* resulting in discipline and instruction. This must be emphasized again and again because we have a natural tendency to wash the outside of the cup.

In other words, if someone gets external hold of these three points, the easiest thing in the world is to turn them into a "system" of works, whereby we, manipulating this covenant machinery, can ensure that all of our kids will "turn out." Not only is this *not* covenant nurture, it is the antithesis of covenant nurture. If someone thinks that saying prayers, providing a decent parental example, and ensuring that the kids have a Christian education will automatically do the trick, he is setting his family up for a grand fall. Believing the promises will result in observable parental faithfulness in these three areas, because faith without works is dead, but conforming externally to these three areas is not the same thing as believing the promises.

Prayer in Covenant Nurture

With all that said, faith in the promises that results in prayer is an essential part of this process of bringing children up in the nurture and admonition of the Lord. Like all prayers, these are not offered up so that God can do something about that lamentable ignorance of His. God knows everything already; He is the source of everything already. The reason we pray to Him is that He wants *us* to learn this.

We should begin by placing a high priority on the public prayers of the church. In our individualistic era, we have a tendency to think that all efficacious prayer must be hidden away from others. Jesus did forbid showboating in the public prayers of the church, but we are called to corporate prayer together. In our service of worship, one of the regular things we have included in what we present to God as

a church is the task we have of educating our children. Certain petitions should be offered up by Christian churches regularly   prayer
for persecuted saints around the world, for kings and all those in
authority, for the cause of missions, and so on. In addition to this, our
liturgy includes regular prayer for home educators and private Christian schools. We are seeking to honor God in what we do, in how we
bring up the kids, and we present this request together.

In the family, the prayer should be more specific and particular. A
husband and wife should pray regularly for their children, for their
specific temptations and struggles, the tasks they have before them,
their future spouses, and so on. Parents should talk to God about
their children before talking to their children about God.

Parents should also use prayer as an investigative tool. Suppose the
parents suspect that one of the children has lied about something to
them, but they cannot prove it. It is important that parents not discipline blindly because the Bible teaches that every fact has to be established in the mouth of two or three witnesses. But God knows the
truth about the matter, and the
parents should pray, asking God to
provide them with all they need to
know in order to be godly parents.
If there is a hidden lie that needs to
be brought into the light and dealt

> *Parents should talk to God about
> their children before talking to
> their children about God.*

with, the parents should ask God to do it. And of course, such a
prayer offered in all honesty is a prayer that is offered up in the will
of God. How would our loving Father *not* answer such a prayer? But
too often the reason we don't ask is that we don't really want to
know. We belong to that shortsighted school of car maintenance and
repair—don't lift the hood if you don't want to know.

In all this, parents are praying over the details. But they should not
forget to pray the big picture. This means asking God to supply what
God has promised to supply, and in doing this, we pray His words
back to Him. In substance, this means that parents should pray to
God, regularly, asking Him to ensure that the children walk with Him

all of their days, and that they bring up their children with the same demeanor of faith. Parents should not hesitate to ask God for their children, grandchildren, and great-grandchildren. We should dare to pray as far as the promises will take us, and as we have seen, the promises take us for a thousand generations, which is a longer period of time than the human race has been around. We have not yet gotten close to a thousand generations.

You don't know whether any of your ancestors prayed for you, but wouldn't it have been glorious if they had? So apply the golden rule, and pray for your descendants. Most of the readers of this book will be, in the providence of God, an ancestor for tens of thousands of people. So pray for them. Ask God to give them His grace.

These descendants, however, are not visible to us—the only visible link we have to them are the faces we see around the dinner table every night. And because it is important to link what we ask God for to what we do, this brings us to the importance of personal example.

Personal Example in Covenant Nurture

Personal example is important because children learn an enormous amount through imitation. Parents teach constantly, whether they are "teaching" or not. Paul assumes this when he tells us as Christians to be imitators of God: "Be ye therefore followers of God, *as dear children*; And walk in love, as Christ also hath loved us, and hath given himself for us an offering and a sacrifice to God for a sweetsmelling savour" (Eph. 5:1–2). We are to be imitators or followers of God, "as dear children." In other words, loved children gladly imitate their father and mother, the ones to whom they are dear.

In the last section, I will be addressing the question of formal education and discipline, but it is important for us to place a *stronger* emphasis on the instruction and discipline that comes through the process of setting an example for imitation. Virtually everyone recognizes the value of a personal example that does not contradict the formal instruction that is given. Hypocrisy can be a difficult hurdle for kids to get over. If parents who smoke cigarettes are telling their children that they cannot smoke, the charge of inconsistency is an easy one to level, and children who want to disobey will have no problem taking advantage of that inconsistency. "Do as I say, not as I do" can be a real stumbling block to children. Jesus had to warn His followers to listen to the doctrine of the Pharisees (because they sat in Moses' seat) but not to live in the same way they did (Mt. 23:3). This warning is necessary whenever the teaching is sounder than the practice. Paul takes note of it when he says that Gentiles blaspheme God because of the bad example of the Jews (Rom. 2:23–24).

But while this is an important part of setting a good example, it is, in my view, not the most important part at all. Setting a consistent example that dear children will instinctively follow is the way to get instruction down into the bones. The rationalism that we inherited from the Enlightenment has trained us all to think that everything that we really "know" is that which can be objectively measured and doled out in credit-hours. We have created a great illusory mechanism for making ourselves think that we know how people actually know things. And we identify what they know in terms of what we can measure. We quantify knowledge in such a way that at a parent/teacher conference a teacher can say, without any sense of embarrassment, that a child received an eighty-seven percent on his last English assignment in poetry, as though a poem were like six yards of fabric, or five pounds of flour. This is *not* to say that there is no quantitative element to

> Setting a consistent example that children will instinctively follow is the way to get instruction down into the bones.

knowledge. On a vocabulary test with one hundred words on it, if a student were to get six of them wrong, it would make poetic sense to say he got a ninety-four percent. But this kind of knowledge, the easily measurable kind, is the *least* important knowledge we have. And it is not the kind of knowledge that children acquire in the home by imitation.

This is a point that is worth pursuing. If I were to tell someone in passing that the Greek word *kai* means "and, even, or also," this would probably tell most people that I know some Greek. What it ought to tell them is that I don't know it very well at all. That predictable little list of "and, even, also" comes right off a list of vocabulary words memorized for an introductory class, and does not represent the speech and thought patterns of someone who was fluent. Compare what I just wrote to what a native speaker of biblical Greek would say if asked what *kai* meant. He would probably be as flummoxed as I would be if someone asked me for all the definitions of *but*. I have no earthly idea how many different definitions *but* has. Having written that previous sentence, I have gone to the dictionary and looked it up. It appears that as a conjunction it has nine different definitions (according to the *American Heritage Dictionary*). As a native speaker of English, I recognized them all and understood all the examples given. But I would have failed a pop quiz that requested me to supply the nine definitions of *but*.

Knowledge is embodied, not distilled and abstract. Abstract principles off a page are a kind of dehydrated knowledge, but they are not true, incarnational knowledge. To shift the example somewhat, allow me to illustrate with dogs, children, and grandchildren. Over the course of our marriage, Nancy and I have had several dogs in our home for several short tenures. When it came to disciplining and training these dogs, I was about as worthless as it gets. The dogs would regularly leave me nonplussed and then just sit there panting with that impervious look on their faces. But when my wife and I were disciplining and teaching our children, everything went much more smoothly. With the dogs, I knew that I did not know. With the kids, the confidence was there. I have concluded that the reason for the great difference was that my family had no pets when I was a child, and so I had no *embodied* notion of what I was supposed to be doing. But my parents were effective and diligent parents, and I had countless opportunities to see how they loved and disciplined me, my brothers, and my sister. Most of the lessons I learned from watching in this way I have forgotten (that is, "forgotten" if my memory were to be tested with a quiz), but the real reason I can't summon them up as conscious recollections is that they are all down in the bones. And now, the really strange thing is that my wife and I currently have the privilege of watching our children teach and instruct and discipline our young grandchildren. In watching the wisdom our children have with this age group, we see them applying things that they *cannot* be consciously remembering. How do they know to do that?

Personal example in the context of personal relationship is God's appointed means for imparting wisdom. By personal example parents teach tone, facial expression, kindness, sacrifice, unspoken assumptions, and so on. It is the personal example that sets the aroma of the home. And tragically, many conservative Christian parents rely entirely on rigorous discipline and teaching (covered in the next section), but by their personal example they ensure that their children will not really love or understand what they have been taught. This is because the tone of the home contradicts the words that are formally imparted.

Formal Instruction and Discipline in Covenant Nurture

My emphasis on faith and personal example does not mean that formal instruction and discipline are unimportant; they are in fact very important in bringing up faithful covenant children. But in my experience as a pastor, most parents who try to build a one-legged stool try it with this leg. I have never met parents who just prayed for their kids and did nothing else. Neither have I met parents who just provided a personal example. But I have met numerous parents who disciplined and taught regularly while neglecting prayer and holiness in the home. Perhaps this is because this is the leg of covenant nurture that our neighbors and fellow church members can see.

Instruction is really a form of discipline. Both of them place the children under a regimen. Formal instruction is a positive form of discipline, and what we usually call discipline is negative, seeking to prevent the kids from doing "that" again. Both forms are applied from the earliest days. A one-year-old is learning both vocabulary and limits. He is told that this is a "light," and that is a "table," and that the vase on the coffee table is a "no touch."

In the discipline and instruction of the kids, the children should be learning that the parents are living sacrificial lives that overflow with gladness. The regimen that the children experience is not there so that the parents might have a plausible excuse to "take" from their children. It is there because the parents are *giving* to them. For example, a parent who requires a child to do the dishes should not be doing it in order to get free labor but rather to bestow a work ethic. And this means that the parents must establish from the very first the principle that the children must gladly obey their parents in the Lord, for this is right (Eph. 6:1–4). No discipline seems pleasant at the time, but later on the harvest is enjoyed (Heb. 12:6–12).

The direction of discipline and the direction of instruction are the same direction—maturity and wisdom in grown children. This means that the discipline and the instruction should presuppose increasing responsibilities and weight for the children as the years go by. But we often get this backwards.

When sin in children is little and somewhat cute, it is frequently indulged. The world did not come to an end because the three-year-old pitched his fit. But as the years unfold, sin gets more and more serious, with weightier consequences. A decade after the three-year-old's fit, he is now capable of getting someone pregnant, or smoking dope, or joy-riding in a car with a bad set of friends. When this becomes apparent, the parents often panic and start laying down the rules. Thus we see kids grounded, with curfews and additional restrictions, all of which provoke additional rebellion because glad obedience is an alien concept.

Wise parents reverse this order. Little children should live under careful and close oversight. They should not be able to do anything *significant* without permission. This is not because the parents are control freaks, but rather because parents want to instill the concept of glad obedience when the concrete is wet. After the cement truck has left is a bad time to start discussing whether you wanted a patio or a garden wall. As children get older, parents should gradually remove rules and *lift* restrictions. A reluctance to do this is often one of the great indicators that parents are not really trusting God for their children. Their faith is in their own abilities, and as the children get older it becomes harder and harder to maintain that faith. But wise parents know that preschool children are shaped, elementary-school children are taught, teenage children are directed, and adult children are advised. Faith knows that the point of bringing up children is to make them wise and mature in bringing up their own children. This means that the goal is true maturity.

In all of this, it should go without saying that the education that such children receive should be thoroughly and completely Christian. Fathers are told to bring up their children in the nurture and admonition of the Lord (Eph. 6:4). Parents are commanded to bring up their children in an environment dominated by the Word of God (Deut. 6:4–9). The greatest commandment says that we are to love the Lord our God with all our hearts, souls, *minds*, and strength. Loving God with all our minds means loving Him when we do math,

> *Preschool children are shaped, elementary school children are taught, teenage children are directed, and grown children are advised.*

biology, languages, history, and so on. It means loving Him in the learning of the catechism. It means loving Him in how we hear the Scriptures read and how we receive sermons preached at church. Formal instruction is required by the Word of God and not to be despised. Part of respecting it is knowing the limits of what it is intended to do.

In summary, the grace of God is the foundation of the promises and faith is the foundation of all righteous appropriation of the promises. This faith is itself a gift from God, lest anyone boast. Parents who have been given this gift of faith will show that faith by how they bring up their children. But they are showing us something invisible by means of that which is visible. They are not showing us something visible *instead* of that which cannot be seen. Such faith manifests itself throughout all of life. But when it shows particularly in prayer, example, and teaching, it shows us the heart and soul of covenant nurture.

Revitalizing Reformed Culture

Doug Jones

Embracing covenant succession forces one immediately into the future. It highlights the connection between faithful children and a healthy Christian culture, showing us that the path to a mature Christian culture is primarily through our children. Malachi famously emphasizes the new covenant promise that the new Elijah "will turn the hearts of the fathers to the children, and the hearts of the children to their fathers, lest I come and strike the earth with a curse" (Mal. 4:6). Culture involves time and maturity. We most certainly cannot disciple the world if each subsequent generation takes a step backward.

The irony we run into, however, is that though the Reformed faith has been the largest contributor in Christendom to the topic of covenant reality, our tradition is still apparently pretty clueless as to how to live out this theology. The question "Why do Reformed cultures repeatedly fail?" should constantly haunt us. The Reformed faith has several centuries of *ideological* children. We generate disciples primarily by means of ideas—by people reading Reformed writings. But where are the biological grandchildren delighting in the faith over centuries? That's the key to Christian culture.

Most strikingly, Reformed thought has been an important contributor not only to the discussion of the covenant but also to that of the antithesis. We have long excelled at identifying the line between belief and unbelief, light and darkness, true faith and pagan infiltrations. For centuries, the Reformed faith has marked the antithesis against Romanism, pietism, scientism, legalism, egalitarianism. More than anyone else, it seems, the Reformed have been there pressing the key questions: "What fellowship has righteousness with lawlessness? What communion has light with darkness? What accord has Christ with Belial? What part has a believer with an unbeliever? And what agreement has the temple of God with idols?" (2 Cor. 6:15–16).

Why the Failure?

And yet we must be missing something writ very, very large. Why is it that, for all our important talk about antithesis and covenant, generation after generation of our children betray us and abandon these realities?

All the great Reformed cultures of centuries past, which we praise for heroism and loyalty, have left us plenty of books but no great lineages of children. Sure, we can point, once in a while, to some descendant of Jonathan Edwards and some three-generation line of Scottish pastors, but the fact that we can actually point to them confirms the problem. If what we have been teaching is true, there should be so many lines of faithful descendants that there would be no need to be stingy and pick out rare lines. We should be overwhelmed with faithful descendants.

> *All the great Reformed cultures which we praise have left us plenty of books but no great lineages of children.*

Where are the faithful children of the Puritans, Scottish Covenanters, Southern Presbyterians, Dutch Reformed, Huguenots, and Swiss and German Reformed? These were all powerful Reformed cultures. Their children should be persevering, expanding, and dominating culture. These cultures were once the cutting edge. Why have they vanished? Why did the hearts of the children not turn to their fathers?

And, of course, we have to answer this sort of question in the face of several cultures within Christendom that have, perhaps however weakly, shown more cultural stamina than the Reformed. Even granting their obvious weaknesses, many Roman Catholic cultures have persevered in numerous parts of the world for centuries. Though the Reformed might certainly have complaints with the expressions and tendencies of these cultures, we surely have to grant Roman Catholic cultures some serious praise for passing down some version of the faith for more than one generation. Reformed cultures rarely get past that first generation, let alone dream of six or seven. In a parallel way, the eastern portion of Christendom gave us Byzantium, the longest-lasting Christian culture the world has yet seen. It lasted over a millennium—a feat (though again despite various failings) that has to silence any Reformed boast. Do they have something we lack? Surely we don't want mere formalism, but that doesn't inspire children anyway. What are we lacking?

Weak Answers

When we Reformed consider the question of why our cultures fail so quickly (and the evidence that we even raise that question is slim), we tend to answer rather too neatly by invoking some line about martyrdom, namely, that these Reformed people were like those of Hebrews 11:38, "of whom the world was not worthy." In other words, we suggest that they were so great that the enemy had to wipe them out: "The world has hated them because they are not of the world, just as I am not of the world" (Jn. 17:14).

There is some truth in this, and I think it fits some Reformed groups like the Huguenots, who were scattered abroad by enemies and brought some life for a while to other Reformed cultures. Surely, the faithful have faced martyrdom, but the Reformed pattern of failure seems too constant to be explained away so easily. After all, the Lord promises the opposite for faithfulness: "The Lord will cause your enemies who rise against you to be defeated before your face;

they shall come out against you one way and flee before you seven ways" (Deut. 28:7). Our enemies are normally supposed to fall, not triumph over us.

But notice that this martyrdom explanation doesn't address our main failing—the rebellion of our own children. The martyrdom passages focus on the understandable hatred of the "world" against faithfulness, but they don't suggest that having one's own children turn against you is a sign of holiness. Martyrdom doesn't explain treason.

The loss or captivity of our children is in fact often a sign of a cultural curse. The Lord promises "it shall come to pass, if you do not obey the voice of the LORD your God" (Deut. 28:15), then "you shall beget sons and daughters, but they shall not be yours; for they shall go into captivity" (Deut. 28:41), and "your sons and your daughters shall be given to another people, and your eyes shall look and fail with longing for them all day long; and there shall be no strength in your hand" (Deut. 28:32). No strength in our hand—what a telling expression. Though our children have avoided the relatively easy captivity of Assyria or Babylon, where one's loyalties tend to become very clear, they have fallen headlong into the far subtler captivity of modernity—individualism, egalitarianism, rationalism, sentimentalism. And our eyes "look and fail with longing for them all day long." Notice, though, the promise for faithfulness and imagine its cultural consequences: "He will prosper you and multiply you more than your fathers. And the Lord your God will circumcise your heart and the heart of your descendants, to love the Lord your God with all your heart and with all your soul, that you may live" (Deut. 30:5–6).

So the question remains: Why have the children of Reformed cultures not carried forward the faith faithfully? Is it something about us, about Reformed culture, that produces this end? Our ecclesiastical opponents will answer quickly in the affirmative (and truth be told, we do have our own house to clean).

The most common solution we offer is doctrine, more doctrine. Doctrine saves. So we do everything we can to download Reformed ideas into our kids' heads. We hope in catechisms, memorization, apologetics, and worldviews, all of which are important and have their place. They can't, however, bring the blessings of faithfulness on their own. God hasn't set up the universe in that way: "You believe that there is one God. You do well. Even the demons believe—and tremble! But do you want to know, O foolish man, that faith without works is dead?" (Jas. 2:19–20). The road to apostasy is riddled with ideas.

Harriet Beecher Stowe, author of the infamous *Uncle Tom's Cabin*, one of the most powerful pieces of romantic propaganda ever written, once presented a telling snapshot of Reformed life. Her parents were Calvinists, her older brothers were Calvinists, and her husband was Calvinist. Later in her life, Stowe complained that her father's doctrines were made of "hair-splitting distinctions and dialectic subtleties" that "were as unintelligible to me as . . . Choctaw."[1]

Those Reformed with a more sacramental perspective (I count myself among them) are quick to point, not to doctrine, but to the tragic history of the Reformed neglect of the sacraments. Many Reformed churches still staunchly oppose weekly communion, and we have a long history of rejecting not merely paedocommunion but even young-adult communion.[2] To place teenagers outside the Lord's Supper is to beg for apostasy. Certainly,

> *The most common solution we offer is doctrine, more doctrine.*

these sorts of traditions are key players in our failures. Naming is deathly important. The Lord's Supper names those who belong to the triune God. You can't name and rename a child, early and often, as "outside the covenant"—alienated from God—and then be surprised

---

[1] Cited in Gregg Camfield, *Sentimental Twain: Samuel Clemens in the Maze of Moral Philosophy* (Philadelphia: Univ. of Pennsylvania Press, 1994), 45.

[2] The subject of paedocommunion is controversial in the Reformed community and by no means agreed upon by the contributors of this volume. One need not have a position on paedocommunion to grapple with the issues of covenant succession. Indeed, covenant succession demands much more.

when he or she later keeps the name of alien, spiritually shriveled from the lack of God's feast. If we "train up a child" to act like a non-Christian, then "when he is old he will not depart from it" (Prov. 22:6).

My sympathies easily lie in this sacramental direction and much reformation is needed, but the sacramental answer alone still falls short. Though crucial, it can't do it alone. There are, for example, plenty of paedocommunion churches where the children are a mess, addicted to modernity and the "cool," heaping greater curses upon themselves. Byzantium, too, practiced paedocommunion for centuries, yet God brought an end to that empire.

No solution to the problem will be simple, and neither the doctrinal nor sacramental solutions would generally claim to stand alone, and even the suggestions I offer won't be sufficient by themselves. But we can err even in what we gather into the package.

Discerning Deeper

We need to reexamine Deuteronomy 27–30, that momentous passage cited above in regard to enemies, children, and culture. What does the Lord point to there as the fulcrum between blessings and curses? Faithfulness, obviously, but what sort? What sort of personality does this faithfulness have? Faithful in doctrine? Faithful in evangelism? Faithful in spiritual disciplines? Faithful in the sacraments? All of these are important, but what is the divine priority?

In the midst of the long, detailed, and humbling list of cultural blessings and curses, we find an intriguing line. We're told that "all these curses shall come upon you and pursue and overtake you," but not for failures in any areas that the broad Christian community tends to value—evangelism, prayer, doctrine, sacraments, etc. The divine priority says that all the curses will fall "because you did not serve the Lord your God *with joy and gladness of heart,* for the abundance of everything." Because you lack "joy and gladness of heart . . . you shall serve your enemies" (Deut. 28:47–48). What is God saying?

"Joy and gladness"? Since when has that been the pivot of reality? Certainly this has to be a divine typo.

I don't pretend to understand the full weight of this claim, but we should be obsessed with finding it out, obsessed with making it the very center of our lives and cultures. Nothing else appears as important, given the stark context of Deuteronomy 27–30. At the very least we should better grasp the place of joy and gladness of heart in the Christian life.

The broad Christian community has many, many books on joy, but few of them appear to grasp the weight of joy. They tend to talk rather stoically about how to feel pleasure in the midst of dysfunctional relationships. Joy is just a marginal psychological trait, not the center of the universe. How is it that, for centuries, Christendom can write creeds and theological tomes that don't tell us this simple point

> *The divine priority says that all the curses will fall "because you did not serve the Lord your God with joy and gladness of heart."*

from Deuteronomy? Why haven't we had giant church councils on the nature of joy? Or different schools of thought that wrestle over the intricacies of joy? Why don't our creeds dedicate long sections to expositing the nature of joy for the people of God? Is there a systematic theology that has this sort of joy as its chiastic center?

Even the answer to the great first question of the Westminster Larger Catechism doesn't line things up in the simple and earthy manner of Deuteronomy. The catechism exhorts us that "Man's chief and highest end is to glorify God, and fully to enjoy him forever." Wonderful—but Deuteronomy is far more earthy: we are to serve with "joy and gladness of heart, for the abundance of everything." The stated motive for joy, here, could have understandably pointed explicitly to the grand character of Jehovah, and meditating spiritually on that, but it doesn't. It just speaks about joy for all the great stuff God has given us—joy for the abundance.

The words used in Deuteronomy for "joy" and "goodness" (*simchah* and *tov*) work as synonyms in much of Scripture. The earthiness of their use in Deuteronomy shows up in their repeated use in celebratory contexts. These words rarely show up in the context of pure meditation. They are predominately surrounded by loud parties: "And all the people went up after [Solomon]; and the people played the flutes and rejoiced with great *joy* (*simchah*), so that the earth seemed to split with their sound" (1 Kgs. 1:40). "For how great is its *goodness* (*tov*) and how great its beauty! Grain shall make the young men thrive, and new wine the young women" (Zech. 9:17). These are the sorts of joy and gladness about which God's curses and blessings turn.

In a deeply profound sense, the lesson of Deuteronomy turns out to be the earthy center of Ecclesiastes as well. There the exhortation becomes "So I commended enjoyment [*simchah*], because a man has nothing better under the sun than to eat, drink, and be merry; for this will remain with him in his labor all the days of his life which God gives him under the sun" (Eccl. 8:15). Even more pointedly,

> *Joy carries a tremendous amount of weight in Scripture, though it gets scandalously little attention.*

Ecclesiastes says, "Go, eat your bread with joy [*simchah*], and drink your wine with a merry heart; for God has already accepted your works" (Eccl. 9:7). This is the joy that continues from Deuteronomy as the pivot of blessing and cursing: eat, drink, and be merry in the Lord.

Earthy Joy is Life

The earthy joy that knows "nothing better" than to "eat, drink, be merry," and receive the blessings of God serves as a part-for-whole connection to the theme of "life" so central in Scripture. Earthy joy becomes a picture of divine life itself: "You will show me the path of *life*; in Your presence is fullness of *joy* [*simchah*]; at Your right hand are pleasures forevermore" (Ps. 16:11). In David's vision, joy is not some pleasant, marginal feature of our existence on earth. It characterizes the personality of the Godhead, joy is life, divine life is joy. Interestingly, it is this same passage, connecting joy and life, that Peter cites in the Pentecost sermon for the new church (Acts 2:28). We often speak of the centrality of such distinctions as Creator/ creature, fall/redemption, and faith/works, but all of these seem to ride on the more basic Scriptural contrast between life and death. In the beginning God breathed life into man and set a Tree of Life in the midst of the Garden, promising death for violating it. This wonderful "obsession" with life continues throughout the story. Here is just a sample:

For the *life* of the flesh is in the blood. (Lev. 17:11)

See, I have set before you today *life* and good, death and evil, in that I command you today to love the LORD your God, to walk in His ways, and to keep His commandments, His statutes, and His judgments, that you may *live* and multiply. (Deut. 30:15–16)

I call heaven and earth as witnesses today against you, that I have set before you life and death, blessing and cursing; therefore choose *life*, that both you and your descendants may *live*; that you may love the LORD your God, that you may obey His voice, and that you may cling to Him, for He is your *life* and the length of your days. (Deut. 30:19–20).

The LORD is my light and my salvation; whom shall I fear? The LORD is the strength of my *life*; of whom shall I be afraid? (Ps. 27:1)

Who is the man who desires *life*, and loves many days, that he may see good? (Ps. 34:12)

In the way of righteousness is *life*, and in its pathway there is no death. (Prov. 12:28)

The law of the wise is a fountain of *life*, to turn one away from the snares of death. (Prov. 13:14)

The way of *life* winds upward for the wise, that he may turn away from hell below. (Prov. 15:24)

In the beginning was the Word, and the Word was with God, and the Word was God. . . . In Him was *life*, and the life was the light of men. (Jn. 1:1, 4)

But you are not willing to come to Me that you may have *life*. (Jn. 5:40)

Then Jesus spoke to them again, saying, "I am the light of the world. He who follows Me shall not walk in darkness, but have the light of *life*." (Jn. 8:12)

Jesus said to him, "I am the way, the truth, and the *life*. No one comes to the Father except through Me." (Jn. 14:6)

And so it is written, "The first man Adam became a living being." The last Adam became a *life*-giving spirit." (1 Cor. 15:45)

He who has the Son has *life*; he who does not have the Son of God does not have *life*." (1 Jn. 5:12)

And He said to me, "It is done! I am the Alpha and the Omega, the Beginning and the End. I will give of the fountain of the water of *life* freely to him who thirsts." (Rev. 21:6)

Many of these verses, though, could be read as merely upholding life as mere spiritual/biological existence, rather than life in any heightened, joyful sense. The following collection, then, should help frame the one above. These verses all assume mere existence and go on to emphasize the aspect of quality over that of mere existence, as if there were a heightened life within the life of mere existence:

You will show me the path of *life*; in Your presence is fullness of joy; at Your right hand are pleasures forevermore. (Ps. 16:11)

So they will be *life* to your soul and grace to your neck. (Prov. 3:22)

For whoever finds me [wisdom] finds *life*, and obtains favor from the Lord. (Prov. 8:35)

A sound heart is *life* to the body, but envy is rottenness to the bones. (Prov. 14:30)

The fear of the LORD leads to *life*, and he who has it will abide in satisfaction; he will not be visited with evil. (Prov. 19:23)

For wisdom is a defense as money is a defense, but the excellence of knowledge is that wisdom gives *life* to those who have it. (Eccl. 7:12)

And this is eternal *life*, that they may know You, the only true God, and Jesus Christ whom You have sent. (Jn. 17:3)

You have made known to me the ways of *life*; You will make me full of joy in Your presence. (Acts 2:28)

For to be carnally minded is death, but to be spiritually minded is *life* and peace. (Rom. 8:6)

He who would love *life* and see good days, let him refrain his tongue from evil, and his lips from speaking deceit. (1 Pet. 3:10)

I have come that they may have *life*, and that they may have it more abundantly. (Jn. 10:10)

The list could go on, and we might have exegetical quibbles along the way, but at the very least the emphasis on this thing called life, connected with joy, should be a far greater subject for theological reflection. It carries a tremendous amount of weight in Scripture, though it gets scandalously little attention.

My main contention, then, is that here lies much of the failure we witness in Reformed culture. Life—as depicted in Deuteronomy,

Ecclesiastes, and the Gospel of John, along with the rest of Scripture, with all its connections to divine life and earthy joy—is not the central reality of Reformed culture. We traditionally have various other emphases that we find most central, and we allow these to drive our child-rearing, education, and worship. Of course, the same charge can be leveled at many other portions of Christendom, but it has particular sticking power for Reformed cultures.

Reformed Weaknesses

Theological critics over the years have pointed out various internal problems—some genuine, others not—that the Reformed faith faces. I'm choosing a representative critic because I think that his criticism clearly sticks, and yet it is not the sort of criticism that the Reformed faith has no natural means to handle—just the opposite, in fact.

Jeremy Begbie raises the line of criticism below within a discussion of aesthetics, focusing on the "Neo-Calvinistic" aesthetic theory that grows out of Kuyper and Bavinck and gets filled out in Dooyeweerd, Rookmaaker, and Seerveld. The criticism is not limited to the domain of aesthetics; it easily applies to other areas of the Reformed faith. Begbie writes,

> The Neo-Calvinist concept of God is insufficiently shaped by the self-disclosure of the Trinity in the history of Jesus Christ. God is portrayed fundamentally as the powerful Lawgiver, whose absolute and sovereign will is enacted in the establishment of precepts which we are summoned to obey; his love is a secondary attribute, reserved for the elect. . . . God's demands logically precede his grace; Adam's standing before the Fall sets the scene for all that follows. Grace, in whatever form it appears, is introduced to meet the requirements of God's law. . . .
>
> The Neo-Calvinists expound human destiny primarily in terms of *duty* and *obedience* to God. The human condition before the Fall casts its shadow over all that follows. Elect and reprobate all stand

under God's law. . . . The essence of humanity is defined in terms
of obedience. . . . [Neo-Calvinists] speak of our calling principally
in terms of obedience to divine law (humanity's condition prior to
the Fall) rather than in terms of being invited to share in the life and
purposes of the triune God. Culture centres around the concept of
obedience. In contrast, I suggest that a more satisfactory approach
would view cultural involvement chiefly as a gift rather than a legal requirement.[3]

This criticism that the life of the Trinity—self-giving love—has not
been central in the development of Reformed thought has been
raised in this century against much of the Christian tradition. Back
in the sixties, Karl Rahner rightly and famously complained that most
believers in the Trinity are practical unitarians in day-to-day life. The
charge stands.

Without love as the personal, intertrinitarian bond of Father, Son,
and Holy Spirit, *power* and *law* easily fill the vacuum. That is the default relationship between a superior One and unequal subordinates.
The problem is that odd permutations arise when the Reformed tradition combines a practical unitarianism with a legitimate appreciation of Old Covenant law, the sovereignty of God, predestination, the
decrees, and providence. When these traditional, biblical commitments of the Reformed faith work within a proper trinitarian framework, the result is lovely and rich. But when combined, as they have
been, with a default unitarianism, the results are quite ugly (again,
the best contributions of *any* Christian tradition combined with unitarianism will always be gruesome).

Drawing, then, on my prior discussion about joy and life, we find
that Reformed traditions tend to produce a culture in which the
metaphors and frameworks of power and law are central rather than
those of trinitarian joy and life. When decree and law are more fundamental to the character of God than joy and love, we find Reformed

---

[3] Jeremy Begbie, *Voicing Creation's Praise* (Edinburgh: T & T Clark, 1991), 150–51, 158,
159.

cultures driven by law, principle, duty, precision, obedience, logic, reason, simplicity, and power. All of these have their good and proper place within biblical ethics, but as a consequence of divine joy and love, not as the starting point. In the Trinity, law flows from love. That is why the Lord can readily say, "I desire mercy and not sacrifice, and the knowledge of God more than burnt offerings" (Hos. 6:6).

When we think of the Godhead as being power and law *first,* we create a brand of rationalism that pervades contemporary Reformed churches. The sort of rationalism that I'm speaking about here echoes the secular version of ancient Greece and the Enlightenment. Both of those secular traditions held that the highest reality was law, namely the laws of thought and essence which dictate (note the power relation) the nature of reality. In those traditions, ideas, contemplation, immateriality, politics, and mathematics are all valued more highly than action, body, earth, sacrifice, and aesthetics. To the extent that the Reformed tradition duplicates their exaltation of law over joy, we'll repeat their rationalism at the heart of our cultures, with all the good things we do merely taped loosely on the outside. More devastatingly, though, we will continue to lose our children.

In the Trinity, law flows from love.

Reformed rationalism exalts the alleged precision of intellect over imagination and the mysteries of bodily sense, with the result that an anti-aestheticism dominates Reformed people. Aesthetic appreciation becomes at most a marginal, high-brow practice, not a feature of day-to-day life. Rationalism has to exclude whatever it can't efficiently capture—namely, the most interesting parts of life. And we wonder why our children turn away.

Reformed rationalism exalts principial order and law over joyous celebration, with the result that a boring orderliness dominates Reformed people. We find Presbyterians defining themselves first in terms of their books of discipline and church government (just look at our websites) rather than a celebration of life and redemption. And we wonder why our children turn away.

Reformed rationalism exalts ideas over action, with the result that we produce far more arguments, books, and magazines than hospices, trades, and technologies, with the result that a latent Gnosticism cripples our hands. We are forever learning and teaching but never building. An unnatural devotion to ideas sets us at odds with what our bodies were designed for. And we wonder why our children turn away.

Reformed rationalism exalts cynicism over nobility by turning a biblical notion of total depravity into a hatred of all imperfection, with the result that every corner of life is somehow dirty, clouded, and deserving of scorn. Our perfectionism makes this life inherently evil and so we look away from the glories of the present to some geometrical heaven. We don't know how

> *Rationalism has to exclude whatever it can't efficiently capture—namely, the most interesting parts of life.*

to raise questions about what a good and beautiful life is, and so we trudge, ox-like, through life, never looking around. And we wonder why our children turn away.

Reformed rationalism exalts control and carefulness over adventure and noble risk, with the result that a bureaucratic cowardice dominates Reformed life. We're too often so concerned to play by all the social, academic, safe rules that we would probably tsk-tsk Christ for being too hard on the Pharisees. This isn't a call for an ignoble, secular wildness—just a Davidic version. Instead, we crave safe reputations for the sake of being acceptable to all the wrong people. And we wonder why our children turn away.

Reformed rationalism exalts duty and obedience over love and joy, with the result that a deep seriousness dominates Reformed people. Seriousness is often taken to be the supreme Reformed virtue, and playfulness and childishness get pushed aside as inappropriate, as not reflective of the ultimate, serious reality, the God of gavels. Why is there no grand and wide Protestant tradition of comedy? The Jewish community has a wonderful tradition in this respect. But we can't produce what we don't value deep down. Pure duty allows no room for the exhilaration of play; it's too messy and superfluous. And we wonder why our children turn away.

Rationalism is unnatural and unsatisfying, striving against the naturally sublime joy at the center of the Godhead and creation. We insist on trying to pass this anemic faith on to our children, and they drop it very quickly.

Concluding Thoughts

Why do Reformed cultures fail so quickly? The short answer I've sketched is not intended to be exhaustive, just suggestive. Many other issues and qualifications could be included. But Scripture itself embraces a certain sort of simplicity. Simple, grateful, earthy joy for "the abundance" is a picture of the self-giving life between Father, Son, and Holy Spirit. Earthy joy should characterize us; it is supposed to permeate our family life throughout our decades. That is the life we are supposed to have as a community and as individuals. That is what it's all about. Yet a neglect of the Trinity combined with a rather unitarian interpretation of law, decree, control, power, duty, principle, intellect, and so on produces the sort of suffocating rationalism common to too many expressions of the Reformed faith. Why do our cultures fail? "Because you did not serve the LORD your God with joy and gladness of heart, for the abundance of everything" (Deut. 28:47). Revitalizing Reformed culture begins with trinitarian gratitude for the abundance, with drinking our wine with a merry heart, for God has already accepted our works (Eccl. 9:7).

The great wonder of the New Covenant is the outpouring of the Holy Spirit, a "much more glorious" ministry (2 Cor. 3:11) with the promise, "I will put My Spirit in you, and you shall live" (Ezek. 37:14). Christ has "obtained a more excellent ministry, inasmuch as He is also Mediator of a better covenant, which was established on better promises" (Heb. 8:6). Compared to the relatively weak saints under the Old Covenant, we are far more enabled to live and show the joy of God to our children: "I will give you a new heart and put a new spirit within you; I will take the heart of stone out of your flesh and give you a heart of flesh. I will put My Spirit within you and cause you to walk in My statutes, and you will keep My judgments and do them" (Ezek. 36:26–27). The Holy Spirit is the perfecter and beautifier of the Trinity's work, and it is only in close communion with the Spirit that we can show our children the utter beauty of God, creation, and all the abundance—the earthy joy God shares with us. Our rationalism quenches the Spirit, resenting the life He gives. We shouldn't expect Him to bless the next generation regularly and broadly if we despise the joy He loves.

Can Reformed culture come alive? Is it worth the effort? Can it become truly trinitarian? Why not just give up and opt for another Christian tradition? The problem is that things are weak all over. Some traditions of Christendom, like Roman Catholicism and Eastern Orthodoxy, are so deeply and creedally entrenched in Hellenistic categories that they have little hope of ever breaking free. Biblical, covenantal categories—the broad metaphysic of covenants—is unnatural to their traditions. Other Protestant traditions tend to be undermined by individualism and/or hostility to the Old Testament. We can't expect our children to be a people "after God's own heart" if they can't sing David's songs and share his thirst for God. Of course, I speak as a participant of the Reformed tradition, but the Reformed faith, of all traditions, seems to have the least to fix. Even with all its weaknesses, it gives the most hope in the long run for a rich Christian culture, a great expression of trinitarian life. But Spirit-enveloped, earthy joy must be at the center of any renewal, or else we face the same cultural curses of the past. "I have come that they may have life, and that they may have it more abundantly" (Jn. 10:10).

Raising Children in Christ-Centered Truth, Love, and Beauty

Benjamin K. Wikner

The promise is to you and to your children and all afar off. (Acts 2:39)

Train up your children in the nurture and admonition of the Lord. (Eph. 6:4)

[W]hatever is true, whatever is honorable, whatever is right, whatever is pure, whatever is lovely, whatever is of good repute, if there is any excellence and if anything worthy of praise, dwell on these things. (Phil. 4:8)

"The thrill of victory, the agony of defeat." That phrase could well describe the experience of many parents in the raising of their children. Without a doubt, parenting has many highs and lows. Birth is typically a great high; a seemingly endless string of sleepless nights to feed and change the new baby is a quick low. Baby's first steps, first words, first catch with the baseball mitt are all pretty good highs; at times these are replaced by the lows of moodiness, melancholy, or even outright rebellion in children. The thrill of a loving parent-child relationship, the agony of a broken one.

Every parent experiences these highs and lows in some measure. In this life, there is nothing nearer, dearer, or greater than the raising of our children. That's what makes the highs so wonderful and the lows so wretched. Such has been the experience of parents from the beginning of time. Just ask Adam and Eve—they could have written a book on the joys and sorrows of parenting. As the first family they were first to experience the thrill of parenting as well as the agony of family breakdown—rebellion, fratricide, and spiritual exile. Did they set the tone for all parents of all time? Is their experience normative for all parents? In a way, yes. The original sin of Adam was imputed to all men, making all his posterity after him, born by ordinary generation, sinners in him. For this reason, parenting will forever be a gut-wrenching challenge full of highs and lows.

So shall we just hope for the best and believe that God will take care of the rest? Should we just be thankful for the highs and resign ourselves to the likely lows, the impending despair? Shall we take comfort in the fact that so many others will be able to commiserate with our pain? In the language of Scripture, "May it never be!" God has introduced something wonderful into the equation, something which has an exceedingly greater impact upon parenting than did Adam's first sin, something which is able to stop the pattern of agony in the home. God has introduced the gospel of His Son—the grace of the New Covenant—into the world. As the Scripture says,

In parenting, shall we just hope for the best and believe that God will take care of the rest?

> Just as through one man's disobedience the many were made sinners, even so through the obedience of the one, the many will be made righteous. And this gift is not like the transgression. For if by the transgression the many died, much more did the grace of God and the gift of grace of the one man Jesus Christ abound to the many. Indeed, where sin increased, the grace of Christ immeasurably exceeded it. (Rom. 5:15–20)

Without a doubt, in our sinfulness, parenting is a challenge. But with even greater certainty, in the light of Christ, it is a glorious challenge in which God has enabled every Christian to triumph over agony, to have victory over sin. We are not ill-equipped for this challenge but have received all that we need for life and salvation (2 Pet.

1:3), both for us and for our children. Our children are too precious, our calling as parents too important, God's Word too clear, and His grace too excellent for us to compromise our godly desire as Christian parents. Our response as Christian parents to the great task of *Christian* parenting must be to step forward in faith—faith in God, faith in Christ, faith in His Word.

God has graciously provided the covenant as both the foundation and the tool for Christian parenting. The covenant provides fertile soil for the spiritual upbringing of our children. In the covenant exist all the spiritual nutrients needed for growth in wisdom, maturity, and godliness. Included are the promises made by God to the children of believers, that He is their God and they His children. As Jesus looked favorably upon and called the little children unto Him to be blessed, God bestows His grace and calls our children unto Him-

> The key to Christian parenting is a Christ-centered life.

self. So much more is this the case today in the New Covenant in which it was foretold by the prophet Malachi that God would turn the hearts of the fathers back to their children and the hearts of the children to their fathers (Mal. 4:6). Therefore, Christ has become the sure foundation for the New Covenant, on which the entire household of God dwells.

As a result, far from being discouraged or defeated, Christian parents (of all parents) should take hold of their parental responsibility with joy, expectation, and exuberance. To us has been given grace upon grace to aid us in our calling. And truly, what greater calling is there on this earth than to bring up God's own children to love, serve, and worship the Lord of glory?

The purpose of this essay is to help you, a Christian parent, to rise to the challenge of faithful Christian nurture, grasp the grace of God's covenant, and apply its blessing to you and to your family. This is a task you can ill afford to neglect—the blessings are too marvelous, the consequences too grave. By apprehending the grace of God's covenant in Christ, not only will you be better equipped to be a more faithful parent, but simultaneously you will be a more mature, fruit-bearing believer as well.

The key to Christian parenting, then, is a Christ-centered life. Jesus Christ and His gospel should so saturate Christians' lives and parenting that it transforms them and their children more and more into the very likeness of Christ. For the purposes of this essay, I will summarize what a Christ-centered life looks like through the lenses of divine truth, love, and beauty.[1]

Stating the Obvious, Obviously Needed

Every solid building needs a foundation. Building a godly, spiritual home requires the same. That foundation for the family is God's covenant, of which Christ is the chief cornerstone. It is essential to look to Christ in our parenting, not as a mantra that will supernaturally make us better parents and spectacularly spiritualize our children, but as a foundation and a starting place. In Christ is all the fullness of wisdom, righteousness, holiness and redemption (1 Cor. 1:30). From Him flow the riches of God's grace and the glory of our eternal inheritance (Eph. 1:7; 2:7). Therefore, the Christian, in order to be a vibrant, faithful disciple, needs to be steeped in Christ from beginning to end.

This may seem so obvious that it hardly needs to be said. Yet my experience as a pastor and as a Christian is that often the obvious things get neglected simply because they are so obvious. In fact, they become boring, and one thing we hate to be is bored. However, if we really understood and appreciated the beauty and glory of Christ we

---

[1] I fear that in laying out the above thesis, some readers may be tempted to tune out, having often heard preachers admonish, "Just look to Christ." I agree that this idea has become almost mantra-like, a panacea for every spiritual ill and want: "Whether over-eating or under-self-esteemed, weak in faith or strong in sin, just look to Christ and you will eventually improve." But what does it mean to "look to Christ"? I wonder sometimes whether those who so ardently proclaim it really know themselves. Nevertheless, the idea itself is both true and necessary. I hope to clarify in a practical way what it actually looks like in parenting.

could never be bored. Unfortunately, sinful hearts easily become distracted from that which truly strengthens to the things that merely excite. When we really need meat and potatoes, we often turn to desserts and candies. Within the innumerable details and responsibilities of nurturing a child, parents can easily lose sight of Christ and neglect the foundation on which their home was built.

What does this look like practically? For one thing, we have a tendency to turn minors into majors, thus minimizing the major things. Instead of *centering* on Christ, concentrating on His love, mercy, justice, and the weightier matters of the law, many believers focus on various peripheral issues. Truth be told, as finite creatures we have only so much room in our hearts for devotion, so much space in our heads for contemplation, and so much time in our lives for service. Therefore, we need to be careful as

> *We all intend to be Christ-centered, but often intention and fulfillment are disparate realities.*

to what will be at the core, the heart of our Christian life. If Christ is not the center of our spiritual being, we will inevitably become unbalanced, misshapen believers. If our hearts are full of Christ, our lives will flow forth the things of Christ: love, joy, peace, patience, kindness, goodness, faithfulness, gentleness, and self-control. Such things win the hearts of our children for the Lord.[2]

Another practical imbalance is when we make methodology more important than message. We all employ various methods in our parenting. There is, however, no divinely inspired method in the particulars of parenting. While the message of Christ should be clear and consistent, methods may vary from church to church, from family

---

[2] This is not to suggest that Christians should avoid or be disinterested in such issues as eschatology, predestination, politics, etc. It's not either/or. The Christian life must never be *either* Christ *or* name-that-issue, any more than either God is one or God is three. Instead, we must begin with Christ preeminent in all things and then, because of and in light of Christ, consider whatever issue is at hand. Another way of putting this is that we should consider all things spiritually in Christ, yet not over-spiritualize by making Christ of no effect in the many issues of life.

to family, and from culture to culture. This is not to say that some methods are not better than others, but when parents become more absorbed in method than in message, they have become dangerously imbalanced. When methods become sources of tension at the expense of the message, the result will be an unstable home built on something other than the solid foundation of Christ.

As Christians, we all *intend* to be Christ-centered. But often intention and fulfillment are disparate realities. Upon reflection we wonder, How did we ever end up where we did? With our children, we always intend to be diligent in nurture and discipline, but after years of parenting, many find themselves with irreverent, cantankerous, unbelieving children. What went wrong? Too many parents look back to their good intentions and absolve themselves of responsibility from the present mess.

Unfortunately, this is altogether too typical in the church today. Well-intentioned Christian parents must navigate through a maze of complicated and competing parenting ideas. As parents, we can ill afford to be ignorant and asleep at the wheel. Our vision must be fixed on Christ; our life fueled by God's promises; and our spirit regularly maintained by God's Word. Let us now consider what Christ-centered parenting looks like.

Christ-Centered Truth

The Centrality of the Gospel

How does the gospel affect your parenting? Can you articulate specific ways in which it shapes your daily parenting regimen? It is not enough that you go to church every Sunday (if you do) to hear the preacher preach the gospel (if he does), or to send your children to a Christian school (if you can afford one). Do not be fooled into thinking that just because your son or daughter is able to recite the children's catechism, memorize an entire chapter of Scripture, or take copious sermon notes, he or she has necessarily understood or accepted the gospel. As James says, the demons are able to do those things. While all of them are wonderful in the right setting (and not puffing up the religious pride of the parent), they are not of the essence of the gospel and it is the gospel that must fuel our parenting—and that we hope will ignite our children's hearts.

Sadly, many parents, in their effort to get their children to memorize the catechism or accomplish some other religious discipline, will actually hinder their gospel intentions. I have heard of parents who wake up their children early in the morning for "catechism drills" in which children are subjected to a barrage of semi-militaristic, in-your-face instruction. Of course, the excuse/reason for such strenuous measures is the desire to teach the children the things of the Lord. Indeed, much *is* taught, but what is taught actually damages the parent's spiritual goal. We might ask, what profit is it to gain the Westminster Shorter Catechism and lose your child's soul? Furthermore, while family devotions are an important and even essential part of covenant nurture, they are not an automatic mechanism for producing spiritual children. Done poorly and unspiritually, they will actually further harden the hearts of children who are struggling with the things of the Lord.

The gospel, first and foremost, is a message of grace; that's what makes it *good news*. In the gospel is revealed the love of God, His mercy and His divine goodness in giving us the gift of His Son, Jesus Christ. Furthermore, we see His powerful provision for our greatest need—the forgiveness of sins. The gospel is the most beautiful truth known to man. We do well to conform our lives and our parenting to its excellent attributes.

But the gospel is also a reality check. To appreciate the glorious grace of the gospel demands that we acknowledge the wretched sin for which the Son of God gave Himself as a sacrifice. Our children must understand their sinfulness and their separation from a holy God *apart from Christ*. This is not a particularly difficult task. Just as most nonbelievers agree they are imperfect (and most will even acknowledge they are sinners of some sort), covenant children have little difficulty grasping that they are woefully imperfect, needy, and prone to error.

Gospel-grounded parenting, however, goes further than impressing the children with *their* sinfulness; it also includes parents admitting their own sin and their need for Christ. A family cannot live in the close confines of the home without sin plainly revealed to every member. When we blow up in a fit of anger at our spouses or our children, when our children observe our failure to act with integrity in a given situation, or when we are lazy and irresponsible in our duties (all of which children have an amazing ability to discern), it is incumbent upon us as Christian parents to repent, seek forgiveness, and be restored in grace. We must lead the way in this even as we lead our children in all the various things of the Lord. Public sins require public repentance. Private sins require private repentance. If a sin is known by the children in the family, repentance should be made by the parent to the children. This requires humility, transparency, and grace before our children. Do we expect any less from them? Indeed, if anything, let us expect more from ourselves as "mature" Christians. Such basic gospel living speaks volumes to our children. Know for sure that they are watching and learning from everything we do, both good and bad.

The noble and most excellent truths of the Christian faith must be faithfully taught to our children. Faithful instruction requires much more than verbal or academic transferal of knowledge. It requires "lifestyle instruction" in which our children not only read and hear the truth, but see it lived out in those whom they naturally look up to as their teachers and models of that truth, namely their parents.

The Centrality of the Church

Christ-centered parenting also seeks to keep all God's truths in proper perspective. Our children must be taught to "seek first the kingdom of God and His righteousness" (Mt. 6:33). Just as Christ came to earth to preach the gospel of the kingdom, so also covenant nurture should hold up the kingdom of God as a priority for our children. Every institution made by man—including governments, schools, corporations, foundations, and organizations—will pass away. The only institution that will transcend the present worldly existence is the church of Jesus Christ, the kingdom of God.

Christ-centered parenting, therefore, must be kingdom-minded simply because Christ is the King of God's kingdom. In light of this, covenant nurture must train up children *in* the church and *for* the church. With the term *church* I am not speaking primarily about your congregation or another church down the road. I am speaking about the entire sum of all who sincerely believe in the Lord Jesus Christ as well as their children. We typically call this the *visible church*.[3] On this earth the church is sadly,

> *Covenant nurture must train up children in the church and for the church.*

though not surprisingly, beset by all sorts of troubles both of the world's making and our own. Yet despite all the problems we find in the church, God's Word is clear: it is precious and beloved, even compared to a beloved bride (Eph. 5). Therefore, to serve the church is to serve the Lord of the church. Conversely, to despise the church is to dishonor the Lord Jesus Christ.

In recent years there has been an unhealthy and unfortunate error in some sincere Christian homes, where households have so focused on themselves that they have nearly forsaken the local church. Much truth is being taught, but the encouragement and opportunity to exercise the outworking of the truth is truncated. At creation God declared the family the foundation of *earthly* society. But the spiritual family—the church—supercedes the earthly family. The spiritual bonds in the church transcend this world and reflect the next.

---

[3] This term, along with its counterpart *invisible church,* is a means of making a distinction between all those who profess faith and those who are genuinely saved. In reality, the term *visible church* is somewhat redundant since we can only know of sincere faith by what we can observe. Therefore, on this earth, a visible believer is a part of the church and the church is only visible.

Marriage, for all its preciousness and virtue in this world, has no place in heaven (Mt. 22:25 ff.). Jesus himself "denied" His earthly relations in order to demonstrate to His disciples the priority of His spiritual family (Mt. 12:48 ff.).

Simply put, despite the vast importance of the earthly family, Scripture nowhere speaks of the nuclear family in the same tender words as it does the eschatological family of God, the church. Instead, the earthly family is a means to an end, the means of nurture to grow covenant young people into spiritually mature adults, ready to serve the Lord. The place wherein that service must be centered is in the church. If we are not training our young people to serve Christ in the church, we not only dishonor the Bridegroom of the church, but we fail to give our children the divine purpose for their godly nurture. Spiritual maturity, godliness, and training in righteousness are not means of personal gain, much less of prideful congratulations for the parents. God's purpose is for the edification and equipping of the church. We are created for good works in Christ Jesus, blessed to be a blessing, for the furthering of the kingdom of God.

Sadly, we find ourselves today in a precarious situation in the church. There seem to be fewer and fewer churchmen, a lamentable want of spiritually qualified and mature men to lead the church of Christ. Many churches have resorted to ordaining women to office, others to ordaining less-than-qualified men who in their immaturity, either through naiveté or malice, damage the peace, purity, unity, and reputation of the church. As a result, many Christians have simply given up on the church altogether. The church is desperate for godly men, men of faith, virtue and spiritual zeal. This grave situation crosses all theological, denominational, and cultural boundaries—the church desperately needs more faithful servants, and especially men qualified to lead.

One of the things we are striving to do in our family is to purposely raise our children to be servants in the church, including preparing them for leadership when and if that time should come. While

God calls those whom He chooses to serve, He uses the means of the covenant to equip His people, for them to present themselves as ready to fill the offices of His church. For our daughters, we hope, pray and train them so that they may be used of the Lord to be highly profitable helpmeets for their future husbands in their service to Christ's church.

Kingdom-mindedness in covenant nurture also affects how we view other churches, denominations, and theological perspectives. It should not be our goal or practice to inculcate in our children a scornful attitude toward churches other than our own. Our vision should be one that includes the whole church and not just our own communion. Our children should be taught to love the bride of Christ and not simply our little finger of the entire body of Christ. Critical and discerning thinkers (which is what we should be training our children to be) will eventually see through the many holes of sectarianism and myopic arrogance. A spirit of sectarianism, which divides believers and fosters disunity among the brethren, must be rejected. Raising our children, either in our instruction or our example, to be spiritually or theologically arrogant is neither kingdom-minded nor edifying. As Paul wrote to the Philippians, "Let us be of one mind, maintaining the same love, united in spirit, intent on one purpose" (Phil. 2:2).

Christ-Centered Love

Gracious Discipline

One of the most regular and important areas of practical application in Christ-centered parenting is that of discipline. We all discipline our children; it comes with the territory as sure as sin to the human soul. Scripture reveals its necessity: "They who love their children discipline them diligently" (Prov. 13:24). In fact, an undisciplined son is an illegitimate son inasmuch as a true son will receive loving discipline (Heb. 12). So the question is not a matter of *if* but *how.* How should discipline be administered? While the manner of discipline can, and often should, vary with the diversities of any given situation and any given child, Christian discipline must in principle be grounded in the foundation of the gospel.

Discipline itself results from the breaking of a law, whether it is the law of the home, school, church, or society. We believe that our laws should be governed by God's law, His moral precepts. While law demands discipline, the gospel reveals the end of the law, not meaning that law no longer has value, but that it finds its completion in and points to the gospel. Only in the gospel does the law make full sense. Only through the gospel will the law of discipline bear spiritual fruit.

Every transgression of the law of God requires just punishment. All mankind stands guilty and deserving of eternal hell at the judgment of a holy God. Yet we know that all who are in Christ will not receive what they deserve, but will receive instead the free gift of salvation. Therefore, all who are in the covenant of grace are no longer objects of divine wrath but have entered into a new relationship with God, wherein as our heavenly Father He cares for us as His beloved children. This fatherly, covenantal relationship, embedded in the gospel, should transform the earthly discipline of our children. Our heavenly Father has already modeled for us how covenant discipline should look—holy, gracious, corrective, restorative, and bound by love.[4]

First, as *holy*, discipline seeks to train a child in the way that he *should* go, the way of righteousness and truth. Discipline must instill knowledge of God's commands and a reverent fear of His holiness. Sadly, however, I think Christian discipline often ends there. Children grow to well appreciate what's right and wrong, and they may

---

[4] Divine discipline is also sacrificial and atoning. While this should affect our discipline inasmuch as we are all recipients of that gracious atonement (Mt. 18:21 ff), I do not believe a principle of vicarious discipline is normative for earthly parenting. It is a unique divine prerogative. Attempted application of this divine prerogative can lead to some absurdities.

tremble at God's power and justice, but they never really come to love God nor rest in His tender mercies.

Second, in modeling the Father's discipline as *gracious* disciplinarians, parents do not need to "punish" every infraction. Indeed, our discipline does not look to the letter of the law, but is willing to pardon transgressions, even significant ones at times, in order to teach the greater law of Christ. But don't get nervous contemplating such grace, thinking, "Will my children sin all the more presuming that grace will abound?" Certainly not! Let us be clear: Gracious discipline does not disregard the law of God. Rather it honors it more fully inasmuch as it seeks to implement it in the fullness of Christ. Surely this is how God deals with us.

Third, having been called to holiness, gracious discipline seeks to be *corrective*, to bring about more godly conduct in our children. But are we (or our children) motivated by the law and punishment? Do we look to Sinai or the wooden spoon to derive our sanctification? Again, may it never be! True, we ought and do fear such things, but such fear does not produce the righteousness of God, that is, genuine sanctification. As young believers, our children must be disciplined to look to Christ, to see the beauty of the gospel, and to revel in God's grace. Corrective discipline points the child's eyes to Christ, which stimulates faith that apprehends God's promises and spiritual blessing. This is a lesson every Christian must learn and we will do well to instruct our children early in the spiritual means of personal growth in holiness.

Furthermore, gracious discipline is *restorative*, that is, it seeks to mend a heart and relationship broken by sin. Sin rends relationships. Every time your child disobeys, he breaks covenant with you as his covenant head, having dishonored your authority as a parent. You, as a gracious disciplinarian, are called to restore that broken relationship. Your instruction and discipline should lead towards restoring a child to full standing in grace and innocence. That means, of course, that a ready spirit of forgiveness must attend the whole discipline process and grant forgiveness at the appropriate time. There should not be a long, drawn-out process of anguished repentance and half-hearted forgiveness.[5] A child needs to know that, having repented of his sin, he has truly been forgiven and can move on with his conscience unburdened and free from guilt. This does not mean that temporal consequences need be removed. For instance, if a child disobediently plays ball in your neighbor's sand lot and breaks the neighbor's window in the process, it would be reasonable and even advisable to make him work for your neighbor

> *If you spank proficiently, instruct knowledgably, and provide diligently, and yet have not love, you have become a noisy gong and a clanging cymbal.*

(mowing the lawn, cleaning the house, and so on) for a wage until the window is paid for. The goal is full restoration in grace, for a broken relationship to be reconciled, and temporal justice to be served, if possible.

Finally, gracious discipline *abounds in love.* Love directs, covers, and grounds discipline. If you spank proficiently, instruct knowledgably, and provide diligently, and yet have not love, you have become a noisy gong and a clanging cymbal. If you are a leader in the church, a teacher of the Bible, and focus on your family, but have not love, you are worse than nothing. Indeed, you are a menace to the gospel and a stumbling block to your children. Love never fails and is the key to covenant parenting.

In our home formal discipline is an event. Informal discipline—the countless opportunities to set a good example, give a word of instruction, or reminder of some basic virtue—takes place throughout the day, but corporal discipline is set apart as a special event. These events may be infrequent,[6] but we try to make the most of

---

[5] Herein lies the danger of "grounding." While the taking away of privileges is certainly a reasonable means of discipline, extended grounding can prolong the pain of discipline and thus the separation between offender and offended.

[6] Though at other times they come in batches, in what Doug Wilson has termed "a reign of terror" that takes place for a few days to compensate for laxity on our part and significant bad behavior on our children's.

them when need and opportunity arise. Upon an infraction serious enough (and circumstances amenable) to warrant formal discipline, we will send our child to the bathroom where he will have to wait until I or my wife is ready to deal with him both emotionally (cooling off as necessary) as well as practically (we may be finishing the dishes or changing a diaper, etc.). During that time it is important that you think rationally about the genuine seriousness of the offense and the warranted measure of discipline. The child has an opportunity to think as well, both in remorse of the misdeed and in dread of the impending discipline.

When I arrive in the bathroom, I will typically sit down on the "throne of judgment" (that is, the toilet) and look seriously at the offending child. I begin by inquiring as to the child's understanding of their sin and build the case for the seriousness of the offense. Having established guilt (in *the child's* mind—you should already have established it in your mind prior to sitting on the judgment seat), you render judgment, which *may* include a specific amount of swats from the spanking spoon. By this time the child should be given the opportunity to repent and say he is sorry for the disobedience.[7] At this point I express my sincere forgiveness and my love which has not in the least been diminished by the transgression. Once the child has

---

[7] A few notes on spanking are appropriate here. First, at certain times you may feel it more profitable to withhold the rod for some reason, but the expectation of the child upon being sent to the "room of judgment" should be that a spanking is forthcoming.

Second, be very careful that discipline does not become physical abuse. When discipline becomes more about you and your anger than about your child and his or her relationship with Christ, it has become abusive. Physical abuse is intolerable and will do great, and often irreparable, emotional damage to a child. The controlled demeanor of good discipline will avoid abusive tendencies; nevertheless, I would not recommend ever giving more than five swats for the worst of disobedience. Typically, we administer two or three.

Finally, most young children will readily express their repentance. Nevertheless, some will fight strenuously to keep from getting spanked. The slower, more methodical method I am suggesting (versus the "eruption" sort) will help in this, but with some children, only a consistent pattern of proper discipline over many occasions will achieve what I have described. "Taking" a spanking is part of a child's acknowledging his or her offense. If they refuse to take their spanking, then there can be no substantive reconciliation.

calmed down emotionally and is ready to listen I may take a few minutes to give some spiritual instruction specifically dealing with the current offense in order to exhort and guide the child to greater obedience in the future. This also is usually a good time to reiterate the gospel, to impress upon the child once again the grace of God's forgiveness and His endless mercy to him as well as myself. Finally, I often like to end in prayer and a confirmatory hug for good measure. The whole event may take five minutes to half an hour. It is time well invested and by the grace of God will return an abundance of spiritual dividends.[8]

Shepherding the Hearts of Our Children

A few years ago, Ted Tripp wrote a significant book on Christian parenting called *Shepherding a Child's Heart*. The book has been a Christian bestseller and has spawned various related volumes. The premise is so simple: We seek to *nurture* the hearts of our children, not merely to achieve certain behaviors. The wonder is that this needed to be highlighted at all. Yet experience reveals that such an emphasis on the heart does regularly need to be pronounced. As sinful humans, in our fleshly weakness we tend towards that which is easier and more comfortable to the flesh. In parenting, this means that while we all desire our children to turn out "good," on account of our weakness and the rigors of parenting we cut corners to achieve merely *good behavior*. Therefore, instead of disciplining and training children to be repentant, we are satisfied with an apology; instead of

---

[8] Keep in mind that I am presenting an ideal here. Obviously we are not always able to have such an orderly session of discipline (would that we could!). Oftentimes circumstances and time constraints inhibit such discipline. We should, however, have a plan and strive to incorporate that plan in our regular discipline of our children.

I do not recommend spanking older children. By the time children are ten to thirteen years of age, alternative means of discipline should predominantly be used—taking away of privileges, public restitution, and church discipline being primary examples. If adolescent children choose to rebel, there is not much a parent can do but take the child before the church or civil magistrate. This is a plea to parents to discipline their children early so that they can enjoy them in years to come.

helping them discern how to choose their friends, we just tell them they can't watch sitcoms like *Friends*.

The popularity of *Shepherding a Child's Heart* suggests the prevalence of parents *training a child's behavior*. Children are expected to submit and obey, and in most Christian homes they do for the most part—at least while in the home (out of fear, shame, positive peer pressure, or simply in biding their time till an expected "release"). But as soon as they leave the home, the true hearts of the children quickly become evident in worldly living. Not that there weren't some obvious clues of such rebellion while the child was in the home. A heart-sensitive observer would have been deeply concerned about the passive rebellion, the sullen and surly attitude, and the general disconnectedness of the child. But if he or she is outwardly "in line"—going to church, attending youth group, not doing anything too terrible—then things must be okay. Or so thinks the naïve, overly busy, or willfully ignorant parent. Such careless parenting often leads to disaster.

It's not enough that our children don't curse, get drunk, or engage in premarital sex. Parenting behavior may well squelch such obvious sin, but if the discipline of the heart has been neglected, such sin will still remain, though hidden, and will in all likelihood manifest itself when the child experiences the liberty to do as he or she pleases. The duty of Christian parents is to train their children to desire to please God in holy obedience. As adults, our primary constraint is our conscience before God. That is also what must constrain a child's behavior, and that requires training the heart, not merely behavior. Parenting for good behavior flirts dangerously with the heart of phariseeism. To salve the religious conscience with good behavior only puffs up our religious pride with outward conformity to a law of flesh. Such an outcome was intolerable for Jesus and should be for us as well.

Christ-centered parenting seeks to impress *the Savior* upon the hearts of the children. Our children need the gospel according to Jesus Christ. From the heart of gospel grace grows the fruit of the spirit as well as the streams of eternal life. Nothing else and nothing less should be the purpose and goal of Christian parenting.

Of course, some may excuse themselves by saying, "Only God can change the heart." While true enough by itself, this needs to be qualified in two important ways. First, the heart of a covenant child does not need to be "changed" in the same way as does that of an unbeliever. One who exists outside of Christ and the covenant needs a radical heart transplant. The covenant child, on the other hand, has been shown God's grace and favor as a member of the covenant from birth, even as evidenced in his baptism.[12] There is no necessity of a radical conversion experience for a covenant child. Indeed, the ideal "conversion" of a covenant child is the process of growing in the nurture and admonition of the Lord.

Second, while we fully recognize that God alone can work spiritual grace upon a sinner's heart, God's Word reveals that He has ordained means to that end. For covenant children, the primary means is *nurture*—the training of the heart of a child in the grace of God so that he will be inclined to conduct his life in a godly manner for God's glory. Just as God has seen fit to use the

> *God has ordained covenant nurture as the means of training the hearts of the little ones to become mature believers.*

preaching of the gospel as the ordained means of saving the lost (Rom. 10:14), He likewise has ordained covenant nurture as the means of training the hearts of the little ones to become mature believers. Such spiritually instrumental nurture is grounded in truth, infused with love, and surrounded by beauty.

---

[12] This, of course, assumes the affirmation of infant baptism. For those of you not in agreement with this view of baptism, consider the alternative—that our children are unholy and need to be converted like the heathen. If so, it is not covenant nurture they need, but radical revival of their souls through evangelism. If infant baptism is wrong, with all that it signifies, this entire volume of essays makes no sense.

Christ-Centered Beauty

We have in this essay already covered the importance of God's truth and love in Christ-centered parenting. But there is yet another highly important aspect to Christ-centered parenting that can easily be overlooked—more so than truth and love, it seems—namely that of beauty. Whereas most Christians tend to quickly appreciate the necessity of truth and the importance of love, the subject of beauty can seem too subjective, ephemeral, or mysterious to grasp. Thus it tends to be neglected, for what we cannot understand we tend not to appreciate.

Beauty is essential to the Christian life. The psalmist declares, "One thing I ask of the LORD, this is what I seek: that I may dwell in the house of the LORD all the days of my life, to gaze upon the *beauty* of the LORD and to seek Him in His temple" (Ps. 27:4). In Psalm 96 we are exhorted to "tell of God's glory among the nations, His wonderful deeds among all the peoples. . . . Splendor and majesty are before Him, strength and *beauty* are in His sanctuary" (vv. 3, 6). Jesus Himself begins His famous Sermon on the Mount with declarations of *beatitude*—that is, things that are blessed, good, and beautiful.

God is the source of all beauty and all blessing. The more we know about the divine and the more we allow ourselves to be consumed by it, the better we appreciate and reflect His divine beauty. Divine beauty is most fully revealed in Jesus Christ, the Son of God. If we truly abide in Christ, we can see what His glorious beauty looks like and are accordingly called to reflect it. A life of spiritual beauty displays a divine aesthetic. It is not an epicurean love of pleasure or a bohemian rhapsody of humanistic virtues.[13] True beauty is grounded

---

[13] The recent film *Moulin Rouge* captivated audiences with the humanistic and materialistic philosophy of bohemianism—the exaltation of truth, beauty, freedom and above all, love. While such ideas are indeed noble, unfortunately for the secular mind they are grounded in nothing more than human inspiration, which ultimately leads to chaos and degradation (which ironically is truly ugly). Such noble things can be properly understood and fruitfully applied only within a divine context. Otherwise, you end up precisely where bohemianism went: the corruption of French society and government, the

in transcendent truth and supernatural glory. It is our privilege and duty to reflect that beauty in our own lives.

Harvard professor Elaine Scarry, in her short book *On Beauty and Being Just*,[14] outlines four ways in which beautification influences social justice. I believe they are applicable to life in general and parenting in particular. First, beauty displaces the observer from the center of things, even from the center of his own existence. It places God at the center, who maintains much better equilibrium than the human self ever could. Such displacement of self-centeredness, making way as it does for divine goodness and truth, redirects our focus from ourselves to God and then to others (such as our children, for instance) whom we are called to serve. Christ himself exemplified such beauty in His life, for "although He existed in the form of God, He did not consider equality with God something to be grasped, but He emptied Himself, taking on the form of a bond-servant and being made in the likeness of men" (Phil. 2:6–7).

Second, beauty inspires and tends to propagate more beauty: we remember a beautiful sunset so we paint it; we want to recollect the image of a beautiful moment, so we photograph it, frame it, and put it on our wall; we are so moved by an event or words that we write it down as a story or poem to be read and reread for ages. Beauty furthermore makes us want to share such good things with others, particularly those we love, which in turn affects them with the enjoyment of beauty as well. Again, the Savior has given His example to us. Jesus, in His high priestly prayer (Jn. 17), prays "that they may all be one; even as You, Father, are in Me and I in You, that they also may be in Us. . . . The glory which You have given Me I have given to them, that they may be one, just as We are one; I in them and You in Me. . . . *Father, I desire that they also, whom You have given Me, be with Me where I am, so that they may see My glory which You have given Me, for*

---

excess of the sexual revolution, and the nihilism of postmodernism. (I think one can argue that the bohemian "values" of France, wherein they most significantly took root, played a dramatic role in France's decay from being a proud nation of Napoleonic sophistication and warrior-spirit to Vichy-like corruption and effeminate spirit.)

[14] Princeton, N. J.: Princeton Univ. Press, 1999.

You loved Me before the foundation of the world" (vv. 21–24). Here we see Christ praying to the Father that He might share with His people the glorious fellowship He enjoys with God the Father.

Third, beauty awakens us to pay attention to things and people we might otherwise ignore. If you have seen the wonder of a child's eyes as he investigates the constant motion of an open anthill, or carefully examined with all your senses the glory of a fragrant red rose, or marveled at the incredible musical intricacy of an orchestral masterpiece, then you can understand the beauty of details. Life goes by so quickly; beauty compels us to pay attention to, and enjoy, things we might otherwise miss. This intensifies our delight, broadens our enjoyment, and enlightens our perspective, all of which makes life that much more profitable.

Finally, Scarry writes that beauty demonstrates symmetry, fitness, balance, and proportion, all of which leads to harmony, peace, and rest. Beauty tends to keep our feet on the ground without allowing them to get stuck in the mud. The fullness of beauty exists in heaven; living a life of beauty appropriates heavenly qualities and applies them to life on earth.

How important is appreciating beauty for parenting? As sinful creatures, the reminder and exhortation to keep Christ front and center in every aspect of our lives is a daily necessity. Sin ever impedes and corrupts the beauty of our Christian existence. Sin destroys, stains, sullies, and pollutes, leaving behind ugly scars. The glory of the gospel is that God sent His Son to save sinners and cleanse them of their spiritual pollution. In terms of parenting, it is altogether too easy to get lost in the details of discipline, diapers, finances, household chores, and innumerable other necessary things. Such concerns can sap all the energy and spirit from a parent, draining any interest in (or time for) aesthetics. Parenting becomes more about survival and sanity than truth, love, or beauty.

Philippians 4:8 redirects us to the proper perspective: "Finally, brethren, whatever is true, whatever is honorable, whatever is right, whatever is pure, whatever is lovely, whatever is of good repute, if there is any excellence, and if anything worthy of praise, dwell on these things." A mind set on these things makes a world of difference in our daily lives and in our witness to others. Conversely, a great hindrance to the promotion of the gospel is the constant ugliness of Christian misbehavior as well as the seeming lack of interest in a life of true beauty. Sometimes we are our own worst enemies. Yet it doesn't take a rocket scientist to know that ugliness repels and beauty attracts. As John Stackhouse writes in *Christianity Today,* "If we neglect beauty in our homes, in our churches, and in the education of our children, we will be cultivating, and propagating, a deficient religion: the heresy of an unbeautiful Christianity. To preach and to live the whole counsel of God, including the beautiful—this is the best apologetic we can offer."[15]

> *A great hindrance to the gospel is the constant ugliness of Christian misbehavior and seeming disinterest in appreciating a life of true beauty.*

This is especially true in regard to our witness to our own children. If an ugly witness to the world, which sees us on occasion, can negatively impact interest in spiritual things, how much more terrible an impact must an ugly witness make upon our children, who see us every day! I fear this has become the stumbling block for countless rebellious and spiritually apathetic covenant children. Instruction, instead of being a positive means of education, becomes tiresome lectures. Discipline, instead of being a loving tool for training in righteousness, becomes an abusive tool of personal wrath. Religion becomes a tiresome laundry list of rules, prohibitions and constraints upon fun, joy, and personal authenticity. Is it any wonder that so many young people leave the faith on account of such a witness?

---

[15] "The True, the Good, and the Beautiful Christian," *Christianity Today,* January 7, 2002 (http://www.christianitytoday.com/ct/2002/001/4.58.html). One thing worth mentioning is that we should thank God that in His grace He continues to grow His church despite our unattractive—at times hideous—witness.

Our children must see Christ for who He truly is, the author of all that is good, lovely, and perfect. If they do not, they will not desire Christ rightly. If our lives and our parenting are not representative of genuine divine beauty, we make the faith we desire to teach into a lie, and a grievous one at that. As parents we powerfully model Christ to our children. God has given us that responsibility and authority. We must exercise great care and diligence in carrying out this duty.

One specific application of beautiful Christian parenting is to teach our children to live *for* Christ. Too many Christian parents fall into the fleshly trap of teaching their children to be *against* things rather than to be *for* Christ. Christian education and nurture begin with constructive instruction in Christ-centered faith and practice, in seeking first the kingdom of God and His righteousness. What we are *for* will guide what we must stand *against*. A false priority of being against certain evils will in the end be personally unfruitful and unsatisfying, and produce a spirit of hatred, spite, malice, and bitterness. Christ's own example speaks volumes. His response to His disciples who asked permission to rain down fire to destroy a village that would not receive them was to rebuke the disciples' harsh attitude of condemnation and to tell them, "The Son of Man did not come to destroy men's lives but to save" (Lk. 9:56). Jesus had all the reason in the world (much more than any of us) to rail against all the problems in this world. Instead, He set the blessed example of living for the glory of God. We, like Christ, should celebrate the good inasmuch as it is truly good, even if not perfect. Therefore, we can rejoice in the good accomplished by both Martin Luther and Martin Luther King Jr.; we can sincerely enjoy and glorify God for the sacred compositions of Bach and the secular music of Mozart; we can marvel at the accomplishments of both Michelangelo and Michael Jordan. This is not to suggest that we don't exercise proper judgment

> *Our children must see Christ for who He truly is, the author of all that is good, lovely, and perfect.*

in discerning the bad and the pagan elements that may exist therein, but it does not allow the bad to diminish the genuine beauty and excellence of anything.

Keep in mind that on this earth nothing is truly perfect. We seek divine beauty within the limitations of our present existence. To deny beauty its rightful place of significance, however, would be to cheat ourselves and our families of great blessing and joy. A man who does not desire or appreciate God's beauty is not truly living, even though he is alive. To be so consumed by the vain and fleeting demands of this passing life that no time or thought is given over to contemplating and living out that which is true, noble, pure, and beautiful, is more than a shame; it is a tragic waste.

In this life, true love can only be known amid the constant threat of loneliness and eventual loss. True peace is comprehended only by faith. Beauty is apprehended alongside much chaos. Yet such things make life more than livable; they make life enjoyable. It also makes parents more capable and parenting more profitable, as well as children more agreeable to the message of the gospel.

Conclusion

Our goal in covenant parenting should be to train up our children to the fullness of the sons of God, to lead them in paths of righteousness and eternal blessing. Who is capable of such things? You are! As Christian parents, you have been given the riches of wisdom and knowledge and blessing in Christ Jesus. To you have been given the promises of the covenant, the means of grace in the church, the Scriptures of the Old and New Testaments, and the leading of the Holy Spirit in you and in your children. God has granted to you and your family all that you need for life and for salvation.

How shall we respond to such grace? With faith in our hearts, leading to obedience with our hands in the work of covenant nurture. Let us trust fervently and work diligently towards this godly end. At the end of the day and on the Day of Judgment will we take credit for the godly outcomes of our children? Assuredly not, any more than we would expect glory for the promises and grace of the covenant.

If God builds you a house, gives you the keys, and then supplies you with strength, wisdom, and material to keep that house well maintained and clean for the next however many years, so that at the end of those years, having gained a bountiful appreciation in equity, shall you then boast, "What a great house I have built. It's to my credit that this home is so beautiful and worth so much today"? Of course not. Instead, you will say, "Thank the Lord for His gracious provision and blessing and for the grace to be a good steward of this home." Still, we would all understand and agree that you were responsible for its upkeep and would be accountable if it had become rundown in spite of God's gracious provision.

The same is true for covenant nurture. God will receive all the glory in saving our children. In reality He has done all the work; we merely follow His lead and steward His prized possessions. We cannot force a child to love Jesus, but we *can* nurture and stimulate that love. Our children have the immeasurable privilege and advantage of being members of God's covenant. They belong to Jesus. We simply need to nurture them by continually and ever more clearly showing them Christ. By presenting Christ to them according to His truth, beauty and love, we are showing them Jesus as He is, the glorious Son of God, Savior of the universe, Lord of the covenant, one with the Father and Spirit, who together are alone worthy of all trust, worship and obedience.

The Church's Ministry of Nurture to Children, Youth, and their Families

G. Mark Sumpter

Church historian George Marsden rightly observed in 1984,

> Evangelical successes have been mixed blessings. During the past decades the gospel has been advanced, many persons have been brought into the Kingdom, and vast numbers of institutions have funneled American abundance into diverse channels of evangelism, education and social service. Yet success has taken its toll.[1]

One costly success is evangelicalism's world of ministry to children, youth, and families. We have been "successful" at Vacation Bible School, catechism clubs for kids, Sunday School, youth groups, youth evangelism, and university ministry. Particularly with children and youth, our success has been the orchestration of programs of evangelical noise and numbers (appealing, attendance-building events) and Reformed needlepoint (catechetical training). This "success" has allowed young people to grow up in a youth ministry program of nurture and teaching, but sadly this is done with an emphasis that isolates the younger age groups from the rest of the community of the congregation. Therefore, we have seen a growing absence of young adults in the local church when they arrive at their early and mid-twenties. We lose our youth in their young adult years because the

[1] *Evangelicalism and Modern America* (Grand Rapids: Eerdmans, 1984), vii.

church never had them. John H. Westerhoff did his part to sound the alarm in his *Will Our Children Have Faith?*[2] More recently, authors such as George Barna, Mark DeVries, Kevin Huggins, Susan Hunt, and Merton Strommen have addressed the issue.[3]

The story of evangelicalism and her modern methods of ministering to children and youth—her attempts at covenant succession—may be retold as a version of *Cinderella*. Cinderella, the evangelical church, fell head over heels for the prince, the parachurch ministries and their program models (in this parable, Mr. Wrong). While attending the grand ball, she gave her hand to the prince, danced well into the evening, scurried home before the stroke of midnight, and lost one of her glass slippers—the

> *We have seen a growing absence of young adults in the local church when they arrive at their twenties.*

ministry of reaching and teaching the church's young. We know how the original tale ends, but the storybook ending of this parable regarding the church and her stewardship of the nurture and care of her children and youth has yet to be written.

---

[2] John H. Westerhoff III, *Will Our Children Have Faith?* (New York: Seabury-Crossroad, 1976). In this publication, Westerhoff sought to enter into the fray of discussion among Christian educators of the 1960s within the mainline liberal Protestant tradition. *Life* magazine in 1957 had made its own judgment on one of Protestantism's sacred cows—the Sunday school. Such classes were seen as so ineffective in transmitting the faith that the time spent there was said to be the most wasted hour of the week. Widespread admission about this stirred concerns about the mission and ministry of Christian nurture and education. Westerhoff expressed concern that certain aspects of the classroom paradigm for nurture was contributing negatively to the transfer of the faith: "My contention is that the context or place of religious education needs to be changed from an emphasis on schooling to a community of faith. No longer is it helpful or wise to emphasize schools, teachers, pupils, curricula, classrooms, equipment, and supplies. Instead we need to focus our attention on the radical nature and character of the church as a faith community" (51).

[3] These authors address the vanishing young adult population in local churches: George Barna, *Generation Next* (Ventura: Regal Books, 1995); Mark DeVries, *Family-Based Youth Ministry* (Downers Grove: InterVarsity Press, 1994); Kevin Huggins and Phil Landrum, *Guiding Your Teen to a Faith That Lasts* (Grand Rapids: Discovery House, 1994); Susan Hunt, *Heirs of the Covenant* (Wheaton: Crossway Books, 1998); and Merton P. Strommen

The goals of this chapter are to examine, first, what the Bible teaches about a coventantal approach to the nurture of our children and youth, and second, what covenant succession looks like when expressed through the church as the metaphorical family of God. Putting into practice the biblical notion of being a covenant community, the people of God as an extended family is to carry out Scripture's charge to the church and the covenant home to nurture the next generation. This practice will serve as a fruitful means of conveying the faith and life of the covenant walk with God.

Historical Influences on the Church and Her Nurture of Children and Youth

Let's consider two items for historical perspective. We will see how both the parachurch movement and the societal changes wrought by the Industrial Revolution influenced the church regarding the care of her young covenant members.

The parachurch movement had its origins in the early nineteenth century. Voluntary societies became a near-substitute for the church. This happened due to an entrepreneurial spirit found in society and in the thinking of Christians. In terms of church ministry, some referred to the "Protestant form of association" which conveyed a decentralization of the work of congregational ministry, a lack of denominational administrative constraints, and openness about both sexes and all ages volunteering to take up Christ's cause. In short, this spirit of voluntarism confirmed the growing understanding that the

---

and Richard A. Hardel, *Passing on the Faith* (Winona: St. Mary's Press, 2002). I acknowledge that several mainline denominations are compromised by impurity in doctrine and life, but nevertheless their situation signals alarm for all professing Christian churches. Tom Gillespie, president of Princeton Seminary, tells the story of the disappearance of young adults from the Presbyterian Church (USA) in these words: "The truth of the matter is that the chief cause of our membership decline is our inability over the past quarter of a century to translate our faith to our children. Put simply, we are unable to keep our children in the church when they become adults" (qtd. in Mark DeVries, *Family-Based Youth Ministry*, 25).

church is akin to a voluntary society. This voluntary society mentality paved the way for the contemporary view of the church and her
ministry to Christ's lambs.

Bruce Shelly cites the example of Herbert J. Taylor. When Taylor
discovered that a whole generation of children was being spiritually
overlooked in Chicago during the 1930s, he determined to help pioneer and finance multiple nondenominational organizations to reach
young people who rarely, if ever, attend worship services and Sunday school. Shelly summarizes the results of Taylor's effort: "These
'non-denominational organizations' turned out to be the Inter-Var-
sity Christian Fellowship, Young Life Campaign, Youth For Christ,
Christian Service Brigade, Pioneer Girls, and Child Evangelism Fellowship—parachurch evangelistic organizations that can be considered the evangelical heirs of revivalism."[4] Shelly's analysis is telling:

> Taylor's line of thinking is significant. Though a Methodist layman,
> he did not turn to his church. He looked instead to new interde-
> nominational agencies. . . . Today, parachurch organizations have
> changed the face of American Protestantism. Many recent observ-
> ers have noted a shift in religious loyalties from traditional denomi-
> nations to the parachurch movements.[5]

The glass slipper of the care and nurture of the church's young is
in the hands of the prince. A blend of passion for ministry and deep
pockets opened the door for people like Taylor to set the American
scene aflame with parachurch fervor. As a consequence, the local
church was seen by many as the runt of a growing litter dominated
by parachurch agencies and movement ministries.

In carrying out our duties of nurturing children after the prolif-
eration of the youth ministry movements of 1880–1950,[6] we have

---

[4] "The Rise of Evangelical Youth Movements," *Fides et Historia* 18 (1986): 47.

[5] Ibid., 47.

[6] The reader may follow the chronological narrative of these movements through this
historical period in Mark Senter, *The Coming Revolution in Youth Ministry and Its Radical
Impact on the Church* (Wheaton, Ill.: Victor Books, 1992).

done so, chiefly, through the traditional instrument of the church youth group. The Reformed are on par with their evangelical brothers in adopting the model of the parachurch and importing it into the local church—our Reformed fathers of two or three generations back adopted their own brand of the parachurch ministry for youth.

> *The local church was seen by many as the runt of a growing litter dominated by parachurch agencies and movement ministries.*

Whether we call it the Walther League or the Luther League for Lutherans, the Young People's Society within the Dutch tradition of the Christian Reformed Church (fueled with ideas from an agency called the Young Calvinist Federation until its recent retirement) or the one-time Machen League of the Orthodox Presbyterian Church, the imprint of the parachurch model can be found in most local Reformed congregations today.[7]

With the practice of the youth group bequeathed to us, slowly, over the past two or three decades, there has been an increase of interest on the part of families from conservative, Bible-believing churches to reevaluate the role of the traditional youth group model of ministry. The result of this reevaluation in some covenant households and churches has strengthened their resolve to retain it; other households and congregations have become leery about the place and practice of it.

The families that embrace the traditional ministries of focus-group nurture like Pioneer Clubs, Youth for Christ, or Young Life measure the success of a church's ministry by how well their home church emulates these kinds of programs. Conversely, there are families that have come to hold that "[c]hildren who are cordoned off into 'age-based herds' develop peer dependency, which makes a child give greater weight to the values of his friends than to those of his

---

[7]See ibid., 98–104 for the background on specific denominational movements within the Reformed persuasion.

parents."[8] Families are solidifying their viewpoints, and the controversy has brought the concept of the youth group and its practices to the attention of church leadership. In the wake of the parachurch mentality, households and churches have been left in a growing quandary, or worse, a rift. The role of the church and her practices and the role of the covenant family and its practices are at loggerheads. Both the church and the covenant family need instruction about this, which we'll pursue below.

The changes wrought by the Industrial Revolution, when combined with the rise of the parachurch and other changes in society and church, contributed to the negative effect. Prior to the Industrial Revolution, most fathers worked at or close to home, often with other members of the family, a situation that invited good leadership in worship as well as work. The head of the household was the leader and pace-setter for the family. Under his leadership, the family functioned as both a little church and a little commonwealth. The father facilitated the growth of his family by taking to heart the responsibilities to "observe God's rule in church, state and home. The father was the instructor. In this, he represented church and state. But more than these, he represented a direct relation to God, mediated by scripture."[9] But all of this soon changed:

> While Christians could sometimes ignore or minimize new intellectual challenges to their traditional beliefs, they found it extremely difficult to neglect the immense social changes that industrialism produced—burgeoning cities, with their poverty, dilapidated housing, drunkenness, prostitution, and crime; massive immigration; and decreased agricultural opportunities that threatened long-established patterns and expectations.[10]

---

[8] Michael Ferris, *The Future of Home Schooling* (Washington, D.C.: Regnery, 1997), 85.

[9] Don S. Browning, et. al, *From Culture Wars to Common Ground: Religion and the American Family Debate* (Louisville: John Knox, 1997), 76–77.

[10] Gary Scott Smith, *The Seeds of Secularization: Calvinism, Culture, and Pluralism in America, 1870–1915* (Grand Rapids: Eerdmans, 1985), 126–127.

Weldon Hardenbrook gives a perspective on what this meant: "This dramatic transition literally jolted the role of men in America. Once farmers and the children of farmers, these men exchanged work around their homes and families for new occupations in factories. And in most cases, this new situation required men to leave their homes for long periods of time."[11]

We can see it coming: the father's isolated employment set up a barrier that proved effective in many cases, even if it was not necessarily insurmountable. His leadership as head of the home became focused on the shop, office, or field. His calling and work of tending to his little church and his little commonwealth shifted out into the mainstream world, away from his family. His former personal responsibilities were often left undone or handed over to social institutions. The result is a fragmentation of the family and specialized ministries for the members of the church. Both institutions have suffered from the loss of multi-generational connectional influence within their respective spheres for covenantal nurture. Obviously I do not want to shift the blame from individual men to social conditions, but we cannot ignore the power of those conditions and the unique temptations they bring. So, even at the risk of oversimplifying things, some comment on the results of industrialization is in order.

For the household, on one hand, there is the Christian man who gives up too easily as he swims upstream against a family-*unfriendly* way of life in North America. In this giving up, he abdicates his charge to oversee and direct the nurture of his children. This man has the inclination to turn to the professional specialists of the church who stand in his place regarding household training. This man's view of the *family* is weak.

On the other hand, there are men who are self-conscious about the biblical mandate regarding household nurture. These men, in the

[11] Weldon Hardenbrook, *Missing From Action: Vanishing Manhood in America* (Nashville: Thomas Nelson, 1987), 11; qtd. in Steve Farrar, *Point Man* (Portland: Multnomah, 1990), 40.

name of a zealous mission to maintain control of their family, have the tendency toward their own kind of isolationism. In a spirit of watchfulness, they can overly isolate their children from both the younger and older generations of the church. This man's view of the *local church* is weak.

The influence of industrialism creates equally important concerns for the church. First, as we said earlier, the local church that excessively isolates her age groups from one another will orphan her children from Mother Kirk.[12] The congregation that practices the traditional model of specialization and isolation, interestingly, is untrained in the biblical image of the local church *as family.* In contrast to this situation, some local churches are keenly aware of the message and practice of the secular world, which is seeking to squeeze the church into its mold of segregating the ages from one another—something often borrowed from educational institutions. Such congregations are moving at warp speed nowadays to showcase a special vigilance about this kind of worldly influence. The families of a congregation like this guard against segregation by answering with a strong—maybe near-exclusive—orientation toward an intergenerational approach to ministry. That is, all the ministries of the church, at all times, must include every generation. This local church, we can rightly say, has a weak view of the local church *as church.*

In summary, the adoption of the parachurch model for the local church, and industrialization and its influence on the covenant home and church, have set the stage for undermining the covenantal model of nurture for children and young people. It is this foundational doctrine of the covenant that enables us to build most solidly a practice of nurture for our children and youth that rightly affects, in a mutually beneficial way, our ministries in the home and church. So it is to the theology of the covenant that we now turn.

---

[12] See Mark DeVries, *The Coming Revolution,* 41–42, 116–118.

Recovering a Biblical Grid for a Covenantal Approach to Covenant Succession

In their book *Reaching a Generation for Christ,* Mark Senter and Richard Dunn challenge the reader with the idea that in order to get pastoral work among teens biblically re-aligned with God's purposes, "youth ministry will need to think more about itself from an ecclesiological perspective—understanding itself within the doctrine of the church. . . . [It] should not be handled as a spiritual parenthesis but as a continuity with biological and faith families."[13] Senter and Dunn are very much on to something. They have at least driven us into the parking lot of the right doctrinal theater: the covenant and the church.

We can rightly say that "to miss the covenant is to miss Scripture."[14] In this portion of the essay I will develop the doctrine of the covenant with an eye specifically toward ministry. First, we confess that the Covenant of Grace

> was differently administered in the time of the law, and in the time of the gospel: under law, it was administered by promises, prophecies, sacrifices, circumcision, the paschal lamb, and other types and ordinances delivered to the people of the Jews, all foresignifying Christ to come; which were, for that time, sufficient and efficacious, through the operation of the Spirit, to instruct and build up the elect in faith in the promised Messiah, by whom they had full remission of sins, and eternal salvation; and is called the Old Testament. (Westminster Confession of Faith, 7.5)

> Under the gospel, when Christ, the substance, was exhibited, the ordinances in which this covenant is dispensed are the preaching of the Word, and the administration of the sacraments of Baptism and

---

[13] Richard Dunn and Mark Senter, eds., *Reaching a Generation for Christ* (Chicago: Moody, 1996), 673–74.

[14] Douglas M. Jones III, "The Beauty of It All" in *Back to Basics,* ed. David Hagopian (Phillipsburg: Presbyterian and Reformed, 1996), 68.

the Lord's Supper. . . . There are not two covenants of grace, differing in substance, but one and the same, under various dispensations. (WCF 7.6)

From Genesis to Revelation, the Bible is a single, unified message of the Father's sovereign plan of redemption, of the Lord Jesus Christ and His work of redemption, and of the giving of the Holy Spirit for applying that work to us (Lk. 24:13–45).

Theologians commonly wed the concepts of the covenant and the church. In the plan of salvation, Jesus Christ, the Covenant-Keeper, brought the triumph of His grace for all those whom the Father had given Him. The invisible church, made up of all the redeemed from every age, trusts in her Head, Jesus Christ. This invisible church is manifest in history, in the world; she is visible as men and women, boys and girls. Multiple images are used in the Scriptures to show what this visible church is like. One prevalent image is that of "the household of God," which is well-suited to inform the church's ministry to children, youth, and families.

Vitally important to a discussion of this image and its meaning is the Old Testament figure Abraham, for he is highlighted as the *father* of the faithful. Various lessons on the Abrahamic covenant could be underscored at this point (e.g., the centrality of the Word, the conditionality of the covenant, Abraham's cleansing by the sign and seal of circumcision as the family-head of the faithful line, and so on). We narrow our focus to certain aspects of the family image of the church as it is featured with Abraham and his seed.

(1) The three parties that are the recipients of God's blessing in the covenant are the believer, Abraham; the seed of the believer, his children; and those who make up the multitude of the families of the earth, those distinct from Abraham's household, the "foreign" Gentile nations (Gen. 17:4–5, 7, 9, 27). The sign of circumcision is the means of inclusion in this corporate, familial relationship within the covenant. Circumcision of the male reproductive organ reminds the people that they are born in sin and no one is saved by the work of

human generation; man needs regeneration (Gen. 17:10–11, 13). *Covenantal Lesson: God's grace to the believing older generations of the church calls for faith and anticipation regarding God's work in the younger generations who are set apart for Him, to be in relationship with Him.*

(2) God called Abraham to separate himself from the earthly family of man. That family has its own worldview and discipling influence of idolatrous worship and pagan living (see Gen. 12:1; Josh. 24:2–3). In terms of covenant nurture, Abraham is to "command his children and his household after him, that they may keep the way of the LORD," for it is his instruction that will be the instrumental means for bringing to pass what the Lord had promised to him (Gen. 18:19). Notice that this covenant nurture is carried out with the world of Sodom in the background (Gen. 19). *Covenantal Lesson: The church as family in covenant with God is commissioned with holy discipleship in contrast to the world's discipleship.*

(3) Significantly, when God establishes the Abrahamic covenant we are told repeatedly that it is an everlasting covenant. This covenant matters today (Gen. 17:7, 9, 19). *Covenantal Lesson: The church as family should expect long-term, fruitful, covenant faithfulness since the Lord has designed this covenant arrangement to extend to "a thousand generations"(Ps. 105:8).*

We will return to these lessons in a moment. For now, remember that this seed of the Abrahamic covenant, with its familial motif, was planted and watered by God throughout redemptive history. One significant text is Malachi 4:4–6:

> Remember the Law of Moses, My servant, which I commanded him in Horeb for all Israel, with the statutes and judgments. Behold, I will send you Elijah the prophet before the coming of the great and dreadful day of the LORD. And he will turn the hearts of the fathers to the children, and the hearts of the children to their fathers, lest I come and strike the earth with a curse.

This text closes out the Old Testament with a succinct reference to the rich Old Testament theology of God's grace upon Israel which includes the Law (Moses) and the Prophets (Elijah). Interestingly, Malachi denotes Israel and Judah's rebellion and God's pending judgment with symbols of *family* (e.g., Mal. 1:6; 2:3; 2:10). The reverse of judgment, the reception of mercy and grace, is put in the same symbolic terms of family (Mal. 1:2–3; 3:6–7; 3:17).

With these familial themes out in the open, the people of God are given the promise of hope in Malachi 4:4–6. How are we to take the oft-quoted familial reference in 4:5–6: "Behold, I will send you Elijah. . . . And he will turn the hearts of the fathers to the children, and the hearts of the children to the fathers"? This reinforces the biblical image of the church as family. In Luke 1:16–17, the angel speaks to Zecharias of the mission of his son, the new Elijah, John the Baptist: "And he will turn many of the children of Israel to the Lord their God. He will also go before Him in the spirit and power of Elijah, 'to turn the hearts of the fathers to the children,' and the disobedient to the wisdom of the just, to make ready a people prepared for the Lord." He quotes Malachi 4:5–6. The announcement of John's coming means the arrival of hope for the new Israel, the church.

The motif of the church-as-family foreshadowed in the Old Testament is fulfilled in the New Testamentwith the gospel, which calls for repentance, a turning "to make ready *a people* prepared for the Lord." John the Baptist's ministry of preparation meant preaching the covenant, the relationship between God and man, and the relationship between men. "The people who are prepared for their God are those who have learned to live in peace and righteousness with one another."[15] Jesus Christ affirms this very purpose. He came to form a new community of faith: "Whoever does the will of God is My brother and My sister and mother" (Mk. 3:32–35).

The theological implications of the promise of Malachi 4:5–6 are not to be understood in terms of the human, biological family being restored by the power of the grace and work of Christ—though

---

[15] I. H. Marshall, *Commentary of the Greek New Testament: The Gospel According to Luke* (Grand Rapids: Eerdmans, 1986), 60.

the gospel *does* provide hope and renewal for the biological household. Rather, we understand the promise in terms of the new, spiritual family, the family of God—the church.

Here the gospel's power is seen in its fruit of turning the hearts of the generations back to one another. *The gospel renews the church as the every-generation people of God. Therefore, applying in practice the familial nature of the church is a sign of the gospel's coming with power into the world.*

To summarize: In light of the Abrahamic covenant, what is important to a covenantal ministry approach and what is lacking in Reformed pastoral practice is that God not only condescends to make Himself known to the believing head of the home and his descendants, but He also makes Himself known *through their familial connection and interaction with one another.* A sign of the age of Christ's redemption is that the generations of the covenant in the church are turned toward one another (Mal. 4:6). With this biblical groundwork in mind, what practical contours for ministry should arise from believing covenant succession? How do we put covenant nurture to work? What does a covenantal approach to ministry look like?

Covenant Succession Expressed through the Image of the Family of God

A moment ago we read from Senter and Dunn that "youth ministry should not be handled as a spiritual parenthesis but as a continuity with biological and faith families." We must plan and execute ministry in a variety of expressions where the generations of the church connect with one another. Our covenantal lessons for ministry (above), based on the Abrahamic covenant, must become operative at this point. They might be recast as five affirmations that should guide a philosophy of ministry to children, youth and families.

1. We Affirm: *Nurture of children and youth is a priority; covenant children and youth help make up the local church of today, not merely the church of tomorrow.* The covenantal cause that we need to champion in our

day is treating our children and young people as full participants in the life of the church, *right now*. If you take up pencil and paper and scratch out a few notes on the book of Ephesians, you see that Paul addresses children and youth as full participants in the life of the congregation. He admonishes them directly in Ephesians 6:1–3, showing that he considers them to be vital members of the community, growing alongside the adult generations of the congregation. The catalog of the household table in Ephesians 5:22–6:9 (wives, husbands, children, fathers, slaves, and masters) gives responsibilities for faith and life in the stations of each group's calling in the home and world; these same groups, moreover, have responsibilities to faithfully, zealously fulfill the general office of baptized covenant disciples in the faith and life of the church.

Consider things this way. We commonly divide Ephesians into two halves, the doctrinal portion of chapters 1–3 and the practical section of chapters 4–6. When Paul goes about unfolding the riches of redemption and the elements of God's mercy to save those dead in trespasses and sins, and speaks of the Lord's gracious work of uniting Jew and Gentile "to create in Himself the one new man" (chapters 1–3), the whole of the household table is in his mind. In this respect, each group of the church is addressed and must take up the work of being a student of the truths of God's Word (the doctrinal portions of Ephesians). Similarly, in chapters 4–6, when he addresses the calling of baptized disciples—a calling of preserving the unity of the church and carrying out the service of the ministry with one another—he is expecting the generations to be at work together as the household of God. This view of the church captures the covenantal practice that concerns us.

Elders, when you visit church families do you inquire about the growing spiritual abilities and talents of the children in the household? How well do you articulate to that household the age-appropriate expectations for service that is engaged with the broader community of the church? What are you doing to lead the congregation to follow through on their commitment to train children and youth in doctrine and *life?* Deacons, when you communicate to certain thirteen- and fourteen-year-old boys that without them important hospital visitations will not be faithfully accomplished, do you realize that you are imparting instruction that paves the way for on-the-ministry-training for the rising generation of the next deaconate? Pastors, is there an every-generational approach in your preaching? Do you address each of the members of the household table regularly? Parents and teachers, do you tell the children of the covenant that their prayers are vital to the gospel power of the pastor's preaching?

This first affirmation of a covenantal approach to ministry addresses our view of, and expectations for, the younger generations of the church. Are we convinced that they help to make up the church of *today,* not just tomorrow? Do we act on our conviction,

> *Are we convinced that the youth help to make up the church of today?*

conveying a ministry of nurture that helps them to grow in doctrine and life, in the full life of the congregation? Putting our children and youth "on hold" only communicates to them that real covenant life and faith is for the older generations of the church. Training and ministry in our congregations must reflect, deep down, the need for the generations to be at work together. There must be ways of pursuing applications for faithful service that align ourselves with a dominant theme in Scripture that displays God's own way of doing things. For as Scripture says, "A little child shall lead them" (Is. 11:6).

2. We Affirm: *Nurture of children and youth is principled—our teaching is guided by the whole counsel of God.* The concept of nurture within the familial teachings of Scripture first appeared when God instructed Abraham, as a recipient of electing grace, to "command his children and his household after him, that they keep the way of the LORD, to do righteousness and justice" (Gen. 18:19). The word translated "command" (NKJV) means "to order, charge, commission, appoint, ordain." The word is common in the Bible and is used, for

example, when Jesse commanded David, his son, in matters of husbandry (1 Sam. 17:20); also, it is used when a king commanded his servants (2 Sam. 21:14). The various contexts show again and again that there is an authority figure involved who serves "in a position to command the people [expecting] their obedience."[16] It sounds like the backbone of a text like Deuteronomy 6:6 and following: "And these words which I command you today shall be in your heart. You shall teach them diligently to your children," or Deuteronomy 11:18–19: "You shall lay up these words of mine in your heart . . . you shall teach them to your children." Our teaching must be deliberate and forthright; we must give attention to the practice of training the rising generation in the Scriptures and in the specifics of applying it for godliness.

Nurture is the key to a methodology for covenant training. While commanding our children and youth "to keep the way of the LORD," we must call for comprehensive training. The texts of Deuteronomy say "these *words* . . . shall be in your heart . . . *teach them* diligently to your children." God indicates that the words of Scripture, as the way of life, must be known, embraced, and practiced.

Today in the local church, we have the tendency to focus teaching and nurture on a narrower range of subjects when we minister among age-specific or gender-specific groups. For youth, we typically focus on subjects like dealing with authority, peer pressure, guidance, and popular culture. The whole counsel of God's Word must be opened systematically, with educational aims and content goals. The whole counsel of God feeds the whole young person. Generally, we should have the same concern for adults. We should nurture them with the whole of Scripture and its doctrine. Our concern should be the same for children and youth.

Regarding covenant succession and the nurture of our children and youth through teaching, Lou Priolo notes, "Someone has said that

---

[16] R. Laird Harris, ed., *Theological Wordbook of the Old Testament*, 2 vols. (Chicago: Moody Press, 1980), 2:757.

a message prepared in a mind reaches a mind, but a message prepared in a life reaches a life."[17] I point this out because in keeping the familial aspect of the church in view as we think about covenantal nurture, we must resist an overly institutionalized or classroom approach to nurture. Of course, we desire to implement a comprehensive plan that includes goals for teaching subject matter that widens and deepens the church's nurture of her children and youth, but here's the sticky part: we must carry out our endeavor in a way that reflects the circumstances of everyday life.

> *We must resist an overly institutionalized or classroom approach to nurture.*

For this reason, our Reformed needlepoint classes for children (catechetical training), as absolutely necessary as they are, if divorced from the earthiness of real life will nurture a generation of drill sergeants for the training ground, not a regiment of footsoldiers for the spiritual battle field. We need sharp drill sergeants, but ones who can also command with wisdom, precision, and skill in the actual warfare of the Christian life.

In the body of Christ, some members of the body have an elevated place and role. These members are elevated by office and calling—recognized by the congregation—and they ought to practice their ministry with service and humility. Considering the apostle Paul's emphasis on the place of leadership gifts and teaching gifts in the execution of nurture in the Word, the growth of the body requires authority figures who are seasoned teachers in doctrine and life (see Eph. 4:11–16). What will build up the body in love (Eph. 4:16)? The body will be built up in love when each part contributes to the work at hand—the older, seasoned generations nurturing the younger ones while speaking the truth in love. Mature leaders, working with the whole counsel of the Word (just as we would expect in the home) foster a pattern of mature discipleship in the way of life in the covenant.

---

[17] Lou Priolo, *Teach Them Diligently* (Woodruff, S.C.: Timeless Texts, 2000), 12.

3. We Affirm: *The institutions of the family and the church should promote worship, edification, and evangelism as means of nurturing covenant children and youth in such a way that both institutions show the complementary, family-like character of the other and promote the distinct mandate of both.* With this affirmation, we get to the heart of implementing a practical, covenantal ministry in the family and local church. Both institutions, the home and the church, are to hold up a mirror that reflects a practice of nurture that the other may see and benefit from. This mutually supportive and at times supplementary relationship will serve powerfully and faithfully to shepherd the hearts of children, teens, and their families. Let us expand this affirmation a bit further.

First, both family and church should provide youth with opportunities for growing in the grace and knowledge of God. Both institutions must work to execute the three functions of worship, edification, and evangelism in a balanced manner. We too easily slip into a default mode of giving emphasis to one over the other two, but all three—worship, edification, and evangelism—require balanced attention.

Next, the affirmation states that our nurture should be done in a way that shows the complementary familial character of each institution. This chapter has tried to set out the familial face or character of the church. The covenant home is ready-made as an institution of multiple generations; the church is called to express that same image. Both institutions must work at displaying this image since the younger and older generations are included in both. How does the family and church work at this? The household head must see to it that his nurture is done in such a way that the church learns from him. In this way, the home complements the church. At the same time, the church's leadership must conduct its ministry of nurture with a design that reinforces the charge given to the head of the home. This is why each institution should carry out its stewardship of nurture as an example for the other; just as I wrote above, each should act as a mirror for the other, reflecting a familial image.

Last, this affirmation implies a way of approaching covenant nurture that promotes the distinct mandate of the respective institutions. Confusion about the mandate of each institution often surfaces at this point. Questions emerge: Shall the church be "domesticated" (i.e., made homelike) by doing away with the nursery, the age-segregated children's classes, and the youth group? Shall the household become an ordained haven for ecclesiastical practice—an insular house church with patriarchally-administered baptisms and "church" discipline? Some elaboration may prove helpful.

In the Scriptures, the first "church" was a family—Adam and Eve. God's establishment of the covenant household as primary, as the building block for the church, shows that the local church is dependent upon the family. Keeping the concept of nurture in mind, consider the particular nature of this dependence: the

> *Shall the church be "domesticated," having no nursery, age-segregated children's classes, or youth group?*

family should model, for the church, *church-like* expressions in its covenant household life. This includes church-like expressions of family worship, edification and training, and household evangelism (i.e., to extended family).

Authority to carry out this mandate is from the Lord. All authority and the exercise of that authority in the church and in the state derives from the triune God; even so all authority in the family is derived from God's lordship (Mt. 28:18; Eph. 1:21–22; Deut. 6).

Considering this structure of God-given authority and sphere sovereignty, how specifically should the family accomplish its mandate of household nurture? Shouldn't we take into account that some facets of discipleship and nurture are the sole responsibility of the institution of the church?

The Bible summons those appointed by God as heads of households to exercise their stewardship in *faith*. The family, in this light, must be instructed by the church about its sphere of dominion and supported in its stewardship of that dominion—and that instruction should orient the family *toward faith in God*. That is, the family must believe God for its own jurisdiction of nurture and the family must believe God for the jurisdiction of the church's nurture. Thus, the family necessarily must show its own kind of dependence, in faith, on the church.

The tell-tale sign of unbelief for the family is taking on a view of itself and its government which is idolatrous—that is, a view of itself which is self-serving and therefore anti-covenantal. The practical expression of this idolatry is one of being satisfied with the family's personal significance. R. J. Rushdoony points this out:

> The family as a social organization is the prime area of dominion. It has far more than personal significance. Originally, and, to some degree, in some areas of the world, the family in the larger sense, as clan and tribe has been extremely important. The weakness of these older forms has been the primacy of blood rather than of faith. By insisting on the primacy of blood, the theological significance of the family has been obscured, and, instead of *dominion*, the clan or tribe has aimed at *power*. . . .
>
> On the other hand, in the modern world, romanticism and pietism have reduced the family to the personal and emotional level, so that marriage and the family become purely personal to the parties involved, and they are indifferent to the theological and social significance thereof. Thus, the pietist sees Christ as King in the personal sense, "my Lord," which indeed He is, but the pietist fails to see Christ as King over Church, state, school, family, vocation, arts and sciences, and every area of life, and the pietist fails to see the social significance of redemption and Christ's kingship.[18]

Unbelief in the family must be overcome. In some households, it results from an abdication of the family's responsibility for nurture and discipleship. Other families fall into unbelief due to overzealous practices of family training that include an excessive restriction on

---

[18] R. J. Rushdoony, "Marriage and the Family" in *Salvation and Godly Rule* (Vallecito, Calif.: Ross House, 1983), 477–78. Emphasis original.

covenant members. In this overzealous practice, covenant members are restricted from most, if not all, training in the church geared specifically for certain generations. This unbelief denies children and youth access to the grace of the variety of the generations of the church. In Rushdoony's words, both of these families are seeking personal significance for the home. Both stand in need of the same biblical teaching for correction.

To overcome the unbelief of family protectionism, a man needs to lead his family with the awareness that the church is more than individual family units called out of the world to worship, provide nurture, and bear witness. The church is the *called-together* people of God. This called-together idea is an arresting concept. As the "called-together ones," we are called together as Christians, as covenant members. John Murray offers help for those who grip tightly to the idea that the individual family unit is the highest-priority institution in God's program. He challenges the parroted phrase that the church is the mere "called-out" ones:

> There is no evidence to support the notion that the church is be defined as the called-out ones. The biblical evidence will show that the idea is rather that of assembly or congregation. It would be more correct to say that the church is the called-together ones. The church is the congregation of the faithful, the communion of the saints, the fellowship of believers. As such it is an institution, an organization which has been constituted by Christ its head. The idea that the church consists of the called-out ones fails to take account of what is central, and one has reason to fear that it has ministered to the individualism which discards corporate responsibility and the necessity of maintaining purity and unity in the body of Christ.[19]

Murray advises us to see the church as the called-together people of God, emphasizing our corporate identity and responsibility. This is

---

[19] "Government in the Church of Christ," *Collected Writings of John Murray,* 4 vols. (Carlisle, Penn.: Banner of Truth, 1976), 1:264.

a summons to a certain kind of allegiance, an allegiance that requires the household to be dependent upon the church.

Practically, we must say that "there is a necessary dependence of the family upon the Church; for no area of its collective life from cradle to the grave is left unaffected by the transforming power of the Church's ministry."[20] And yet, as we have emphasized regarding the church's ministry, "[With the coming of the gospel era], the family is not outmoded or dissolved, but *drawn into* the church community. . . ."[21]

> The church is the called-together people of God.

The church, therefore, has a stewardship of care and nurture of the covenant home; she must treat the covenant family dutifully, supporting and equipping the head of the household to carry out his most significant and fundamental role in the nurture of his family. Following from this, the question of youth groups—yea or nay—may be answered by affirming the need to offer specific ministries to certain generations of the church. There are specific times and occasions to provide ministry to specific groups of children and youth (just as we would offer specific training to individuals in the home); however, it must not be a dominant expression of nurture in the church. There are specific times and occasions for providing ministry according to gender too, but once again, it should not be the dominant expression of the church's ministry.

To sum up this affirmation, as the church maintains its distinctive constitution as the organized called-together ones, it will best serve the institution of the covenant home through ministry that shows the church's family-like features. Nurture in the local church is to serve as a model for the work of nurture in the household whose parents have the primary responsibility to carry out that nurture. And again, we would say that that ministry in the home should be done in such

---

[20] Raymond O. Zorn, *Church and Kingdom* (Phillipsburg: Presbyterian and Reformed, 1962), 166.

[21] Edmund P. Clowney, *The Church* (Downers Grove: InterVarsity Press, 1995), 192. Emphasis mine.

a way that it is a model for ministry for the church. Both institutions should express a model resembling the familial fabric of the covenant, showing their mutual dependence. In order to live out this mutual dependence, our faith must rest in God, who provided these institutional gifts with the mandate to care for His young.

4. We Affirm: *Ministry, in a covenantal approach, is overseen and conducted by members of the household of faith. The nurture of children and youth is most consistent and effective when carried out by a variety of adults.*

The theology of the church requires a theology of delegation, which includes delegation of the authority and the practice of nurture. Delegation is a means of stirring up trust and confidence that God is at work in others. Delegation also serves as a means of grace that summons others to share in faith and life together so that the generations, sexes, and personalities of God's people blend together as the household of faith.

Community—in the church and in the home—inherently requires delegation. Individual parents are charged with the responsibility of bringing up their children in the nurture and admonition of the Lord (see Deut. 6; Eph. 6:4). Notice that both of these commands are placed within the broader context of the community of the covenant people of God. Israel was to write the commandments on the doorframes of their houses and on their city gates. This no doubt was to reinforce the mutual interests between the covenant community (Israel as a whole) and the covenant household. As the institutions intersect with one another, they each gain the wisdom of a multitude of counselors. The people who worship and serve alongside one another share mutual influences of godly living with wisdom and skill.

We recognize that due to the limitations of individual men who lead individual households, there is delegation within the biological family: mom takes many of the household duties, and the children grow into their regular chores. Similarly, due to limitations of church leaders, there is delegation within the church community.

God never intended for there to be a complete and full delegation of a parent's responsibility for his child's nurture to others; nor did

He intend for there to be a complete and full absence of it. Just as there is some measure of delegation within the human family, so there is to be some measure of delegation in the spiritual family. What difference does this make for ministry and nurture in the church?

This means that the church should recruit a wide variety of volunteers to be "family" to her young. For a fictional example, the Burkes and the Willits are the parents who are in charge of Bible teaching. The Smiths and the Harons are in charge of the monthly service ministry at the nursing home. The O'Malleys and the Harpers meet with the Youth Catechism Leadership Team. The Daniels, Tedds, and Cobbs lead the way with the Summer Mission Team. Why the variety? The variety is the family-like face of the church reaching the children and youth of the covenant households. And where are the parents in this model of leadership? They are involved at *different* levels (some in leadership, some not) and at *different* expressions of ministry (different programs and functions of church life). This is covenantal parenting within the community of God's people.

> *The church should recruit a wide variety of volunteers to be "family" to her young.*

This kind of leadership saves on the wear and tear of just one couple serving with a workhorse kind of energy month after month. It also expresses the familial character of the church, for it aims at multi-generational influence (senior adults, younger married couples, singles, etc.) working together to nurture the children and youth. Spiritual talents and abilities are employed and parceled out to meet the needs at hand. Children who grow up in the covenant around the family of the church learn that nurture in the church is family-like; they also learn that a family is serving with them and training them. Therefore they grow up as welcomed participants along with the whole of the congregation. This model of serving together works to correct the notion among our youth that they have to "graduate" into the adult generations of the church. Instead, they know all along that they have been involved in and with the church.

5. We Affirm: *The family and church should expect long-term fruit of covenant faithfulness since the Lord has made this covenant arrangement not with one generation, but a thousand (Ps. 105:8).* In this covenantal ap proach to covenant nurture, we measure success according to God's standards, not ours. We measure success by carrying out ministry according to faith. We trust in the Lord regarding His promise to believing parents. Those who serve in church-based covenant nurture are effectively placed into a position of being a covenant family to the children and youth of the church. To the parents of a biological household and to the "covenant parents" of the household of faith, God says through David, "The children of [My] servants will continue, and their descendants will be established before [Me]" (Ps. 102:28).

We serve in ministry by faith, assuming God's Word to be operative in the hearts and minds of covenant children. One important way of working fruitfully is *acting* on God's promise that He will be faithful to a thousand generations. We serve in faith, trusting in His promise and fully expecting Him to use His ordinary means of fulfilling the covenant promise to our children and to our children's children. One way that this faith is expressed is through living in faith together as a household. The generations are called to walk together in covenant with God. Covenant-based nurture has a lifetime perspective—from the womb to the tomb.

> *Covenant-based nurture has a lifetime perspective—from the womb to the tomb.*

So we set up for our children and youth a *lifetime* of growth and nurture. This is growth and nurture that immerses itself in the variety of generations mixing together, generation influencing generation, representing the full lifespan of a covenant walk with God. Those in their fifties, sixties, seventies, and eighties who have experienced the faithfulness of God for a lifetime make the best workers among children and youth. Their experience teaches that being in the covenant does not warrant an automatic, untroubled faith that never fails. Rather, a strong faith is one that sees the larger picture, one that continues steadfastly to believe our great God's saving promises in Christ over the years of a whole life. With this long view, the younger generations are exposed to a sanctified seriousness and encouraged to walk in the covenant with God and bear the mantle of faith and righteousness right at our side.

As the church increasingly reforms herself, she will faithfully express her identity as the multi-generational people of God and will carry out her calling, looking to God for His blessing up and down the lineage of the generations. Thus we believe Him when He says that He is our faithful God, even to a thousand generations. The Bible, both Old and New Testaments, requires us to plan and provide congregation-driven ministry among the generations of the church. The glass slipper of children and youth nurture finds its most faithful expression on the foot of the Bride, the people of God.

Conclusion

Imagine that you have just visited Anytown Reformed Church, which is practicing church-based covenant nurture for the succession of God's grace and faith to children and youth. You saw something like the following:

1. There is growing leadership base in youth-appropriate expression. Two seventeen-year-old young men serve with the deaconate. They attend meetings and carry out various duties, working with an assigned deacon. You also learned that three high-school-age ladies rotated on and off, every six months, with the ministry coordinating team of the women's Dorcas Society.

2. Special efforts are made to integrate the generations of God's people. The communicants' class for communicant membership at Anytown Reformed requires that the Covenant Partners, a variety of adults from the congregation, attend the classes with the young people who are in catechism and doctrine training. The pastor works hard in that communicants' class to involve the *church* in the training, discussions, and prayer. On the Lord's Day when you visited

Anytown Reformed, the Covenant Partners stood near the young people who were professing their faith before the congregation

3. There is a conscious and visible acknowledgment that every generation is absolutely necessary for the work and ministry of the church. Every Wednesday night at the Missions Ministry and Prayer group, the Minute for Missions Prayer update is wholly in the hands of the young people of the church. They are responsible for the missionary updates, letter-writing, display case of pictures and letters, emails, and the section of the church's web page covering the missions education of the church. Also, every two years, the youth of the church sponsor the Matthew 28:18 Missions Conference—from start to finish. Additionally, you saw in the church newsletter something about Timothy Teams, which are two small groups of nine to twelve youths and parents who are the primary means of outreach down at State College. These Timothy Teams are in charge of a ministry of evangelism to international students. Every September they initiate a ministry called HomeLight. HomeLight makes sure that clusters of international students are partnered with hospitality hosts (families) in the church for the school year. One Timothy Team oversees the teaching ministry to internationals; the other oversees and carries out serving ministries among the internationals. The youth are in key areas of leadership to make this ministry happen.

Wouldn't we want these kinds of service-dominant, nurture-grounding expressions of covenant life in our homes, involving us, our spouses, our children, and our young adults? Wouldn't we want them to permeate the local church?

The church is called to an every-generation ministry; now is the time for us to think and act biblically. The reformation across North America regarding the roles of the church and the family is growing. The instruments are sounding more tuned and the dancefloor is getting more crowded. It's a big dance! Cinderella, the church, sees the glass slipper. Will you be faithful in helping to serve the church and family so that she will rightly keep this slipper of covenant nurture for her great wedding with Christ, the Bridegroom?

A Father's Perspective: Covenant Succession by Grace through Faith

Joel Belz

Some folks attribute the saying to Casey Stengel, and others to Yogi Berra. It probably wasn't original with either one, but in any case it's wonderful: "Predictions are always difficult, but especially about the future." And even more especially, we might add, when we're talking about the future of our children.

What we all long for, of course, is a formula. Take three cups of A, half a teaspoon of B, a dash of C, and stir vigorously for seventeen years. Presto, out comes an absolutely perfect son or daughter. In other words, we want to be able, with a high degree of certainty, to predict the future about our children. And being more inclined toward naturalistic solutions than we are toward supernaturalistic ones, we hurry to formulate our recipes to make sure we are doing everything right at this end, so we can be absolutely sure everything will come out just right on the other end.

And when it doesn't? We hurry back and reformulate our recipes. Two generations ago, evangelicals' recipes for their children included equal doses of parental involvement in the local public school PTA and a vigorous youth group at the local church. And we were always careful to remember how important healthy portions of family devotions and bedtime prayers were. A generation ago, that had been either replaced or augmented for many with a recipe flavored heavily by Christian schools. When Christian schools proved not to have a one hundred percent success rate, home schooling became the new formula. And by the time a new millennium dawned, still another new recipe (which actually was very old) became the new rage. We call them classical schools.

How many more such readjustments will it take before we learn that God doesn't deal in formulas? It might prove to be an embarrassing question. His order for passing on His covenant love from one generation to another is at the same time a far simpler and a far more complex matter.

The Reason for Formulas

It should be no surprise that we tend to look for formulas and recipes. The Bible itself often seems to point us in such a direction. Again and again, God's promises seem at first to be rooted in conditions that strike us as very formula-like. Not least of those, of course, is the Bible's most famous formula of all having to do with child-rearing, found in Proverbs 22:6: "Train up a child in the way he should go; even when he is old, he will not depart from it." Make this cake according to the instructions, we seem to read here, and you can count on its turning out just fine.

Granted, we've been disappointed and dismayed along the way. We've seen kids whose upbringing seemed just about perfect who then strayed from the path. But, holding staunchly to the formula, we've rationalized both to ourselves and to others that probably (a) we didn't know as much about that upbringing as we thought we did, or (b) the child isn't old enough yet to have inherited God's promise. In any case, we reassure ourselves, the formula is intact even if the child and his or her parents aren't.

How many more readjustments will it take before we learn that God doesn't deal in formulas?

Even before the book of Proverbs, we have God's promises to the patriarchs that appear to be heavily conditioned on the behavior and faithfulness of the parents. Deuteronomy 11 seems full of such implications:

> You shall therefore keep the whole commandment that I command
> you today, that you may be strong, and go in and take possession of
> the land that you are going over to possess, and that you may live
> long in the land that the Lord swore to your fathers to give to them
> and to their offspring, a land flowing with milk and honey (vv. 8–9)

On the other hand, the exact nature of these formulas sometimes gets a little cloudy. What do we make, for example, of the apostle Paul's direction in Ephesians when he references Exodus 20 and calls the instruction to "Honor your father and your mother" the "first commandment with promise"? The promise of this Fifth Commandment, oddly, is to the children—not to their parents!

The great point of the biblical record, however, is never to direct us toward heroic people in any generation who have been good at qualifying for God's blessings through their great obedience. The point instead is to remind us that everyone except for Jesus Himself has failed dismally at such an assignment. There have been lots and lots of promises and good-faith commitments from God—but not a single example of anyone who kept his or her end of the bargain. This is exactly why we must be so very careful about trying to engage in "across-the-table" agreements between God and us as if we were business equals. Coming to God about our children is instead a matter of vastly subordinate subjects getting a glimpse of the nature of the largely one-way promises of a supremely faithful Father.

Not Works, but Grace

My father and mother had eight children. Mom and Dad were faithful parents—not just from the perspective of those who watched them from some distance, but also in the minds of those who observed them up close, and in the hearts of us kids. If we knew that Mom and Dad weren't perfect, we never made much of such faults or held them against our parents. So folks aren't surprised now, half a century later, to observe that all eight of the Belz children still "walk with the Lord." The reality is, of course, that that "walk" for some of us sometimes is more a crawl, a stumble, or even a stagger. But that is part of the point.

I remember poignantly, therefore, that as my father lay dying from cancer in 1978, a friend approached him urgently.

"Max," he said, "it's important that you write down whatever it was that you and your wife did right with your children. You've got to pass that on. Maybe it should be a book."

"Oh, no," Dad responded. "If I did, it would just have one line. It would say quite simply that God was faithful."

That was not just weariness on Dad's part. It was an important insight about the main link between a sovereign God and His children.

The problem with formula thinking when it comes to educating and passing our faith on to our children is that it is always too much rooted in works righteousness—and not nearly enough in God's mercy and grace. We properly, and very theologically, reject works as the means by which we ourselves are justified and brought into a proper relationship with God. But then too often we turn right around and act as if that performance (*our* performance) is critical to how God will respond to our children. We may not formulate it that way in our minds, but it's precisely how we spell it out with our practical living. Somehow, we actually think we can earn God's favor for our children—or worse yet, that we can wrestle God into a position where He is in our debt.

> The problem with formula thinking is that it is always too much rooted in works righteousness.

Tragically, the very means by which we do all this tend to become the false gods against which the true God so sternly warns us. The PTA service and church youth groups, the Christian schools, the home schools, the classical schools—even the family devotions and bedtime prayers—all these and more, good and worthy as they are, become that by which we hope our children might be perfected. But like all false gods, we will find ourselves betrayed in the end if that is where we put our trust.

The Waiting Game

It is to remind us not to trust in formulas that God sometimes intrudes into our comfy routines and shatters our neat designs. He spoils our sure-fire recipes and says: "Hold on! Wait up. I want to make sure your trust is properly focused."

My wife Carol Esther and I had that happen to us in 1995. Our formulas had nearly worked. While hearing more than a few of our friends agonize over the difficulty of raising teenagers in such a terrifying culture, things had in fact gone quite well with us and our five daughters. No, I hadn't been as faithful at family devotions and time in prayer as I had wished. But all had profited, we thought, from their years at a good, local, interdenominational Christian school. Two were already through college and happily married; prospects seemed bright for the other three. This was so much easier for us than for some around us; what were they fussing over?

That's when one of our daughters chose suddenly to take a decidedly and blatantly disobedient path. Refusing to hear our counsel, she was disciplined, lovingly but firmly, by our church. But she would not hear the elders any more than she would hear us—and the next couple of years found us agonizing over the meaning of what we had too casually thought were God's great promises. Knowing that God promised to store my tears in a bottle, I told Him several times He might need to get a big tank instead. Don't get me wrong—not once, I think, did my wife and I consider that God had somehow dropped His end of the bargain. It was never a matter of lashing out at Him as though He had let us down. It was instead acute bewilderment, confusion, and for me, at least, frustration at having to wait for God to do what we thought He had promised.

Did I exclude all thoughts about my own deep-rooted disobedience, my slowness to seek God's face, my dull ears, my hard-hearted stubbornness? Of course not. I had to wrestle through all that—and in the process got to learn again that my own sinfulness, while certainly an issue, was not primarily what this all was about. I did experience the freshness of God's mercy and grace directed at me. But I also got to see, in some ways for the first time, how impoverished I was at being able to offer any of my own obedience as a bribe to God for my children. On that count, I was not just broke, but overdrawn. For both myself and my children, I needed mercy—rich and free.

But the waiting was awful, and in talking since then with hundreds of parents who have experienced similar situations, I know how many others have similarly chafed at not being able to snap their fingers and have God do what seemed so right for Him to do. "I've got it now, Lord," I said in a hundred different ways. "Now it's okay for you to take care of this matter." But it was precisely in saying that, in a hundred different ways, that I demonstrated I really didn't get it yet. I was still suggesting it was something I had to get right, and then God could reward me. I was still suggesting it was my works, not God's grace. So the wait went on.

> *I came to see how impoverished I was at being able to offer any of my own obedience as a bribe to God for my children.*

I lost fifteen pounds and for the first time in my life couldn't sleep at night. Both circumstances convicted me. When, I asked myself, was the last time I was so hungry for God that food had lost its appeal? When had my desire for God's presence kept me awake at night? Did this mean I loved my daughter more than I loved God Himself? The evidence was pretty clear that it did. And God, knowing that about me, claimed me anyway as His child.

Two Mountains

Through those agonizing months, I was impressed almost every day with the theological imagery provided by two sets of mountains. On the one hand, my activist "do-something" nature prompted me to suggest to my wife, "Let's go grab our daughter, get plane tickets to some hideaway in the Swiss Alps, and deprogram her for the next six months." But my quietist, pietist nature (not nearly as well developed in my personality) suggested otherwise. "Maybe," I said sometimes, "I should just go up to Mount Pisgah, an hour's drive into the Smoky Mountains from our house, and spend some personal time fasting and praying." Even now, from the distance of more than eight years, I remember that tug-of-war as a picture of the struggle we all engage in as we ask the question: Whose victory is this going to be—God's or ours?

And I do not mean to disparage the active obedience God expects from His children. I am committed, more than I have ever been, to doing those things God commands us, both explicitly and implicitly, in regards to our children. But as I do them, it is with a modesty and humility that always keeps in mind that God owes us nothing at all. We pray with our children and read God's Word to them and seek out godly schooling for them, not because that will then somehow obligate God to show our children favor—but simply because those activities will remind our children, again and again, who they are and who God is. Such blessed life-lessons take hold of our souls. That is ultimately what it's all about.

I know now how much earlier God ended our family's wait than He has that of some others. I have wept even in recent months with some dads and moms who have waited ten and fifteen times as long as the two years or so that we endured. And I don't mean to imply these folks are slower at learning God's lessons than I was. A God whose ways are past finding out simply chose to show His grace to me in a different way. Our daughter returned to us, to her church, and to her patient Lord Himself. She testifies often now about the good—and sometimes mysterious—things God is teaching her as a wife and mother.

Her papa is still learning as well. He's learning that when God assigns waiting periods to His children, it isn't usually so that we'll finally get it right. It is almost always so that finally we'll understand that we'll never get it right. Typically, that takes even longer.

And her papa marvels increasingly at how tenderly, and how unexpectedly, God weans us from thinking we know His ways, or from supposing we can chart the path that would let us wrest from Him exactly what we want, when we want it. Almost certainly, He will teach you with methods quite different from those He used to teach my family and me.

For after all, He's quite determined not to let anybody reduce the great God of heaven to a mere formula. He wants the glory when it comes to the faithfulness of our children. He means for our faltering faithfulness to be a humble response to His faultless faithfulness—never a means of earning His faithfulness in the first place. To get such glory for Himself, and to maximize it, He'll keep making it hard for us to make overly precise predictions—especially about the future.

Contributors

TIMOTHY BAYLY is pastor of the Church of the Good Shepherd in Bloomington, Indiana. Ordained in 1983 by John Knox Presbytery, Presbyterian Church (USA), he served a yoked parish in Pardeeville, Wisconsin, from 1983 to 1991. Since 1992, he has been a PCA pastor serving in Bloomington, Indiana. Bayly and his wife, Mary Lee (Taylor), were married in 1976 and have five children and two grandsons. Bayly received his B.A. from the University of Wisconsin (Madison) and his M.Div. from Gordon-Conwell Theological Seminary.

JOEL BELZ is founder and publisher of *World* magazine and CEO of God's World Publications Inc. in Asheville, North Carolina. Born in Iowa in 1941, he has been active in both publishing and Christian education all his life. He is a graduate of Covenant College (B.A. in English) and the University of Iowa (M.A. in Mass Communications). He has chaired the boards of Covenant College, Asheville Christian Academy, and the Evangelical Press Association. He is an elder in his local church, and in 2003 was chosen as moderator of the General Assembly of the Presbyterian Church in America. Mr. Belz writes a weekly column for *World*, and in 1996 co-authored *Whirled Views: Tracking Today's Culture Storms* with *World*'s editor-in-chief, Marvin Olasky. Mr. Belz and his wife Carol Esther have five married daughters and eleven grandchildren.

RANDY BOOTH received a B.S. in history and has been an ordained minister for twenty years. He is the pastor of Grace Covenant Church (Confederation of Reformed Evangelical Churches) in Nacogdoches, Texas, and currently serves as the moderator of the CREC. He has been married to his wife Marinell for thirty years and they have three grown children and one granddaughter. He has overseen the planting and establishment of five churches and is the director of Covenant Media Foundation, a conference speaker, co-founder of Veritas Classical Christian School in Texarkana, Arkansas, and the chairman of the founding board of Regents Academy in Nacogdoches. He is the author of *Children of the Promise: The Biblical Case for Infant Baptism* and several published articles.

DAVID HAGOPIAN earned a B.A. in History with a minor in Classical Greek from the University of California at Irvine and a Juris Doctorate from the University of Southern California. He has edited or contributed articles to several Christian magazines and journals and has edited or written several books, including *The Genesis Debate: Three Views on the Days of Creation* (editor), *Back to Basics: Rediscovering the Richness of the Reformed Faith* (editor and contributing author), *Always Reformed: A Dialogue of Differences within the Reformed Tradition* (editor and contributing author, two volumes, forthcoming), *Beyond Promises: A Biblical Challenge to Promise Keepers* (co-author with Douglas Wilson). He is a principal consultant with Precept Marketing Group, Inc., a partner with the law firm of Holdsworth & Hagopian, and the co-founder and president of Crux Press. He also helped to found Ancient Hope Reformed Church (member, CREC) in Mission Viejo, California, and is ordained as a teaching elder in it. He has been married to his wife, Jamie, for seventeen years and has four children on this side of glory, Brandon, Kirstin, Anallyce, and Alden, all of whom have been home schooled.

DOUGLAS JONES is a fellow of philosophy at New Saint Andrews College in Moscow, Idaho, and senior editor of *Credenda/Agenda* magazine. He is co-author, with Doug Wilson, of *Angels in the Architecture: A Protestant Vision for Middle Earth* and currently a Master of Fine Arts (Poetry) candidate at the University of Idaho. He and his wife, Paula, have five children.

DR. NELSON D. KLOOSTERMAN is a father of five and grandfather of five. Ordained to the gospel ministry in 1975, he has been associated since 1981 with Mid-America Reformed Seminary (Dyer, Indiana), currently teaching courses in Ethics, New Testament Studies, Homiletics, and Church Polity. He is a minister among the United Reformed Churches. He obtained a B.A. in Greek from Calvin College (Grand Rapids, Michigan) in 1972, and a B.D. from Calvin Theological Seminary (Grand Rapids, Michigan) in 1975. In 1991 he obtained his Th.D. from the Theological University of the Reformed Churches (liberated) in Kampen, the Netherlands. Dr. Kloosterman has translated and published several books, including *The Ten Commandments: Manual for the Christian Life*, *Responsible Conduct: Principles of Christian Ethics* by J. Douma, and *Preaching and the History of Salvation* by C. Trimp.

DR. CHARLES ALAN MCILHENNY received his B.A. from Moody Bible Institute in 1973, his M.Div. from the Reformed Episcopal Seminary in Philadelphia, and his Doctorate of Ministry from Westminster Theological Seminary in Escondido, California. He is the co-author of *When the Wicked Seize a City* and has been an outspoken voice for moral issues, having appeared on hundreds of radio and television shows all over the country. He has been pastor of the First Orthodox Presbyterian Church in San Francisco for over thirty years as well as pastor of their mission work Providence Orthodox Presbyterian Chapel in Castro Valley, California, for the past seven years. He is also an Adjunct Professor of Apologetics, Religions and Cults, and New Testament at City Seminary of Sacramento, California. He is married to his wife of thirty-four years, Donna, who is the Director of the Alpha Pregnancy Center in San Francisco. He and his wife have three married children and five grandchildren.

DR. ROBERT S. RAYBURN has been the pastor of Faith Presbyterian Church (PCA) in Tacoma, Washington, for twenty-five years. He earned his B.A. from Covenant College, his M.Div. from Covenant Theological Seminary, and his Ph.D. from the University of Aberdeen. He and his wife Florence have five children. He is the author of the chapter on Hebrews in *The Evangelical Commentary on the Bible*.

G. MARK SUMPTER (M.A., Westminster Theological Seminary in California) is currently pastor of Faith OPC in Grants Pass, Oregon. He has been involved in congregational youth and family ministry for over twenty-five years. He and his wife Peggy have six children.

TOM TROUWBORST was born and raised in the Christian Reformed Church. Tom now serves as the pastor of Calvary OPC in Schenectady, New York. He and his wife of thirteen years, Colleen, have been blessed with seven covenant children. After graduating from Pace University with an M.B.A, Tom worked as a CPA, eventually forming his own practice with Colleen. Tom earned his M.Div. from Bahnsen Theological Seminary and, prior to ministering at Calvary, served as both a ruling and teaching elder at Messiah's Congregation in New York City.

BENJAMIN K. WIKNER was born in South Korea and raised in Cedar Falls, Iowa, as a Lutheran catechumen. He received his B.A. from Covenant College (1994) and his M.Div. from Westminster Theological Seminary in California (1999). He is pastor of Providence OPC in Temecula, California. He and his wife of ten years, Erin, have been blessed with five covenant children.

DOUGLAS WILSON is the pastor of Christ Church in Moscow, Idaho, where he has served since 1977. He received an M.A. in philosophy from the University of Idaho. He is author of numerous books, including *Reforming Marriage*, *Mother Kirk*, and *The Case for Classical Christian Education*. He and his wife Nancy have three children and nine grandchildren.

Acknowledgments

First of all, I want to thank the Lord Jesus Christ for His truly amazing grace. It is only by this abounding grace that I have been saved and furthermore been enabled to apprehend the promises presented in this book. I am so very thankful that the Lord has promised good to me and my family in His covenant and has favored me with children, giving me the privilege of nurturing a few of His precious souls in this same grace. My wife and I were blessed with our fifth child at the end of this project and even as our lives have continued to become more challenging and complex, we have even more profoundly been amazed by God's grace. Fittingly, our fifth child is named Grace.

I want to thank a few others also—less instrumental than the Lord to be sure, but instrumental nonetheless in making this project a reality. I want to thank my earthly parents. You gave me a stable environment as I was growing up, which I now realize was invaluable in countless ways. As for my wife and children, what more can I say than has already been said in this book? Thank you for your enduring patience and indefatigable confidence in me. I should also thank Kevin Skogen, who was my pastor while I was at Covenant College, who first planted the seed in my head that I should seek the ministry and who modeled a home that faithfully practiced the doctrine of covenant succession. Thanks also to Frank Brock, a mentor in the faith and in life. And thanks to Bob Godfrey, who sustained my confidence in covenant succession while a student at Westminster Seminary in California, even as it flagged under the duress of theological and ecclesiastical cynicism. Thanks also to Doug Jones for his vision and accommodation in publishing this volume, and to Don Poundstone and Ken Montgomery for their helpful editing. I want to thank the people of Providence Church in Temecula for their love, support, and encouragement in the past year and a half as I have labored to finish this work. Finally, a big thanks to each of the contributors of this volume, who have been so patient to see the fruit of their labors made available to Christ's church.

Scripture Index